GOVERNANCE IN ANCIENT INDIAN POLITICAL SYSTEM

GOVERNANCE IN ANCIENT INDIAN POLITICAL SYSTEM

DR. KUMAR JWALA

ABHIJEET PUBLICATIONS
DELHI- 110 094

ABHIJEET PUBLICATIONS
2/46 Tukhmeerpur Extension
Delhi-110 094
Phone: 011-22960492, 65698474
E-mail: abhijeetpublication@gmail.com

GOVERNANCE IN ANCIENT INDIAN POLITICAL SYSTEM

First Published 2009

ISBN 978-81-89886-71-4

PRINTED IN INDIA

Published by J.K. Singh for Abhijeet Publications, Delhi-110 094, Lasertypeset by Gaurav Graphics, New Delhi and Printed at Himanshu Printers, Delhi.

Preface

In the recent past, issues of governance has received increasingly serious attention from researchers, policy makers and student of social sciences. Governance now not only occupies central stage in the developed discourse but is also considered as the central element to be incorporated in the development strategy.

Kautilya, Manu, Sukra, Gandhi, Nehru, Patel and Ambedkar in Indian tradition have directly and indirectly given the theories of how to manage the society and the state. Kautilya's *Arthasastra,* is a classical book on Governance. One must study Kautilya's *Arthasastra, Manusmriti, Ramayana, Mahabharat* and Puranas to know about the Ancient Indian Political System. The need of the hour is to study Ancient Indian Literature without any prejudice. West can learn from Eastern tradition and literature and vice versa. An attempt has been made to fill this gap.

This work would have not been completed without the help of teachers, my friends and family members, who helped me directly or indirectly.

First of all I am highly grateful to Prof. R.R. Jha, my teacher in BHU for constant guidance and encouragement.

I am also indebted to my teachers, Professor M.P. Singh, Prof. S.N. Singh, Prof. Mujtapa Khan, Prof. Bidyut Chakravarty, Prof. Subroto Mukherji, Prof. Achin Vinayak, Prof. Nisarul Haque, and Prof. Rajesh Anand.

Among the friends I would like to thank Sanjiv Kumar Tiwary, Dr. Anil Dutta Mishra and Dr. Sweta Mishra for their help and advice.

My family stood like a rock when I needed them. My father Sakaldeo Tiwary, mother Kanan Tiwary inspired me and provided all help to complete this work on time. I have no words to express my gratitudes and love to them.

Last but not least, I am highly obliged to Sri J.K. Singh M/s. Abhijeet Publications, Delhi for bringing this book in nice form and in short time.

Kumar Jwala

Abbreviations

1. ABORI	-	Annals of Bhandarkar Oriental Research Institute.
2. Adiparvan	-	Adiparvan of the *Mahabharata*.
3. Ait. Brahmana	-	*Aitareya Brahmana.*
4. Amara	-	*Amarakosa.*
5. Anct. Ind.	-	Ancient India.
6. Anusasana	-	Anusasana parvan of the *Mahabharata*.
7. Ap, Ap Dh	-	*Apastamba Dharmasutra.*
8. Arth Kautilya	-	*Arthsastra* of Kautilya.
9. A.S.R.	-	Archeological Survey of India report.
10. AV	-	*Atharvaveda.*
11. BBRAS	-	*Journal of the Bombay Branch of Royal Asiatic Society.*
12. Bhag	-	*Bhagawata Purana.*
13. BMC	-	Catalogue of Coins in the British Museum.
14. Br	-	*Brahamana.*

15. C.I.I.	-	*Corpus Inscriptionum Indicarum.*
16. Ep Ind - E.I.	-	*Epigraphia Indica.*
17. Gautama	-	*Gautama Dharmsutra.*
18. I.A.	-	*Indian Antiquary.*
19. I.C.	-	*Indian Culture.*
20. I.H.Q.	-	*Indian Historical Quarterly.*
21. Karmandaka	-	*Nitisara* of Kamandeka.
22. Kath	-	*Kathopanisad.*
23. Manu	-	*Manusmriti.*
24. Mat	-	*Matsaya Purana.*
25. Narada	-	*Naradasmriti.*
26. NIA	-	*New Indian Antiquary.*
27. Puranic Rites	-	*Puranic Records of Hindu Rites and Customs* of Hazra.
28. Rajdharm kanda	-	Rajdharmkanda of kritya kalpam.
29. Rajniti Prakasa	-	*Rajniti Prakasa* of Viramitrodaya.
30. R.V.	-	*Rigveda.*
31. Sabha	-	Sabhaparvan of *Mahabharata.*
32. Santi, Santiparvan	-	Santiparvan of the *Mahabharata.*
33. State and Govt.	-	*State and Government in Ancient India* by A.S. Altekar.
34. Sukra	-	Sukra *Nitisara.*
35. Vashistha	-	*Vashishta Dharmsastra.*
36. Visnudh	-	*Vishnudharmottara Purana.*
37. Vyavaharakande	-	Vyavaharakande of Krtyakaḷa Patary.
38. Yaj. Yajn	-	*Yajnavalkya Smriti.*

Contents

1

Introduction

The value of the Puranas, as a source of ancient Indian History and Culture, has been correctly emphasized by the eminent scholar the Late Prof. H.H. Wilson.[1] For the first time he has drawn the attention of historians to the importance of the Puranic studies. Prior to the systematic study of the *Visnu Purana,* there was a general belief among the peoples that the Puranas relate only to imaginary stories. But later-on by the sweat of one's brow F.E. Pargiter[2] proved the value of the Puranas as an important source of the dynastic history of ancient India.

Approximately until fifty-five year ago, no systemic study of the Puranas as the source of ancient Indian history had been made. We are indebted to Dikshitar, who wrote two books *Matsya Purana: A Study*[3] and *Some Aspects of the Vayu Purana,*[4] in which he has tried to discuss genealogies, philosophy, music, consmogony, architecture and polity etc. He also published an article[5] 'Polity in the Puranas' in which he utilised the *Visnu,* the *Markandeya* and the *Agni* Puranas. But this article comprised of only four pages. The other book 'Cultural History from the Vayu Purana' was published by Patil. But these two scholars have not taken pains to determine the dates of the Puranas.

The subject matter of their study was based on the facts only. Though F.E. Pargiter and Hara Prasad Shastri have made efforts to fix the dates of the few Puwranas, yet no adequate justice has been done to them. Indeed Prof. Hazra is the first Indian scholar who has taken pains to determine the probable dates and chronology of the extant Puranas. His valuable contribution is published in the shape of two books: *Studies in the Puranic Records on Hindu Rites and Customs*[6] and the *Studies in the Upapuranas*.[7] In these two books he has solved so many problems connected with Puranas. The other works like *Matsya Purana: A Study*,[8] *Markandeya Purana Eka Samskritika Adhyana*[9] by V.S. Aggarwal, *Harvamsa Purana Ka Samskritika Vivechana*[10] by Veenapani Pandey, *Studies in Skanda Purana*[11] by A.B.L. Awasthi, *Polity in the Agni Purana*[12] by B.B. Misra and *Agni Purana: A Study*[13] by S.D. Gyani are of similar nature.

The writers of ancient Indian polity like K.P. Jayaswal, N.N. Law,[14] V.R.R. Dikshitar,[15] Beni Prasad,[16] P.V. Kane,[17] N.C. Bandhopadhyaya,[18] A.S. Altekar,[19] U.N. Ghoshal,[20] R.S. Sharma,[21] V.P. Verma,[22] and A.D. Pushalker[23] have utilised the Puranas as a source for the Political Ideas and Institutions but no adequate attention has been paid to the political institutions of the Puranas. Sri Jagdish Lal Shastri for the first time tried to compile the Political ideas in the Puranas in the year 1944. His work, *The Political Thought in the Puranas* summarizes the political ideas of the *Matsya*, the *Agni*, the *Garuda*, the *Kalika* and the *Visnudharmottara* Puranas only with in thirty-two pages which is undoubtedly very meagre. Afterwards in 1959 Dr. Ghoshal, in his book *A History of Indian Political Ideas* critically examined the political ideas of the Puranas in two chapters. In the chapter 18 he discusses the political ideas of the early Mahapuranas (*Vayu, Brahmamda, Visnu, Markandeya* and *Bhagawata* Puranas) and in chapter 24 he has dealt with the political ideas of the later Mahapuranas (*Garuda, Visnudharmottara, Matsya, Bhavisya, Kurma, Linga, Naradiya* and *Aditya* Puranas) but no serious attempt has been made. Beni Prasad also devoted a separate chapter dealing with the polity of the different Puranas in his book *The Theory and Government in Ancient India.* But this chapter consists of only seventeen pages, which shows that like other scholars he has also not done justice to them. S.D. Gyani and B.B. Mishra are the first scholars who have endeavoured to discuss political ideas of the *Agni Purana.* Dr. Gyani has made an effort to deal with all aspects of the *Agni Purana* while Dr. Mishra has taken pains to discuss the polity in the *Agni Purana* exclusively. In the support of this conclusion he has cited the evidence of the *Matsya* and the *Visnudharmottara Puranas.* But no equal treatment is done with the other Puranas as his main subject of the study was Polity in the *Agni Purana.* The present author has utilised the texts of the *Markandeya,* the *Vayu,* the *Visnu,* the *Matsya,* the *Visnudharmottara,* the *Garuda* and the *Agni* Puranas only. As the subject of his study is based on the above-mentioned Puranas, the other Puranas have not been taken into account. In support of the statements of the Puranas the author has quoted the verses from Smritis, Epics, the *Arthasastra,* the *Nitisara,* the *Manasollasa,* the *Sukraniti* and also other classical Sanskrit literature as well as the epigraphic sources. The author has been generally guided by the indication of the eminent scholar Mr. P.V. Kane, whose *History of Dharmsastra* (Vol. III) is undoubtedly the most valuable work on the subject.

Without fixing the dates of the Puranas it is no use to study the political thought contained in them. Regarding the dates of the Puranas it may be said that no particular date can be assigned to any Purana as each Purana deals with different topics and was compiled at different periods. Prof. Hazra is the first scholar who has made an effort to investigate the probable dates of the Puranas in his work *Studies in the Puranaic Records on Hindu Rites and Customs* in two chapters consisting of 116 pages. His study is based on the contents of the Mahapuranas and Upapurañas.

The *Markandeya Purana* which is considered to be the oldest Purana by the scholars begins with Jaimini, a pupil of Vyasa, who approaches the sage Markandeya for the solution of some doubts raised in his mind by the study of the *Mahabharata*. For want of sufficient time Markandeya does not answer the questions put to him by Jaimini but refers the latter to four wise birds living on the Vindhyas. It is noticeable that in the chapter first wherein Jaimini approaches the sage Markandeya for the solution of doubts, Jaimini praises the *Mahabharata* which shows that at the time of compilation of this Purana, the *Mahabharata* was regarded as the highest Dharmasastra. Prof. Hazra is of the opinion that "this is one of the oldest and most important of the extant Puranas".[24] Regarding the approximate date of this Purana Hazra thinks that this Purana was most probably compiled between 200 A.D. and 500 A.D.[25] The *Markandeya Purana* also states that Lady Madala was about to give instructions to Alarka regarding the duties of Ksatriyas or duties of Kings in chapter 27-35. Hazra opines that from the study of these chapters it appears that "*Markandeya Purana* (except 338, to the end) inserted some time about the third and fourth centuries A.D. It is highly probable that these chapters were added in the third century."[26]

The *Vayu Purana* is also considered to be the older than the existing Puranas. The *Mahabharata*[27] refers to a Purana proclaimed by Vayu, and the *Harivamsa Purana*[28] lays down *Vayu* as an authority. Bana,[28] the author of *Harsacharita*, says that he attended the reading of the *Vayu Purana* is his native village. Alberuni,[29] who wrote his scientific account of India, repeatedly, quotes *Vayu Purana*. Hazra[30] after a chapterwise study give the conclusion that this Purana was compiled between 200 A.D.

The *Visnu Purana* which is considered to be the most important of the extent Puranas is Vaisnava in its teaching from beginning to the end. Like other Puranas it also has several chapters on Smriti matter. Regarding the date of the Purana, there are divergent opinions among scholars. Pargiter opines "It is a late Purana composed as a single whose upon a consistent plan, and not collection of materials of Vedic times, as we fine in the *Vayu, Brahma* and *Matsya*. From its account of Buddhism had recovered its supremacy, so that it could be earlier than about the fifth century A.D., and it is Brahmanical." Farquhar thinks: "*Harivamsa* clearly cannot be dated later than A.D. 400, and the *Visnu Purana* is so like it most of its features that it is probable that it belongs to the same general date."[31] Winternitz further says, "Pargiter may be right in thinking that it cannot be earlier than the fifth century A.D. However, I do not think that it is much later." C.V. Vaidya makes an effort to prove that the *Visnu Purana* is not earlier than the ninth century A.D. on the hypothetical assumption.[32] Hazra after comparative study between the *Kurma Purana* and the *Visnu Purana* and between the *Bhagavata* and the *Visnu* and also between *Visnu Purana* and *Harivamsa* concludes that "It is highly probable that the *Visnu Purana* was written in the last quarter of the third or the first quarter of the fourth century A.D."[33] The arguments given by Hazra are more convincing. So it appears that this Purana was most probably compiled in the fourth century A.D.

The *Matsya Purana*, an encyclopaedia, dealing with different branches of knowledge is supposed to be compiled probably about the last quarter of third century A.D.[34] From the general study of this Purana we come to the conclusion that it borrows some chapters from the *Vayu Purana*. Now the question is from what original source have they borrowed (the *Vayu* and the *Matsya Puranas*) their accounts. In this regard Pargiter is of the opinion that about the last quarter of the third century A.D.. the *Matsya Purana* borrowed from the *Bhavisya* the shorter account (of the future dynasties) which ended in the downfall of the Andhras and the local kingdoms that survived them also "The *Bhavisya* account was then extended down to the time when the Gupta Kingdom has acquired the territories assigned to it, and its language was revised; that would be (say) about 320-325 A.D. The *Vayu* copied from the *Bhavisya* almost immediately and that is the version found in *Vayu*. Afterwards the language of *Bhavisya* version was revised again......about 330-335.......... This second revision was soon adopted by the *Vayu* and is the version found now in *Vayu* manuscript generally."[35] He further says that the date of the *Vayu Purana* may be placed not earlier than the middle of 3rd century A.D. and not later than 335 A.D., and most probably about the last quarter of the third century A.D.[36] Hazra opines that "this Purana was subjected to additions, and also perhaps to alterations more than once."[37] He further says that the *Matsya Purana* borrowed only those chapters from the *Vayu* which is found necessary, without caring for the lines containing references to other chapters of the *Vayu*.[38] So it appears that the date of the *Matsya Purana* also falls either in the last quarter of the third or the first quarter of the fourth century A.D. Though Hazra is of the opinion that the chapters 215-243 and 252-257 of the *Matsya Purana* dealing with specially the polity should be dated earlier than 600 A.D.[39] Thus it is difficult to suggest any probable date of composition of the *Matsya Purana* under these circumstances.

The *Visnudharmottara Purana*, an encyclopaedia and an ambitious work consists of three parts. It does not deal with only various stories and legends but also with various important subjects like Geography, Astronomy and Astrology, Cosmology and Cosmogony, Omens and Portents, manners and customs, results of actions, genealogies of kings, various kinds of gems and donations, law and politics, science of war, administration of Justice, Anatomy, medicine, horticulture, grammar, lexicography, dramaturgy, dancing, music, painting, sculpture, architecture and so on. Regarding the date of this Purana, Hazra thinks that the *Visnudharmottara Purana* cannot be earlier than 400 A.D. and not later than 500 A.D.[40] He is also of the opinion that this Purana is unmistakably influenced by Kalidas's *Raghuvamsa*.[41] Again he says that this Purana has utilised the *Ramayana* and incorporated a large number of verses from the *Mahabharata* and the

Upanisadas.[42] At certain places this Purana also refers to Manu as a Lawgiver and utilises the verses of the *Manusmrti* and *Yajnavalkya-smrti.* Buhler opines that the date of this Purana cannot be placed later than about 500A.D.[43] Hazra thinks that this work must have been compiled either in Kashmir or in the northern part of the Punjab.[44] He further says that from the evidence adduced it is highly probable that the *Visnudharmottara Purana* was composed some where in southern Kashmir. Buhler[45] and Winternitz[46] also take it to be a work written in Kashmir.

The *Garuda Purana* is also a work of encyclopedic character containing almost all subjects of the general study. This Purana specially deals with chapters on astronomy, testing of gems, omens and portents, medicine, grammar, politics, chiromancy and also details of worship of different deities etc. It is noticeable that this Purana devotes a number of chapters on death and the beyond. It also deals with doctrines on fate of the soul wafter death, *Karma* and rebirth and so on. It also summarises and borrows verses from some other works like *Yajnavalkya-smrti, Manu-smrti, Parasara-smrti* and *Brhatasamhita* etc. Regarding the date of this Purana Mr. P.V. Kane after comparing the text of the *Yajnavalkya-smrti* comes to the conclusions "the *Garuda Purana* represents a stage intermediate between Visvarupa and the Mitaksara."[47] Therefore the date of this Purana may be ascertained between 800 and 1000 A.D. Hazra concludes that "it is therefore highly probable that the extant *Garuda Purana* was compiled between 800 and 1000 A.D.[48] Which seems to be correct one.

The *Agni Purana* which is widely known as the Mahapurana is an encyclopaedia in miniature. It claims to be an epitome of all branches of knowledge. The knowledge is divided into two sections—*Para* and *Apara*. The *Para* knowledge is that through which this supreme Brahma is attained and *apara* knowledge consists of four Vedas (the *Rik,* the *Yajur,* the same and the *Atharvan*) their six-fold limbs, *Abhidhana* (lexicography) *Mimamsa*

Dharmasastra, Purana, Nyaya, Vaidaka, Gandharva, Dhanur-Veda and *Arthasastra*.[49] The last chapter of this Purana contains the list of the topics narrated in the preceding chapters. The number of these topics is fifty. This Purana also lays down that it has indebtedness to the *Ramayana*, the *Mahabharata* and the *Harvamsa Purana*. From the study of the first chapter of this Purana it is obvious that the compiler had mind to make it an encyclopaedia. The chapters which deal with different branches of knowledge and belong to the present Agni Purana lead us to think that they have been borrowed from the different sources like the *Ramayana*, the *Mahabharata*, the *Amarkosa*, the *Narada-smrti*, the *Visnu Purana*, the *Harivamsa Purana*, the *Vayu*, the *Matsya* and the *Visnudharmottara* Puranas. Sri P.V. Kane after comparing the text of the Vyuahara section of the *Yajnavalkya-smrti* and those are found in the *Agni Purana* (Chapters 253-258) with those used by commentators Visvarupa and Vijanesvara, come to the conclusion that "the Yajnavalkya preserved in the *Agni Purana* is intermediate between the text of *Yaj*. Current somewhat later, i.e. about 900 A.D.[50] Sri H.P. Shastri is of the opinion that this Purana was compiled between 800-900 A.D. Prof. Hazra thinks that the present *Agni Purana* was compiled some time during the ninth century A.D. He further says that it is difficult to say where the present *Agni Purana* was first compiled.[52] H.P. Shastri thinks that it was compiled in Bengal or Bihar.[53] Hazra says that it originated in the Eastern Orissa or in the Eastern Bengal[54] (most probably in the latter).

Portions Containing Governance Puranas

The exclusively ideal view of Governance is found in the rajadharma sections of the Puranas. The Puranas containing these sections are *Agni*,[55] *Matsya*,[56] *Visnudharmottara*,[57] *Padma*,[58] *Kalika*,[59] *Brahaddharma*[60] and *Nilamata*.[61] A more general treatment is to be found in the Nitisara section of the *Garuda Purana*[62] attributed to Brhaspati and Saunaka, Episodes like those of Balibandha,[63] Vena[64] and Prahlada[65] also embody certain precepts of polity. Short exhortations as that delivered to her son Alarka by queen Madalasa[66] again take an ideal view of polity as traditionally upheld, while the cosmological and cosmogenic accounts furnish the basis for these traditional views of polity. The factual view of polity on the other hand stands revealed in the legends of the traditional history section of the Puranas. Thus in spite of the Purana areas advocacy of the caste system, which the political institutions stand for, these portions still preserve the instances of the frequent change of caste that occurred in former ages.[67] Similarly the highly appreciated principle of conjugal chastity as expounded in Savitri-Satyavan and other episodes of the Puranas could not conceal the hard fact of Draupadi's five husbands, which was, however, in accordance with the old set-up of the accepted values of primitive Indian society where the bride was provided not only to the husband but to the *Kula*—a law which the Sutrakaras denounce.[68]

But factuality is not the only political property of this section. Some cases and incidents of this account also furnish the basis of some well known traditional maxims of polity and have become common illustrations of the treatise-writers. Thus the cases of Nahusa, Pandu and Vrisnis etc. are frequently quoted by writers like Kautilya, Kamandaka and Manu to show the evils of Avinaya, hating, gambling and drinking. Ambrisa and Nabhaga etc. have become ideal kings of legendary history worthy of imitation by the royal aspirants desiring success.[69] These and other side-lights of the traditional history accounts of the Puranas would clarify to a large extent the socio-political background of the age preceding that in which the advocated view of polity was established and recognized. These would further enable us to modify some of the current notions about the development of Indian Political thought and institutions.

The Originality of the Puranic Governance

There is, indeed, little in the ideal view of polity in the

Puranas which cannot be learnt from other sources of knowledge. This is what still gives some weight to the assertion of Dr. K.P. Jayaswal that "the Puranas have no originality. The Puranas merely copy some chapters from some well known authors e.g. *Agni Purana* borrows from an author called Puskara."[70] But the assertion is too sweeping and we do not agree with the statement in its entirety for the following reasons. Firstly the criticism takes into account only the rajadharma sections of the Puranas, ignoring the polity of the episodes, traditional history and cosmology. Secondly the similarity of the ideas expressed at one place with the ideas expressed at several other places does not deprive them of a claim to originality if those ideas have become a matter of tradition like the notes and explanation of the words in the dictionaries and encyclopaedias. In the case of ideas which have already become common-place a thinker is not to be charged for copying some writer or another. The way of presentation and the distinctive context in which it is put instills even his similar matters a welcome originality of approach. Thirdly we fail to understand as to how Puskara is a well-known author. Thus Kautilya does not mention him among his predecessors, nor do Kamandaka and Sukra. The *Apastamba Dharmasutra*,[71] refers to an author named Puskarasadi but we cannot be sure of the identity of the two. Puskara of the Puranas is moreover, a legendary personality as he is said to be the son of the water god Varuna.[72] The sections on Rajadharma have no doubt a secondary importance but that is only in view of their stereotyped reproduction of the traditionally ideal view of polity and not in view of their copying the works of some well-known authors. The *Nitisara* section of the *Garuda Purana*, however, attributes its matter to Brhaspati and Saunaka[73] the former of whom is no doubt a well-known author of polity but the injunctions are too general to have an exclusive bearing on policy or stand a comparison with the fragmentary views of Brhaspati surviving here and these in quotations gathered together by Dr. Aiyanger in the name of *Brhaspati-smrti*. *Saunakiya Nitisara* on the other hand is nothing but a reproduction of the tradition prevalent over generations traceable ultimately to Visnu.[74] Should we for this reason deny the claim of originality to the Puranas. If so we should deny the originality of all other sources of Indian polity as according to Santiparvan[75] and *Kamasutra*[76], the *Arthasastra* or the science of polity is a tradition extracted fro a general compendium of one thousand chapters on Dandaniti composed by Brahma and transmitted through generation. It is hardly of any avail to prolong the discussion. Suffice it to say that with due recognition of the fact that there is very little in the polity of rajadharma sections of the Puranas which cannot be found in any other sources of Indian polity, we deny the other implications of the statement of Dr. Jayaswal.

As to the originality of the polity emerging from the other sections of the Puranas one should notice the fact that besides the practical instances of certain well-known precepts of ancient Indian polity and the survival of some primitive practices forbidden by laws of the orthodox socio-political set-up, there is some thing even in the ideal view of the polity enunciated through the legends and episodes which may claim some amount of originality Episodes like those of Balibandha, fight of Indra and Vrtrasura and the cheating of Jarasandha by Krisna Arjuna and Bhim afford philosophical justification of the observance of the virtues of *dana* and chivalry even at the cost of ones kingdom and life. Thus Vrtrasura, when he is confronted with Indra equipped with his Vajra, says—"By this your Vajra, O Sakra! which is, indeed, sharpened by the lustre of Hari and the penance of Dadhici you should conquer your enemies being duly instigated by Visnu for wherever is Visnu there is victory. I also concentrate my mind on the lotus feet of Sankarsana and being thus pierced by your Vajra I shall achieve the salvation breaking all the mean fetters of this bad world." At this when Indra begin overwhelmed by his bravery and boldness declines to take up the Vajra against him, he encourages Sakra to attack him by assuring that he would not be guilty of anything by his act. In matters of valour, power, birth and death man regards himself as the cause only in delusion to the utter ignorance of that Absolute who makes all of us to dance like he puppets controlled by threads. Man, as a matter of fact, stands nowhere. It is He who creates out of Himself and destroys to assimilate within Himself.[77]

Similarly Bali even after being told of the intentions of Vamana by his Guru declines to break his promise on similar fatalistic grounds.[78] Now although chivarly is a theme of the *Rajadharma* of the Smrtis like that of Manu also it has not been recommended in utter disregard of the expedients. Even Manu asks one who is threatened by great dangers on all sides to save himself by the application of the four expedients either conjointly or separately and not by a suicidal fight for spiritual welfare.[79] But here the Puranas seem to implicitly prescribed the standards of individual morality even for the kings and the warriors as against the concession of expedience granted to them by the *Arthasastra* and Smrtis.

As to the originality of the cosmological and cosmogonic sections of the Puranas the above discussion would suffice. What we need to notice here is the fact that these sections afford materials not only for the inference of the fundamental postulates of the Puranic polity but also of the ancient Indian polity as a whole. In this way we see that the order of importance of the matter going under the name of puranaic polity varies considerably with reference to its context.

Authorship of the Puranic Governance

All the Puranas are traditionally attributed to Vyasa and it is Suta who recites them on his behalf. But strangely enough there are hardly any accounts in the Puranas which can be ascribed directly either to Vyasa or Suta for almost all of them are put in the mouth of other personages. There are a number of narrators whose speeches are merely reported by Suta and which Vyasa is reputed to have compiled together. Many of the narratives are old and many are comparatively new inserted from time to time in the long course of centuries in, which the Puranas assumed their present form. Long after their being first reduced to writing the process of adding new legends besides recasting the old ones continued with the result that the informations of various kind though pooled by innumerable unknown hands have acquired some sort of general unity.

The *rajadharma* sections of the Puranas, as said above, are works attributed to various authors. It appears, however, that the sections are not the actual works of these authors but compilation of the ideas traditionally ascribed to them. Thus the section of both *Agni* and *Visnudharmottara* are ascribed to the same author Puskara but the account in the latter is more elaborate than the former showing the hands of different persons in the process of compilation. The interlocutor of Puskara at both the places is Rama Bharagava. There are some chapters apart from those attributed to Puskara in the *Agni Purana* ascribed to Rama Dasarathi who instructs his younger brother Laksamana in the matter of policy while he was going to kill Meghanada in Lanka.[80] Pt. Jagadish Lal Shastri see to identify the two Ramas when he writes—"It may be stated he that political thought in the *Agni Purana* (chapts. 218-225; 227, 322-35) is put in the mouth of Puskara who is describing the same to Rama (cf. Chapters. 223, 136, pp. 44 of the app.) and it is no wonder that Rama hands down his traditional heritage of polity to his closer brother Laksamana bent upon slaying the demon foe."[81] But Rama the interlocutor of Puskara is a Brahman as he is repeatedly addressed as *dvija*, Bhragava and so on during the discourse and evidently these addresses could not be applied to Rama the elder brother of Laksamana. While thus there can be no link between the two accounts of the *Agni Purana* the two have, nevertheless, several topics in common, as they both are traditional accounts. But while that of Puskara is simple and more comprehensive that of Rama Dasarathi is given to tiresome classification and technical terms which coupled with its shortness only breeds ambiguity. A comparison of the sections of *Agni* and *Visnudharmottara* shows, on the other hand, that besides the essential unity of the two the account of *Visnudharmottara* is more comprehensive.

Manu is probably the earliest legislator known from the other sources of Indian polity but in the *Matsya Purana* even Manu is shown as receiving instructions in *rajadharma* from Visnu in His fish incarnation.[82] But all these claims of originality in terms of authorship reaching back to divine beings are rendered more pretences by the close agreement of the sections of the *Matsya* with those of *Agni* and *Visnudharmottara*.[83] What appears to be the fact of the case is that like the list of the kings 'Vansanucarita' there was evolved later on a fund of traditional polity which was included in the contents of the above Puranas. The *Garuda Purana* polity, if it is polity at all (in view of its *Subhasita* nature) is even later for such type of independent works in the classical Sanskrit are evolved late in the time of Bhartihari and Canakya of the *Rajanitisastra*. It is important to notice that the *Brhaspati Samhita* of the *Garuda Purana* is entirely identical with the *Rajanitisastra* of Canakya.[84] The rajadharma sections of the Puranas, however, are not the works of inspired authors like Kautilya. They are merely a compilation of the traditional knowledge of polity. Although Kautilya also asserts that his treatise is a summary of the works of previous Acaryas[85] still he pronounces his bold disagreement from the views of some of them after station his reasons duly. The Puranakaras, on he other hands, summarize the traditional polity in order to perpetuate its existence besides conveying it to the common people. This is why the treatment of polity in these sections has become more general and less exhaustive than that of the *Arthasastra* treatises. It is not necessary, therefore, that all the contents of these sections should correspond to the age of their finalization. These are, nevertheless, late in as much as they include even the final phase of the development of the ancient Indian traditional polity.

With the polity contained in the historical and cosmological accounts the case is different. Enunciation of the polity is not there the chief object but only an occasional point in the context. These accounts preserve though heavily overlaid by myths and legends, the fundamental premises and assumptions upon which Hindu culture is based and no one whether he is writer on polity or some other subject could question the validity of any of these age worn assumptions much like the poet who can never alter an accepted poetical truth. These, therefore, reflect the mentality of ancient Indians the motive force of their culture. Now as the Puranakars also believed in them they too had no inclination to alter any of these assumptions and basic truths, the preservation of which, as sacred heritage, they regarded as their privilege. This is why wherever these sections occur they agree remarkably well with each other. Like the historical accounts of the Puranas they are the earliest kernel of the Purana class of works and hence the antiquity of the political ideas contained in them may go back to an equally high antiquity.

Date of Puranic Governance

Except for the Rajadharma sections of certain late Puranas of encyclopaedic nature there is no polity in the Puranas, which can be treated as an entirely separate and unconnected accretion to be dated independently of the Puranas. Some of the precepts of the Puranic Governance are so inextricably mixed up with the philosophical and legendary texture of the Puranas that they appear to have been born and developed with original stuff with which the Puranas were formed. To date the Puranic Governance, therefore, means date the Puranas themselves. But that in itself is a big task which neither the space nor the canvass of the subject at our disposal permits. As many of the learned authors have already endeavoured to date the Puranas we may tentatively accept the generally recognized dates. We should, however, point out that we look upon the Puranas as a class of literature and the expression; Puranic Governance or 'polity in the Puranas' signifies Governance as found in it. The dates which are propounded in view of certain specific sections or the parts of the Puranas, therefore, will to suit our purpose and we shall have to explain the views that may happen to deny in any ways the existence of polity earlier than a certain date before which the Puranas existed in any form. This is to say that whatever the form of the Puranas before their present reaction and whatever the date of those forms we are not prepared to accept that they had no relation, however, remote with polity and political theory in any of their forms or at any particular date. The reasons behind this assertion is the fact that the *gathas, narasansis* and *akhyanas* which formed the basis of the Purana class of literature had a bearing usually on the character and exploits of kings and Princes and not of common men. Thus the Urvasi Pururavas Akhyan of the *Rigvada* adopted by the Puranas is about a king and celestial damsel.[86] Yama samvada of the *Rigvada* likewise, concerns one who rules over the world and rewards and punishes men in accordance with their good and bad deed after death. Similarly the legend of flood occurring in the *Satapatha Brahmana* and the Puranas centres round Manu again a royal personage.[87] Harishcandra who figures as an illustrious king in the Puranas is the hero of the *Aitareya Brahmana* story.[88] As the Puranas were recited in great sacrifices like Asvamedha and Rajasuya by Adhvaryu priest they might have embodies some precepts of polity tacit or express from the very beginning.

If polity be regarded primarily as one of the subjects of the Smrtis and Dharmasatra the following remark of Dr. Hazra controverting the view of Pargiter that the Smrti material began to be incorporated in the Puranas from the time of Apastamba may mean that polity could not have any relation with the Puranas from which Apastamba had quoted much less from those forms in which the Puranas existed earlier than Apastamba. "We should not like Mr. Pargiter venture" says Dr. Hazra "to infer that the authors of the Puranas had begun to introduce Smrti matter in the Puranas in the time of Apastamba."[89] But this remark of Dr. Hazra is not very sound instead of giving reasons for his disagreement he hazards the conjecture that "the stanzas quoted by Apastamba in the name of the Puranas might have possibly been *Gathas* which were current among the people in ancient times and received admission in due course into the Puranas".[90] It is curious to notice that elsewhere on the basis of a passage in some of the Puranas the same learned scholar regards *Gatha* along with *Akhyanas, Upakhyanas* and *Kalpajotis*[91] as being utilised by Vyas in compiling the original Puranas. Now it may be asked as to what is there to show that the passages even if they were quoted from a *Gatha* current among the people in the time to Apastamba were not a part of the Puranas in their original form? What is the evidence to warrant the conclusion that the particular *Gatha* from which Apastamba has quoted was a late inclusion in the body of the puranas. That the *Gathas* had concern with the *Smrti* matter is moreover, testified by the same author.[92] One of them is referred to in the *Manusmrti* as sung by Vayu,[93] several others of this nature are quoted in the *Mahabharata* while still others are quoted in the Puranas like *Markandeya*.[94] The antiquity of the *Gathas* is very high. Winternitz testifies to the fact that as early as the time of Buddha they along with *Akhyana, Itihasa* and. *Purana* formed the "literary public property which was drawn upon by the Buddhists and the Jains as well as by the epic poets."[95] The same is also probably hinted at when Apastamba lays down that the rest (of the laws and customs) which could not be included within the Sutras may be consulted from women of all castes according to some.[96] Now the Vedas were forbidden to the women and the only channel through which this knowledge of authority could reach was the same 'literary public property' which "the professional story-tellers (*aithihasikas* and *Pauranikas*) of the ancient times"[97] impressed upon them orally. It is, as such, impossible to hold that the Puranas from which Apastamba has quoted or which were current in his time were barren of the Smrti contents and were strictly *Pancalaksana*. How could (without the Puranas being full of *Smrti* and *Arthasastra* contents) the knowledge *(vidya)* possessed by women and Sudras be the limit *(Mistha)* and the Atharvavedic suppliment, which is dancing, music and other branches of *Arthasastra*—an Upveda of *Athrvaveda*, according to the professedly traditional classification of Madhusudhana Sarasvati?

We cannot, therefore, reject the natural conclusion that the Smrti contents came in the Puranas in the time of Apastamba of earlier since he has quoted them as an authority in the matters of Dharma by preferring a mere conjecture to it, as Hazra has done. Even the cosmological accounts of the Puranas to which Dr. Hazra[98] himself assigns a very high antiquity are not quite devoid of Smrti contents thought he latter are scattered and not presented systematically as a code of injudicious in the proper Smrti style. Cosmological view of a country in ancient times determined the purpose of man's existence in relation to the universe laying thereby the basic for the justification of that country's accepted course of conduct civil, social and religious. If the principles of polity could have been deduced out of the mathematical equations in Pythagorean Greece[99] it is not hard to find, we think, the gear of the professed view of the civil course of conduct along with its governing body—the state as cherished by the Puranakara in the cosmological accounts of the Puranas. Let us take for example the relation between the two sexes as a criterion to clarify this situation.

According to the *Mahabharat* it is Svetaketu probably the person of the same name mentioned in the *Chandogya Upanisad* and *Kamasutra,* who effected a change in the sexual life of the community of formulating new laws insisting on conjugal chastity by virtue of his Rsihood. It is expressly stated in the *Mahabharata*[100] and corroborated duly by the traditional history accounts of the Puranas that before the promulgation of the law of conjugal chastity the sexual life of the community-wise very lax. Like the animal world, it is said, the human community led a free life and a young woman was approachable by any one belonging to the same Varna.[101] The varnas referred to in this context were perhaps sexually exclusive artificial groups or communities formed on the pattern of animal life. This we, indeed a unique pattern of life which the school of Svetaketu is said to have opposed. The rules attributed to Svetaketu in the *Mahabharata* are systematically enunciated in the Dharmasutras.[102] As the Puranas along with the *Gathas, Upakhyanas* and *akhyanas* were the 'literary public property' of the age transmitted by Puranikas and Aithihasikas orally, they also contributed to this cause and afforded justification for conjugal chastity by contending that Prajapati Himself set to live strictly chaste conjugal life was enjoined upon man by nature in the *krta* age in which couples were set by birth.[103] Varnas were interpreted in the light of the division of labour and were regarded as formulated by the Creator Himself. In this way the cosmological accounts succeeded in creating a feeling among the masses that the course of life as upheld in the Puranas and the Sutras is sanctified by its immemorially antiquity. Since the cosmological grounds invented by the Puranakaras to convince the masses against the ancient practices were strong arguments for the common men, the Puranas became an authority in this regard to the Dharmasutras, which did not hesitate to quote the Pauranic explanations of the universe for supporting their legal contentions.

Such a motive of the Sutrakaras is clear from the nature of the lines quoted by Apastamba in the name of *Bhavisyat Purana*. "They (the ancestors) live in the heaven until the next destruction of the created things. At the new creation (of the world) they become the seed. That has been declared in the *Bhavisyat Purana*."[104] A parallel idea is found in some of the present Puranas. Thus it is said that when everything will be consumed by the fire of destruction at the end of the Kalpa those who could not reach *tapoloka* from the *Apnaloka* will be born again in the next creation as the seed of the previous one. They are preserved, as a matter of fact, as the seed of the coming creation.[105] This idea of *Bhavisyat Purana,* now no more extent but surviving in some form in the present Puranas, has been quoted by Apastamba to support the code of righteous conduct in this world to be benefited in the next for the very next sutra declares—"Now Prajapati says—those dwell with us who fulfil the following (duties): they study of the three Vedas, the Studentship, the procreation of children, faith, religious austerities, sacrifices and giving of the gifts. He who praises other (duties) become dust and peristhes."[106]

Since the term Purana has been referred to in the sense of a class of literature in the *Atharaveda,* Brahmanas, Upanisads, *Grhya, Srauta* and *Dharma Sutras, Arthasastra* of Kautilya, and the epics, the beginnings of this class of literature cannot be placed later than the sixth century B.C. if not earlier.[107] That they have assumed some concrete form in about 400 B.C. may be inferred from the recommendation of the recital of the Puranas to the eking by the *Arthasastra* of Kautilya,[108] acquaintance of Megasthenese with 'a part at least' of a Puranic cosmology and with a Puranic description of the upper and lower world[109] and from the fact that Apastamba quotes one of the Puranas by name. They, in their concrete literary forms, may be as old or perhaps earlier than the *Mahabharata* and the *Manusmrti.*[110]

As to the Rajadharma sections of the Puranas we may tentatively accept the dates suggested for those sections in the *Matsya* and *Agni Purana* by Hazra. The date of Rajadharma section of the *Matsya Purana* has been placed between 650-1000 A.D.[111] by him. For those of *Agni* he assign in agreement with Kane a date in the 9th century A.D.[112] The Nitisara section of the *Garuda Purana* may also be placed in the 10th cent. A.D. a date to which Hazra assigns this Purana.[113]

The date of the *Nilamata Purana* in which a section has been devoted to Rajadharma has been assessed by its editor Mr. Ram Lal Manjji Lal as some time after the 6th or 7th century A.D.[114] As the *Visnudharmottara Purana* barrows from *Matsya* and as the Rajadharma sections of the *Visnudha* are more elaborate and in general agrement with those of *Matsya* its date should be placed not far from 1000 A.D. latest by which Rajadharma section of the *Matsya* was added.[115] A clue to the date of the Brhadharma Purana in which a section of Rajadharma also occurs is provided by its reference to *Brahnardiya Purana* which, according to Hazra, had acquired the name and form of *Brhannaradiya* as against Nardiya not later that 950 A.D.[116] The sectional polity of the *Brahaddharma Purana* may thus be generally referred to the later half of the 10th century.

REFERENCES

1. *Visnu Purana*, London, 1864.
2. (a) *The Puranic Text of the Dynasties of the Kali Age*, Oxford, 1913.
   (b) *Ancient Indian Historical Tradition*, Oxford, 1922.
3. Madras, 1935
4. Madras, 1933.
5. *Indian Review*, 1935, pp. 365-368.
6. Dacca, 1940.
7. Calcutta, 1958.
8. Varanasi, 1963.
9. Allahabad, 1961.
10. Prakasana Sakha Suchana Vibhaga, Uttar Pradesh, 1960.
11. Lucknow, 1966.
12. Calcutta, 1958.
13. Varanasi, 1963.
14. *Hindu Polity*, Bangalore, 1943.
15. *Aspects of Ancient Indian Polity*, 1921.

16. *The Matsya Purana—A Study,* 1935.
17. *Theory and Government in Ancient India,* Allahabad, 1927.
18. *History of Dharmasastra,* Vol. III, Poona, 1930.
19. *Development of HIndu Polity and Political Theories,* Calcutta, 1927 and 1938.
20. *State and Government in Ancient India,* Delhi, 1958.
21. *A History of Indian Political Ideas,* Oxford, 1959.
22. *Aspects of Political Ideas and Institutions in Ancient India,* Delhi, 1959.
23. *Studies in Hindu Political Thought and its Metaphysical Foundations,* Delhi 1959.
24. *Studies in Epics and Puranas of India,* Bombay, 1955.
25. *Political Thought in the Puranas,* Lahore, 1944.
26. *Studies in the Puranic Records on Hindu Rites and Customs,* p. 8.
27. *Ibid.,* p. 10, 12.
28. *Ibid.,* p. 12.
29. *Mbh.* III, 191-16.
30. 1, 7, 13, & 25.
31. *Harsacharita,* Chapt. III.
32. Sachau, E.C. *Alberuni's India in two volumes,* London, pp. 41-42, 130 and 168.
33. *Puranic Records on Hindu Rites and Customs,* p. 15-16.
34. Pargiter, F.E. AITH, p. 80.
35. Farquhar, Pit; p. 143.
36. Winternitz, *A History of Indian Literature,* Vol. I, p. 545 foot note 2.
37. *History of Mediaeval India,* Vol. I, p. 350.
38. *Studies in the Puranic Records on Hindu Rites and Customs,* p. 24.
39. Pargiter, *Dynasties of the Kali Age,* Introduction, p. XIII, *Ibid.,* p. XIII.
40. *Studies in the Puranic Records on Hindu Rites and Customs,* p. 51, *Ibid.,* p. 30.
41. *Studies in the Puranic Records on Hindu Rites and Customs,* p. 51.
42. *Studies in the Upapuranas,* p. 212.
43. *Ibid.,* p. 206.
44. *Ibid.,* p. 197.

45. *Ind. Ant.* XIX, 1990, p. 408.
46. *Studies in the Upapuranas,* p. 114.
47. *Ibid.,* p. 216.
48. *Ind. Ant.* XIX, 1890, p. 383.
49. *HDS.,* Vol. I, p. 175.
50. AP. I. 12, 1, 3, 271. 17-18.
51. AP. I. 15-16.
52. *HDS,* Vol. I, p. 172
53. *A Descriptive Catalogue of Sanskrit Manuscripts,* Vol. V, Preface, *Pali Studies in the Puranic Records on Hindu Rites and Customs.*
54. *A Descriptive Catalogue of Sanskrit Manusctipts,* Vol. V, Preface, pp. CXLVI.
55. *Our Heritage,* Vol. I. Pt. I, pp. 232-233.
56. Chapts. 218-235; 227; 233-235.
57. Chapts. 215-243.
58. Chapts. II. 2-7; 18; 21; 24-26; 28; 61-63; 66-72; 145-151; 163-177.
59. Vol. III. Chapts. ccvi-ccxxix (ed. Mahadeva Cimanji Apte) Vide Beni Prasad: *The State in Ancient India,* p. 337.
60. Chapts, 87.
    Pt. II. 3.
    Verses 970-1011.
    (All these sections have been collected together and published in original by Jagdish Lal Sastri in his 'Political Thought in the Puranas' excepts only those of *Padma, Brhaddharma* and NTI amata).
61. *Garuda,* chapts, 108-115. Vide Jagdish Lal Sastri: *op.cit.,* p. 2;6.
62. *Bhag.* Viii, 18-23. See also Puranic Index for reference in other Puranas.
63. *Ibid.,* IV. 13-18 Vide Puranic Index.
64. *Visnu.* II. 19.
65. *Markandeya.* 24., Vide Jagdish Lal Sastri, *op.cit.,* p. 26.
66. *Gargah Sanbhratah Kavya Ksatropeti dvi jatayah. Matsya,* 49.41; 50.4-5 of Vayu II. 37.242.
67. *Kulaya hi stri Pradiyatityupadisanti tadindriya daurbalyadvipratipannam. Ap. D.K.* 27. 3-4.
68. Kautilya. I. 6. 20.
69. Kamandaka. I. 16;56;58;60;59. Vii. 51-54-IX. 12;52;54;62;67;

XI. 7-10; 17; 21-22; 31. XII. 7.XV. 50-53;63-64.
XVII. 57. XViii. 20-23;41;;44;56;58;59;71.

70. *Hindu Polity*, pp. 7.
71. *Suddha bhiksa bhoktavyaikakunikau kanvakutsau puskarasadi. Ap. DH.* S.I. 10.28.1.
72. *Adau eva mahabhaga yadogans nrpatmaja. Visnudh.* 11. 4. 2.
73. *Nitisaram surendraya ayamucuh brahaspatih.*
74. *Sarvajno yena candro bhuddaityan hatvapnuyaddivam. Garuda* I. 108-10.
75. *Saunakiyam nitisaram visnuh sarva vratani ca Kathayamasa vai pruvamtatra susruva Sanskarah.*
76. *Sankaradasrnodvyasah vyasadasmabhirva ca. Garuda.* I. 115. 83. Santi. 53.
77. *Kamasutra.* I. 5-8.
78. *Bhag.* VI.II 21-22; 12.7-17.
79. *Bhag.* VIII. 20.2-13;22.2-11.
80. *Manu.* VII. 214.
81. *Kamastu ravanam htva hyayodhyam praptvan dvijah.*
82. *Ramoktanityendrajitam hatva laksmanah pura. Agni.* 142-73.
83. Jagdish Lal Shastri: *Political Thought in the Puranas*, pp. 26.
84. *Arth.* trans. Shamasastri. pp. 6, 32. 71, 235, 243, 327.
85. *Manuruvaca*

    Rajno bhisiktamatrasya kim nu krityatamam bhyaveta. Matsya. 215.1
86. L. Sternbach: *The Canakya-Rajaniti Sastra and Brhaspati Samhita of the.*
87. *Garuda Purana.* A short XXXVII, pp. 58-110.
88. L. Sternbach: *Canakya a Aphorism in the Puranas.*

    Puranam VI. 1. pp. 113-46.
89. *Arth.* Shamasastr. 1.1.
90. *R.V.*X. 95, *Bhag.* IX, 14.15.49, *Vayu* 91-1-52; *Visnu* IV 6.34-93.
91. *Rv.* X.; *Bhag* VI 6.40, VIII, 13.9. *Brahmanda* III. 59. 38.
92. *Visnu* III. 22.
93. *Satpath.* IV 1.5.

    Ait. Brahmana. VII. 14.2.
94. *Sankhyayan Srautasastra* XV. 17.
95. *Bhag.* IX. 7.7.27; 16. 31.
96. *Matsya.* 12.33. *Visnu* IV. 325.

97. *Vayu*. 88. 117-9. *Bhag*. X. 72.21.
98. *Brahmanda* III. 63. 115, 66.66. *Vayu*. 91.94.
99. Hazra: *Puranas in the History of Smritis*. IC. Vol. I, p. 588.
100. Hazra: *Puranic Records on Hindu Rties and Customs*. pp. *Akhyanaisca upakhyanain gathbhih kalpajoktibhih purana samhitam cakre puranarthavisaradha*. *Visnu*. III. 6.16. Vayu 60.21.
101. Hazra, *Puranic Record*. pp. 4-5.
102. *Ibid*. p. 5 cf. I.C. Vol. I. p. 588.
103. *Atragatha Vayugita Kirtayaanti puravidah*.
104. *Yath bijam na vapsyama punsa paraparigrahe*. *Manu*. IX 42.
105. *Markanadeya*. 29. 31-33.
106. Winternitz: *History of Indian Literature*. Vol. I, pp. 323-314.
107. *Stribhyah Sarvavarnebhyasca dharmasesan prtiyadityeke*. Ap. II. 2.29.
108. *Ibid*., pp. 313-314.
109. Hazra: *Puranic Rites*. pp.
110. Barker; *Greek Political Theory*. pp. 48.
111. Adlparva. Ch. 128.
112. *Ma tat kopamakarsistvamesa dharmah sanatanah*
anavrta him sarvseam varnanamangana bhuvi
Yatha gavasthita putra sve sve varne tatha prajah
tathaiva ca kutumbesu na pramadyanti karhici.
adiparva. 128. 40-41.
113. *Sagaotrasthaniyam na parebhyah samcaksita*. *Kulya hi stri pradyatai tyupsdissanti*. *Tadindriya daurbh Iyadripratipannam*. *pradyataityuam na parebhyah samacaksita*. *Kulaya hi stri Tamsadrasayo varesu na jayante niyamatikramat*. *Srutarsayasea bhavanti*
kechitkarmaphalasesena punsh samhave. *Yath Svetaketuh*.
Ap. II. 10.27. 2-4. I 2.5.4-6.
Brahmanda. 1. 7.153;.51-52. *Markandeya* (bib.Ind.) 49. 75.21.
Ap. Dh. II. 9.24.5-6.
Vayu I. 8.29.24.
Ap. Dh.II. 9.24. 7.8.
Dikshitar, *Puranas—A study IHQ*, Vol. VIII. pp. 747-767.
R.C. Majumdar, *Origin and Character of the Purana literature*.' *Orientalia* III. (A.S.I. Commemoration Vol). p. 7-30.
S.P. Gyani, Date of the Puranas, NAI, Vol. V. p. 131-5 also
115. *Puranam* Vol. I, p. 213-219.
Artha. I 5.36.
Jackson. *BRRAS Centenary Memorial Vol*. p. 72.

Macdonell, *A History of Sanskrit Literature*, p. 299.
R.C. Hazra, *Puranic Recordson Hindu Rites and Customs*. p. 177, 26-51.
P.V. Kane, *History of Dharmashastras*, Vol. I, p. 172.

116. Hazra, *op. cit.*, p. 185, 134-140.
Hazra, *loc.cit.*, p. 144.

2

Nature of Puranic State

The political thinkers of ancient India have stressed the necessity of the State for the efficient protection of human life and for the better realization of its higher ideals, but unfortunately they have not discussed the origin of the State. It is certain that from earliest time the State was in existence but how and when the State came into existence is not confirmed from any source. The old political thinkers like Manu, Bhisma and Kautilya have established some principles about the origin of Kingship. The same principles can also be accepted for the origin of State because after the origin of Kingship the society was divided into two groups. The King and the subjects. From that period it may be said that the State came into existence. Though western political thinkers have laid down four theories about the origin of the State. They are: *(i)* the theory of Divine origin, *(ii)* the Social Contract theory, *(iii)* the Force theory, and *(iv)* the Evolutionary theory.

We have occasional speculations about the origin of State in the *Mahabharata* and the *Arthasastra*. The *Mahabharata* says that for a long time after creation of society, there prevailed a golden age. The people were enjoying a kind of harmonious life, free from cares and anxieties. There was not government to see that the laws of nature were respected and followed. The Santiparva of the *Mahabharata* further lays down that society flourished without the Raja or the Danda for a long time, but this harmonious life could not exist for long and somehow there was a moral degeneration. Then the law of forest began to begin to prevail and the *Matsyanyaya* came into existence. Then Gods became alarmed and decided to remedy the situation. When the people approaches Brahmadeva, the chief god, he composed a comprehensive code and created an asexual son named Viraja[1] and appointed him king and the people agreed to obey his orders. Elsewhere, the Santiparva, further, lays down that when the people were tired of the *Matsyanyaya,* they assembled together and entered into a mutual contract, he who becomes harsh in speech, or violent in temper, he who seduces or abducts other people's wives or robs the wealth that belongs to others, should be cast off by us. For inspiring confidence among all classes of the people, they made such a compact and lived for some time. We are, however, told that people still continued to be unhappy, probably because there was no king or government to force the contract. They then approached the Creator with a request to appoint a king. The Creator asked Manu to become the King. Manu did not assent to the proposal and said: "I fear all sinful acts. To govern a kingdom is difficult, especially among people who are always false and deceitful in their behaviour." The people satisfied his objections and said to him: "Do not fear? The sins that men commit will touch those only that commits them. For the increase of thy treasury we will give the fiftieth part of our animals and precious metals and a tenth part of our grain......."[2] Likewise Kautilya also discusses the problem of the origin of the State incidentally during a discussion of spies among themselves. One party says that the government came into existence to counteract the law of the forest that prevailed in society. People there suffering from anarchy therefore, they elected Manu as their king and agreed to pay him one sixth of the grains grown and one-tenth of merchandise as sovereign dues.[3] Thus it appears that Kautilya does not make any reference to any Golden age.

Like the *Mahabharata* and the *Arthasastra,* the Puranic literature also has some speculations about the origin of the State and references have also been made to the State of Nature. The Puranic text lays down that there was time when the people were enjoying a kind of harmonious life, free form cares, anxieties and greed which shows that in the early stage of nature the institution of the state did not exist. The Puranas further inform us that this harmonious life could not continue for long and was destroyed by the people who discovered the art of cultivation and they came into mutual strife. They, therefore, approached Manu who produced the first two Kings—Priyavrata and Uttanapada form his wife Satarupa. From the study of the above-mentioned view of ancient treatises we can compare ancient theories of the state with the similar theories of the west propounded by Hobbes and Locke in the later period. It is interesting to note that the political thinkers of ancient India have laid down that before the origin of the State there was a kind of harmonious life but owing to infatuation and delusion the same could not continue for long. Therefore, the people came into mutual contract and the king and the State came into existence. The puranic literature has thrown a flood of light on this subject will be dealt with in the next chapter.

Though the political thinkers of ancient India are silent on the origin of the State yet they have accepted an account of the organs of the State. Kautilya,[5] who is styled the father of politics, was the first political thunder of ancient India who gave complete definition of the State for the first time. According to him the State consists of seven elements such as Swami, Amatya, Janapada, Kosa, Durga, Danda and Mitra. These seven limbs of the State are mentioned in the most of the texts dealing with polity.

The Puranas are no exception to it and most of our Puranas[6] have accepted above mentioned essentials of the State, (Saptanga Rajya) though some works on polity increases the number of its elements. For example, the Santiparva[7] of the *Mahabharata* in its critical edition enumerates eight limbs (Astangika Rajya) but does not specify the eighth one anywhere. Likewise, some manuscripts of the *Abhilasitarthachintamani* mention nine elements of the State and added/*pauras* and *srenis* to the seven limbs. The *Visnudharmottara Purana*[8] enumerates two new elements—*Sama* (pacification) and *Dana* (Charity) in place of *Swami* and *Amatya* respectively. Thus it is clear that the Puranic literature has accepted the traditional enumeration of the seven elements of the State.

Swami—This element of the state which means the ruler enjoying sovereignty has been regarded as an important limb and given the first place in the order of their mention. The *Matsya Purana*[9] holds that of these seven elements, the king is the root of the kingdom. Therefore, he must be protected. The same attitude has been taken by the *Agni Purana* at three different places.[10] According to this Purana the king is the central figure of an empire and is also the fountain source of all laws and authorities. Therefore, he must be protected. So the puranic literature further dilates the requisite qualities for the Swami at some length. The *Agni Purana*[11] enumerates that the king should be endowed with qualities of wisdom, fortitude, knowledge in different branches of learning, skilfulness, confidence, retentive memory, enthusiasm, eloquence, generosity, patience during bad hours, influence, purity, friendship, self-sacrifice, gratefulness, knowledge of the Vedas, character, and control of senses. It has been further stated in the same text that the king who possesses these qualities is sure to acquire a solenoid fortune. Thus it shows that our Puranic leterature requires sound qualities for being the head of the State.

The second element *Amatya* is also held as an important limb. Usually the word Amatya is translated as minister.

But it would be wrong to accept this connotation. Kautilya has clearly differentiated between these two terms. In the case of Mantrins, he lays down the limit at three of four but in the case of Amatyas he stated that their number should be depended upon the capacity to employ them.[12] We find in the post Mauriyan period that the Amatyas were more commonly known as sachivas. The inscription[13] of Rudradamana clearly mentions the terms—Matisachiva and Karmasachiva. These were a general cadre of officers from whom high functionaries were appointed both advisors and executive officers. The Puranic literature require high and sound qualifications for Amatyas as they are placed after the king in the order of their importance.

The Janapada,[14] according to the Puranas, is the third element of the state. The king is, therefore, asked by the Puranic text to protect and nurse his kingdom.[15] According to the Puranas, is the third element of the state. The king is, therefore, asked by the Puranic text to protect and nurse his kingdom.[15] According to the *Agni Purana*[16] the territory should possess abundant food, mines, minerals and grazing grounds for cattle, holy places beautiful scenes, forests, and should not depend on God for rains. It is, further, said that it should be inhabited by Sudras, Artisans, merchants and industrious peasants. Finally, the people of the kingdom should be devoted to their own king, hostile to their enemies, capable of enduring hardship and be widespread, pious and rich in cattle-wealth. The *Visnudharmottara,*[16] the *Matsya*[17] and the *Agni* Puranas[18] state that the king should live in that country which is mostly populated by Vaisyas and sudras, a few Brahmanas but many hired labourers. Thus it indicates that our Puranic literature requires mainly producing class inhabiting the State. It is noticeable that the *Agni Purana* recommends that the kingdom should be inhabited by foreigners and be ruled by a king who is neither a fool nor addicted to passions. Undoubtedly, the recommendation made by the *Agni Purana* was in practice in ancient India. The history of the period tells us that during the reign of ancient

India. The history of the period tells us that during the reign of ancient kings, foreigners came here form time to time. We are informed that Megasthenes, Fa Hien, and Hiuen Tsang came to India during the time of Chandra Gupta Maurya, Chandra Gupta II and Harsa respectively. The account which has been left by them is very valuable from historical facts about ancient India. The *Visnudharmottara*[19] and the *Agni Puranas*[20] lay down that the king who does not protect his kingdom and its inhabitants remains in hell for a long time, and even he destroys it. (kingdom) our Puranas further express that these seven elements should be mutually interdependent and helpful like and organic wheel. The *Visnudharmottara Purana*[21] further more asks the king to banish all those who create disturbances in the normal functioning of any element of the State and to kill those who are dangerous and revolting against the constituents. The same views are expressed by the *Matsya Purana*[22] and it states that the king should guard the other six components of his empire and if any one revolts against any of these constituents he should be killed immediately. The same text advises the king not to be milked and simple hearted because a liberal sovereign is always despised. Further, if he is hard and grim, the people would be against him. Therefore, it is advised that the king should be neither very mild nor very hard and the king who is both liberal and strong according to the circumstances should be prosperous in this life as well as in the next one.[23] The *Agni Purana,* further, suggests that the creater of troubles among the components of the state should be punished with severe punishment—either death or annihilation.[24]

Thus it seems that great importance was attached to the protection of the kingdom against external troubles which were common in ancient India when small and big states were troubling and fighting with each other. Unfortunately, our Puranic record does not mention the actual population of the State as Kautilya does, who is of the opinion that in the settlement of new territories the village should comprise one hundred to five hundred families and that the *Sthaniya* which is the largest unit in the Janapada should consist of eight hundred villages.[25]

The fourth element mentioned by the Puranas is Durga which should be understood in the sense of fortified capital.[26] Our *Matsya*[27] and the *Agni* Puranas[28] state six type of forts such as the Dhanua Durga, Mahi Durga, Nara Durga, Vraksha Durga, Ambu Durga and Giri Durga. Among these forts, the Giri Durga is regarded as the best one[29] and the king is advised to live with his assistants in it. The *Agni Purana*[30] informs us that the fort should be inhabited with the members of the commercial and the servile castes and of various guilds of artisans. It is suggested that the fort should be situated in a country watered by large rivers and not depending on atmospheric supply of water. The planning of the capital is discussed in detail elsewhere.[31] In short, the capital should be built at a central place and areas should be allowed the temples of the different Varnas and artisans as well as the temples of gods.[32] It is noticeable that our Puranic literature provides a long list of articles mainly consisting of king daily requirements in the time of both war and peace which are kept in the fort. The *Matsya Purana,*[33] particularly, lays down chapters consisting of about 125 verses dealing with the things to be kept in the fort by the king. Probably this long list due to the consideration of defence.

The fifth component of the state in our Puranas is treasury *(Kosa)*. *The Agni Purana* repeats the old theory that the king is the root of the state and the treasury is the root of the king. Kautilya[34] lays down that without treasury it is not possible to maintain army to keep it loyal. Other ancient political thinkers,[35] too, realised the importance of this limb an included prosperous treasury among the essential constituents of the State and declared that if any deterioration is made in this limb, it would be disastrous to the State.

Danda or army is the sixth element which according to the *Arthasastra* of Kautilya,[36] consists of hereditary, hired, wild and corporation soldiers comprising infantry, chariots, elephants and cavalry. The Puranas lay down a vivid description on this component elsewhere.[37] Manu, even allowed the Brahmanas and Vaisyas but not the Sudras to hold arms in the time of emergency.[38]

The last and the seventh element of the state, according to the Puranic literature, is Mitra, which relates the relation between the sovereign state and the numerous feudatories. In other words this constituent tells us about the inter-state relations in war and peace. The *Visnudharmottara* and the *Agni* Puranas[39] have given a vivid description of this element. The *Matsya Purana*,[40] particularly, mentions three types of friends: (i) Hereditary (ii) The enemy's and (iii) An acquired friend arising out of necessity, but it prefers hereditary only. Kautilya and other political thinkers including the compilers of the Puranas is a unique contribution of the early Indian thought to the history the political theory. Though the great Greek political thinkers like Plato and Aristotle speculated on the origin of the state in their works Republic and Politics respectively, the definition propounded by them is not so sound and clear as has been made by early Indian thinkers.

An important contribution made by our Puranic literature in connection with the discussion of the seven components of the state is weaknesses affecting the various prakritis. According to the *Agni Purana*[41] the king may be addicted to use of harsh and cruel words, infliction of cruel punishments, spoliation of the sources of revenue, drinking, women, gambling and hunting, idleness, disinclination for all sorts of work and boastfulness.

The weaknesses of the ministers described in the Puranaic literature are more elaborate than those of the king. The ministers are required to be free from irresolution and blunder, drinking, gambling, hunting, idleness and woman. They are further required to avoid the use of harsh and cruel speaking, dissipation of treasury and boastfulness.

The *Agni Purana* states that drought, epidemics and famine are natural calamities which usually befall the country.[42] Silting of the ditch, tumbling down of its wall and battlements, rotten state of the engines and battering apparatuses, an empty arsenal and a small garrison are described as the defects of the fort by the *Agni Purana*.[43]

The treasury may be undermined by man-made calamities such as shortage of money, and not making up with daily shortage or not keeping proper account. The treasury which is situated at a distance and not capable of easy conveyance is also to be considered a weakness, according to the *Agni Purana*.[44]

In regard to the weakness of the army, our literature states that the army which is obstructed, scattered, dishonoured, insulted, existing in name only, disease-stricken, fatigued, newly recruited, arrived from a distant country, excessively thinned, repulsed, badly disappointed in its hopes, deceived, abounding in pregnant wives, or not connected with its base, recruited with false enticement and bribed by a hostile king, should be deemed as dangerous.[45] Allies overtaken by an adverse father or attacked by an enemy or indulging in impotent rage and void of all vigour and energy should also be deemed as enemy.[46] These weaknesses of the elements of the state undoubtedly destroy the kingdom and its rulers. Therefore, the king is asked to protect his state from these feebleness. It is noticeable that the weaknesses of the different limbs represented by the Puranic literature are merely the summarised statement made by Kautilya,[47] retaining the same words in most cases.

Let us now compare the constituents of the ancient Indian State with those postulated by western political thinkers. The western political thinkers have ascertained the four constituents of the State: *(i)* Territory, *(ii)* Population, *(iii)* Government, *(iv)* Sovereignty. But by scrutinizing the constituents we may conclude that basically there is no difference between the two. Whatever is termed territory by the western political thinkers has been named as Rastra by ancient Indian political thinkers and the word sovereignty stands for the king. It is interesting to note that king in the western political philosophy may also be taken for feudal lords whereas the Swami cannot. According to the ancient Indian political thinkers the Swami was the head of the State whether it was monarchical or republican. The *Amatya, Kosa, Durga* and *Bala,* the other essentials of the state, stand for the government. It is evident that the ancient Indian political thinkers have not mentioned population in this context but it does not necessarily mean that without population that state was in existence. It is self-defining that they did not attach importance to the population. The other probability is that they consider the population as an integrated part of the kingdom (Rastra). Elsewhere the Janapada refers to the Rastra. In the *Nitisara* there is a reference of population in place of Rastra that makes it clear that Rastra included both territory and population. The *Mitra* has rightly been introduced by ancient Indian political thinkers in the constituents of the state. To maintain the balance of power, in the various parts of the country, was the significant point before the kings of ancient India since the country was divided into many states and it is because of its significance that the old political thinkers of ancient India have given the same recognition to the Mitra as was given to the Amatyas and Kosa in the functioning of the state. With the facts mentioned above, it is evident that basically there was no point of controversy between western and ancient political thinkers but it was simply a question of difference of opinion which does not give birth to any grave problem to be discussed here.

As regards the relative importance of these organs of the state, the political thinkers of ancient India have regarded them as the limbs of the body politic. Manu, for example, says that body politic cannot stand if one of them is missing just as three sticks poised properly against one another will collapse, if one of them is taken away.[48]

Sukra[49] compares the seven elements of the state to the organs of the body viz., the king is the head, the ministers are the eyes, ally the ear, treasury the mouth, the army the mind, capital and rastra are hands and feet. It is emphasized by Kamandaka[50] that each of the seven elements is complementary to the others that if the state is defective even in one out of the seven elements it does not pull well. The Puranas[51] also aver that the king is the root of the Saptanga Rajya, therefore, he amongst all elements should be chiefly protected, so that he may also guard the other six elements. Further, as regards the other elements, the *Agni Purana*[52] states that each of the seven elements is complementary to the others. Thus it seems that the organic concept of the state propounded by ancient works on polity was intended to stress the importance of the other components in relation to the head of the state. It is noticeable that the Greek political thinkers Plato and Aristotle, the founder of western polities, clearly expounded the organic theory of the State.[53] Plato compares the state to the human body and says that when a finger of the body is hurt, the whole body feels pain, like wise where a member of the state is hurt, the state in general suffers. He further says that state is best in which unity exists as it does in the natural human body. Hence it may be said that the ancient conception of the state is, in character, followed by the modern theory of the state.

REFERENCES

1. *Mbh*. Santi, 59. 14-29, 88.
2. *Mbh*. Santi, 67.·17-26.
3. *Arth*. I, 13.
4. V.P. Chat. 8; VSP. B.K. I. Chapt. 6; MKP Chapt. 46; MP. Chapt. 6 & 10.
5. *Ibid*., 8.48, 49, 52, 63, 65.
6. *Arth*. VI.I.
7. *VDP* II. 65. 20-21, III, 323. II, *MP*. 220. 19. *MKP*. 24.6.
8. *AP*. 225.11..
9. 122.8.

10. II 143.
11. 220-20.
12. 225.12,233.12& 239.1
13. 238. 4-5. *Arth.* I. 9-10., 15.
14. *Select. Ins.* 1965, p. 180.1.17.
15. *VDP.* II 20-21. III. 323.II; *M.P.* 220. 19; AP. 225.11.
16. *Ap.* 239.2.
17. 239. 24-26.
18. II. 26.2
19. 21.7.2.
20. 222.1-2.
21. II. 65. 70.
22. 223. 7&225.31.
23. II. 145.4.
24. 220. 21-24, *VDP,* II 65. 22.25.
25. *MP.* 220. 20-23.
26. 225. 12 and 223. 13.
27. *Arth.* II.1.
28. Sharma, R.S., *Aspects of Political Ideas and Institution in Ancient India.*
29. *India,* 1959, p. 9.
30. 217.6-7.
31. 222, 4-5.
32. *MP.* 217, 57, *A.P.* 222.5.
33. 222. 1-2.
34. Chapt. VI.
35. *M.P.* Chapt. 217, *A.P.* 222.
36. Chapt. 217-218.
37. *Arth.* VIII. I.
38. *Mbh.* XII. 119. 16, *KNS*XIII. 33-34, *MDS,* IX, 295, *Arth.* II, 8.
39. *Manasollasa* II. 4,540., NVM. 217, 21.5.
40. IX.2.
41. Chapt. VI.
42. VIII. 348.
43. *VDP.* II. Chapt. 145. AP. Chapts, 233, 240.
44. 220. 17-18.
45. 241. 25-26.

46. *A.P.* 241, 27.
47. *Ibid;* 241.28.
48. *AP.* 241.29.
49. *Ibid;* 24130-33.
50. *Ibid;* 241.34.
51. *Arth.* VIII, Chapts. 1, 4 and 5.
52. *MDS.* IX, 295-296.
53. *SM.* I. 61. 62.
54. *KNS.* IV 1-2.
55. *MP.* 220.20, *VDP.* II. 65.21-22.
    239.1.
56. Barker, *Greek Political Theory,* London, 1952, pp. 232-33.

3

Monarch and Governance During Puranas

The importance of the king has been emphasized in the graphic language by several ancient political thinkers, *Aitareya Brahmana*,[1] for example, says that the Gods thought that they were defeated because they had no king, that, therefore, they elected one by consent. Manu,[2] says that the Creator created the king for the protection of all this world when every thing ran through fear hither and thither, as there was then no ruler in the world. Manu,[3] further says that the creator created the king with the essentials parts taken from Indra, the Wind god, Yama, the Sun, Agni, Varuna, the Moon and Kubera, the lord of wealth and therefore, he surpasses all beings by his majesty. He goes on to say that one should not disrespect a boy-king with the thought that he is human being (like others) for it is a great deity that stands (before people) in human form as a king. Narada, too, emphasizes the superiority of the king at different places and in different contexts. At one place, he declares that three persons are independent in this world, a king, a spiritual teacher and.... a householder in his own household. All subjects are dependent, the ruler of the country (alone) is independent.[4]

The *Matsya Purana* holds that the king is the root of the kingdom. The same attitude has been taken by the Agni Purana[5] at three different places. The text of the same Purana lays down that the king is the central figure of an empire and is also the fountain source of all laws and authorities. Hence, the king has been invariably assigned the first place amongst the Prakritis of the State.

As regards the origin of Kingship there are divergent opinions amongst the ancient Indian political thinkers. *Aitareya Brahmana,* for example, states that when the gods and the demons were fighting. The latter were victorious and then the gods decided that because they did not have a king they were loosing the battle. Hence they decided to make Indra as their king and leader and then they succeeded in winning the victory.[6] The Santiparva of the *Mahabharata*[7] contains two theories of kingship—the one associated with the name of Manu and the other with that of Viraja. In both theories the emphasis is made on the theory of divine origin of kingship and of original compact between the king and the people. Manu[8] has also stated the divine origin of kingship. Kautilya[9] has classic passage on the theory of the social contact of kingship. Kautilya[9] has classic passage on the theory of the social contact of kingship. He says, "people suffering from anarchy, as illustrated by the proverbial tendency of a large fish swallowing a small one, first, elected Manu, the Vaivasvata, to be their king, and allotted one-sixth of the grains grown and one-tenth of merchandise as royal dues. Fed by this payment, kings took upon themselves the responsibility of maintaining the safety and security of the in subjects, and of beign answerable for the sins of their subjects, when the principle of levying just punishments and taxes has been violated. Hence, hermits, too, provide the king with one-sixth of the grains gleaned by them, thinking, "it is a tax payable to him who protects us."

The Puranic literature like other works on polity has some speculations about the origin of kingship and reference have been made to the state of nature. From the study of the Puranic sources,[10] it is conspicuous that not only they do furnish an idea of the early state of nature but also throw new light on the circumstances that led to the origin of kingship. The *Vayu Purana*[11] lays down that in the beginning of the Kritayuga people used to reside near rivers, lakes, sea and mountains. They did not feel much cold or heat and used to wander form one place to another in search of their food. The means of their subsistence were fruits, and roots. They wre enjoying a king of harmonious life, free from cares, anxieties and greed.[12] It would not be wrong to say here that during this state of nature, man was a food-gatherer and not a food producer. The same text further informs us that there was nothing like the institutions of family, *Varna-sramadharma*[13] and recognized monogamous marriage.[14] Thus according to this Purana it can be inferred that in the early stage of Nature the institution of the state did not exist. The *Vayu*[15] and the *Markandeya Puranas*[16] further inform us tht this harmonious life could not exist for a long time and was destroyed by the people who discovered the art of cultivation which enabled people to produce more than they could consume. The people appropriated to themselves by force and violence, rivers, fields, hills, trees, shrubs and plants and for the first time they established their separate houses.[17] We are further told that when the means of subsistence were provided, the people were divided into four Varnas according to their occupation.[18] The Brahmanas were meant for praying, Ksatriyas for fighting and protection. Vaisyas for producing and sudras for menial work.[19] Though the duties of the different castes had been settled yet they did not perform them owing to infatuation and delusion, they came into mutual strife.[20] The same text[21] further lays down that the Lord Bhahma prescribed *danda*, (inflicting punishment) force, administration and making war as the profession of Ksatriyas, learning, devotion and conducting sacrifices for Brahmanas, cattle-keeping business and producing for Vaisyas and menial labour for sudras. The *Vayu Purana*[22] at another place asserts that god Brahman also established the institution of *Varnasrama* but the people did not observe their respective duties and came into conflict with one another.[23] They, therefore, approached Manu who produced the first two kings—Priyavrata and Uttanapada from his wife Satarupa.[24] These two kings were the first sovereigns on the earth and from that period the kings came to be vested with Danda.[25] Therefore, it is evident from this Puranic record that the state arose to check mutual conflict between the different varnas. The literature further credits the first traditional king Manu Svayambhuva with the establishment of the Varnas and the moral rules.[26]

Besides Manu, Prathu is represented as the first trditional king by the *Visnu Purana*.[27] According to this text Prathu was born from the arms of Vena who was famous for milking the earth for the advantage of his subjects. The story runs like this that Vena who was the son of Sunitha and grandson of Mrityu inherited the evil propensities of his grandfather. When Vena was consecrated by the great Rishis, he caused it to be proclaimed everywhere; tht he was the lord of the earth. No one would undertake any sacrifice, offer any oblation or make any gift. He was the king, the lord of sacrifice. No one was entitled to oblation except himself.[28] Thereupon, the Rishis assembled and worshipped the lord of earth and said, "O king, O lord, do thou hear, what we speak unto thee, for them thy health as well as the interest of the subjects shall be secured. We propose to worship, for thy welfare with protracted rites, Hari, the lord of the celestial and sacrifices. And thou shalt also be entitled to a share in it".[29] But Vena did not agree and ordered, you all obey my commands and should not make gifts or offer oblations to anyone except me and should not worship anybody else." He further stated, "As to serve one's own husband is the prime duty of women, so it is incumbent upon you, O twice-born ones, tó satisfy my behests only." When the vicious king Vena did not accept the request of the Rishis they had decided to kill him. The ascetics slew that king with the blades of kusa grass.[30] After killing the vicious king Vena, these ascetics saw dust on all sides. When they enquired the cause of disturbance from the people they were informed that the kingdom was without the king and hence the robbers and thieves had engaged in their dishonest work of encroaching upon the property of others." To end this state of things the ascetics after consulting each other, created a prince by rubbing the right hand of that childless monarch. This newly born child was named Prathu, who was resplendent in person and burning like the fire itself. The original bow of Hara named Pinaka, the celestial arrow and armour fell down from the walking. These sastras i.e. weapons were presented to him and he began to protect his subjects. In this way, when the king Prathu was consecrated, he removed the grievances of the people. The same theory of the origin of kingship is repeated in the *Vayu*,[31] the *Matsya*,[32] the *Visnudharmottara* and the *Agni Puranas*.[34] Thus it is clear from the above that the golden period or the *krita*-age disappeared owing to the advent of selfishness, avarice, hatred and malice. Probably, property, family and the caste gave rise to such feelings. So it is obvious that the Puranas like the *Mahabharata* have accepted the divine creation of kingship.

Titles of the King

The head of the administration was the king and he was designated as *Mahibharita*,[35] *Naradhipa*,[36] *Narendra*,[37] *Narendra Chandra*, *Nripati*,[38] *Mahipala*,[39] *Mahikshita*,[40] *Manujesvara*,[41] *Chakravarti*,[42] *Prithavipati*,[43] *Vasudhapati*,[44] *Parmesvara*,[45] *Svami*,[46] *Maharaja*[47] etc. Besides thse he was being called *Murdhabhisikta*,[48] *Rajanya*, *Bahuja*. *Ksatriya*, *Virat*, *Adhisvara*, *Sarvabhauma*,[49] etc. He was called *Bhattaraka* and *Deva*.[50] The *Agni Purana*, at one place, mentions that by performing rituals one becomes *Rajarajesvara*[51] and *Mandaladhipati*.[52] But unfortunately these terms are not explained in our literature either in terms of grades or powers. Study of the general titles given in our literature leads us to think that some of these titles were unconditionally used for paramount sovereignty and the rest were for other kings and feudal lords. Titles like *Rajarajesvara,* (the King of kings), *Narendra Chandra, Samrata* and *Chakravarti* seems to have been used for the paramount sovereigns. On the other hand, we find that kings claiming themselves to be vested with super-human qualities and using titles definitely date back to at least the Gupta period when the kings are found to be designated as *Parmesvara, Paramadaivata* and so on.

Coronation Ceremony

The coronation ceremony, which was performed at the time of the king's accession, has been regarded as a very important function of the State from very ancient days. Most of the ancient literature, therefore, discusses this ceremony. The Vedic literature, undoubtedly, throws a flood of light on this subject. Though the later literature of our period describes its different procedure, yet from the study of the same one may conclude very easily that the procedure of the coronation which has been described in the text is qvoted from the *Aitareya Brahmana* and the *Gopatha Brahmana.* The Puranic literature, too, attaches a great importance to this ceremony. The *Visnudharmottara*[53] and the *Agni* Puranas[54] suggest that after the death of the king no time should be taken in anpointing the king's successor as the king for fear of anarchy. The *Agni Purana* describes five types of coronation, which are as follows:

1. Consecration of the crown-prince *(Yauvarajayabhiseka)* by the reigning monarch;
2. abdication of the throne by the king in favour of a prince;
3. provisional installaiton of the prince on the throne without waiting for an auspicious occasion in the event of the king's death;
4. permanent anointiong of the king-elect; and finally;

5. the annual consecration of the reigning monarch.

The *Agni Purana* uses the term consecrated (*murdhabhisikta)* as a synonym of the king.[55]

The first two-consecration of the crown prince by the king and abdication of the throne in favour of a prince are discussed when the *Agni Purana* summarizes the two great epics the *Ramayana*[56] and the *Mahabharata*.[57] The coronation of Ramachandra as the crown-prince is not discussed fully. Only three or four stages of this ceremony are dealt with and afterwards Rama soon goes to the forest. But from the study of the extant verses it is evident that people's will was to install Rama as the king, and the reigning king was required to follow the popular will of his subjects. It is also known from the text that before the installation of the crown-prince the king was asked to consult his council of ministers including the chief priest. The chief priest was required to make necessary arrangements. Finally, instruction was given to Rama to exercise self-control in relation to his wife on the night preceding the coronation.[58] Thus, we find that in the consecration of the crown-prince, the public will was considered more important and it was due to the public will that Dasaratha could not please his queen Kaikeya and nominate Bharata as his heir-apparent.[59] It indicates that the law of primogeniture was prominent during the *Ramayana* period but in the later period this law was not observed strictly and rigidly. The history of ancient India has stray references which advocate that from time to time the nomination of the prince as heir-apparent was made in practice. The Allahabad Pillar Inscription[60] clearly lays down that Samudra Gupta anointed as heir-apparent by his father Chandra Gupta I before the royal princes and the council of ministers. Thus the Allahabad Pillar Inscription would suggest that this ceremony was performed in the Gupta dynasty. We are further told from the Rastrakuta records[61] that Govind III was consecrated by this ritual at the time of his formal selection as a crown-prince. The reign period of the king Rajendra Chola of the Chola dynasty was counted from his coronation as Yuvaraja.[62] Even in the eleventh century A.D. a Kalachuri king named Karna himself performed the coronation of his crown prince Yasakarna.[63] Bhima II and Vijayaditya III of Eastern Chalukya dynasty were consecrated as crown-princes.

The abdication of the throne in favour of the prince by the king is only referred to in the *Agni Purana* but, unfortunately it does not discuss the procedure of this ceremony. It only lays sown that Yudhisthira installed Pariksita on the throne before going to the Himalayas for final emancipation with other Pandavas.[64] The *Visnu Purana*[65] records the consecration of Kalayavana by Yavanaraja before going to the forest whcih shows that according to the Ashrama theory a glorious king, in his old days, was asked to hand over his office to the crown-prince and retire to the forest with or without his wife.

The third type of coronation is described both in the *Visnudharmottara*[66] and the *Agni Puranas*[67] with slight variations. This Puranic literature states that in the event of the king's death, a tentative consecration of the heir-apparent should be made without any delay. This provision was made, probably, to avoid the speculation of succession and confusion upon the death of the king. The *Agni Purana* refers to the old story of the *Ramayana* that in the absence of rightful successor Ramachandra, his sandals ruled and Bharata acted as its regent.[68] There are numerous references in history that in the absence of a rightful successor even the mother, brother etc., ruled as the regent. We are told that after the death of Satakarni his wife Nayanika or Naganika, was proclaimed regent during the minority of the princess Vedasri (? Khandasiri or Skandasri) and Sakti-sri (Sati Sirimat) or Haku-Siri.[69] Prabhavati Gupta ruled as regent of her minor sons after the death of her husband Rudrasena II.[70] Similarly, Govind III of the Rastrakuta dynasty appointed Karkka as regent for his son Amoghavarsha, who was a boy of 13 or 14 years.[71] Further, during the interregnum of eighteen days between the death of the Chaulkya king Siddharaja and the accession of Kumarapala, the sandals of the former king reigned parhaps on the same analogy.[72] Thus it is clear that the throne was never kept vacant perhaps owing to the fear of anarchy of a Kingless state. Kautilya, the father of Indian politics, is of the same opinion and advises the ministers to guard the secret of the king's death till the accession of the successor to the throne or till the heir-apparent is able to settle down to administration.[73] The Puranic literature, therefore, asks the priest and astrologer to consecrated the successor of the dead king without waiting of rthe auspicious occasion.[74] This ceremony is described very simple in the Puranas. The priest and the astrologer are asked to sprinkle sessamum seeds *(Tila)* and white mustard along with water over the head of the prince. The shout 'Victory' to the newly consecrated king should be made afterwards. After ascending the throne the king announces protection of his subjects, peace, security and general amnesty to prisoners.[75]

The final coronation of the king takes place after a year of his accession to the throne.[76] The Agni Purana[77] informs us that the king should elect his astrologer, the royal priest, ministers and his chief queen before his proper coronation. The chief queen (Mahishi) is consecrated with the king.[78] According to the Hindu scriptures a sacrifice is not successful without the presence of the wife. The Puranas, therefore, prescribe the nomination of the chief-queen before the actual coronation of the king. The *Visnudharmottara Purana*[79] specifies, at great length, the qualities of the principal queen (Agra-Mahishi). According to it the chïef queen should be gracious, virtuous, sweet-spoken, free from anger and greed and able to engage herself in the works which please the king. Further, she is required to have equal treatment with the co-wives and their children and having bounteous treatment with ministers, astròlogers and brahmanas. Furthermore, she is expected to have the knowledge of supervising the works of state servants and the nature of their work and also acknowledge their good deeds.[80] It is remarkable that the *Visnudharmottara Purana* further advises the king to marry a lady of noble family, of the same caste, of charming appearance, affable, modest and possessing good qualities.[81] The symbols of royalty viz., the Chowries and umbrella brought into the king by principal ministers. According to the tails of deer and must be all white with a handle of gold or silver. It is further said that the handle should be made of either sandal-wood, wory or miloh tree but it should be decorated with gold and gems.[82] The length of the handle should not be less than one foot. It is suggested by the same text that the Chamara of ministers, the purohit, the astrologer, the queen and the crown-prince should be yellowish and that of the rest of the people should be black.[83] The same literature further describes the requisites of a royal umbrella. According to it the royal umbrella should be made of the wings of the swan, the peacock or the parrot,[84] and should be ornamented with precious gems. It is further suggested that the length of the stem of the king's umbrella should be six hands. That the umbrella and the chamara were inseparable emblems of sovereignty is emphasized by Kalidasa in *Raghuvansa*.[85]

The proper coronation of the king as described in our Puranic literature may be summarised as follows:

(i) taking bath with water in which sessamum and mustard are mixed;[86]

(ii) seating on *bhadrasana* (Throne);[87]

(iii) proclamation of protection of all;[88]

(iv) amnesting to some prisoners;[89]

(v) propitiation of Indra (Aindrisanti);[90]

(vi) fasting by the priest;[91]

(vii) oblations to sacrificial fire with spells relating to eminent gods;[92]

(viii) sanctifying the head and other limbs of the king's body with earth taken from the summit of a

mountain, from the top of an ant-hill, from a temple of god Keshava, Indra, and from other places such as the court-yard of a royal palace, etc.[93]

(ix) washing his head with Panchagavya;[94]

(x) sprinkling of water from four jars of gold, silver copper and earth by ministers of the four castes accordingly with clarified butter, milk, curd and water from east, south, west and north;[95]

(xi) sprinkling of honey and washing of Kusa grass by brahmanas belonging to the Rigvedic and Somavedic schools;[96]

(xii) chanting of spells (mantra) which are recited by brahmanas at the time of Rajasuyabhiseka;[97]

(xiii) wearing costly dress and seating on the throne;[98]

(xiv) sprinkling of water by a brahmana who is well-versod in the Yajurveda over the head of the king from a golden jar having hundred holes;[99]

(xv) reciting the mantras of the *Yajurveda* and the *Atharvaveda*;[100]

(xvi) touching the king's head and throat with the yellow pigment known as the Rochana by brahmanas well-versed in the *Yajurveda* or the *Atharvaveda*;[101]

(xvii) pouring waters, collected from all the holy places, over the king's head by the chiefs of brahmanas, Ksatriyas, Vaisayas, Sudras and by a harlot;[102].

(xviii) singing and playing of musical instruments;[103]

(xix) holding of chowrie and fan before the king;[104]

(xx) looking at auspicious things such as a pitcherful of medical herbs, mirror, clarified butter etc.[105]

(xxi) worship of the gods such as Visnu, Brahma, Indra, etc. and planets;[106]

(xxii) sitting on a tiger-skin below which there are four skins viz., of lion, cheeta, cat and bull;[107]

(xxiii) tying of a fillet to the king's head;[108]

(xxiv) placing the crown on his head and making him sit on a cushion made of the skin of five animals;[109]

(xxv) introductin of amatyas, ministers, traders and subjects, etc. to the newly-crowned king by the Pratihara (warder);[110]

(xxvi) giving presents to the priest, astrologers and other brahmanas and worshiping the brahmanas and ministers assembled there;[111]

(xxvii) going round the fire, doing obeisance to elders; touching a bull, worshiping a cow with calf, riding the horse, honouring an elephant;[112]

(xxviii) coronation-procession and military parade through the main streets of the capital with the chief minister;[113]

(xxix) return of the procession to the place and closing the ceremony after honouring all peoples and making gifts;[114]

The whole description of the ceremony was followed by the Mantras which were used at the time of the coronation[115] of the king. The *Visnudharmottara Purana* discusses, at great length the auspicious and inauspicious occasions for the coronation.[116] It further states that the king should be anointed by the four castes along with the chief courtesan while the *Agni* Purana lays down that the brahmanas are to anoint the king.[117] From the study of the Puranic literature it is evident that provision of permanent coronation of the king which should be head within a year of his accession makes necessary to select an auspicious occasion and preparation for necessary arrangements. It also indicates that it was, probably, a test for his efficieency of his administration whether he was able to get the affection and loyalty of the people.

The *Agni Purana,* further, recommends that the king on the occasion of his coronation ceremony should release prisoners.[118] This idea was recommended by Kautilya[119] probably for the first time and was actually followed by Asoka for the first time. The Pillar edict V of his epigraphs clearly informs us that he made twenty-five jail deliveries within twenty-six years of his coronation.[120]

The *Agni Purana* states that God Hari and Brahma[121] anointed Prathu as the first consecrated king with Rajasuya rituals, which made him the over-lord of the whole universe.[122]

Qualifications of the King

As the personality and position of the king was of supreme importance in the administrative machinery of the State, it was essential that the person occupyping the throne should be highly qualified. The Puranas refer at various places to these requisites of kingship.

According to the *Visnudharmottara Purana*[123] the king should be versatile, polite, of a pleasing personality, religious-minded, free from anger and indolence, of great self-control, firm in devotion and decision, courageous, sweet-spoken, handsome, of a noble birth, quick in action and perception, powerful, devotee of brahmanas, free from covetousness, grave, sparing of words, neither very strict nor very lenient, the same in dealing with friends and foes, skilled in the wielding of the chariot, elephant, horse and bow, and diligent in gymnastics, observer of fasts and penances, performer of sacrifices, dear to the guru, acting on the advice of ministers and astrologer, understanding time and task, revering the revered and punishing the culprit, and conversant with the six-fold policy. The Visnu Purana[124] lays down that the king should be truthful, bounteous, reputed, modest, noble-hearted, pardoning, valorous; terror to the wicked, religious, merciful, sweet-spoken, respecting the respectable, performer of sacrifices, honoured among brahmanas and saints and in administering justice equal to foe and friend. The *Agni Purana*[125] states that the king who possesses nineteen qualities is sure to acquire a splendid fortune. These qualities consist of knowledge in different branches of learning, wisdom, fortitude, skillfulness, confidence, retentive memory, enthusiasm, eloquence, generosity, patience durig bad hours, influence, purity, friendship, self-sacrifice, honesty, gratefulness, knowledge of the Vedas, character, and control of senses. The *Markendeya Purana* informs us that the king, Ritadhwaja, son of Shatrujit, was endued with beauty and simplicity, heroic, honourable and sweet-spoken, quiet-spoken clever-spoken, learned, friendly, and man of accomplishments. He honoured the hourable, 'was intelligent, modest and had humility for ornament.[126] The Puranic literature further enumerates that the king should follow some general rules of social order which are known as the moral code. They are non-violence, truthfulness, honesty, purity, forbearance and kindness.[127] We are further told by the *Agni Purana*[128] that certain good qualities of a good person should also be adopted by the king. It is said that the king possessed of such qualities could serve as an ideal for his subjects. The *Markandeya Purana* says, at one place, that the king Uttama, the son of Uttanapada was famous for his great strength, powers, righteousness and nobility and was endowed with the wealth of manliness, who also having surpassed all beings, became as glorious as the sun. He was impartial between friends and foes, and just to sons or servants; to the agents of iniquity. He was even as the god Yama, and to the virtuous even as the moon.[129]

For efficient handling of public affairs the king was also required to be fully conversant with the sastras. The Puranic literature suggests that the king must be well-versed in different branches of learning and is required to study *Anviksiki* (the knowledge of self), *Trayi* (The vedic literature), *Varta* (economics) and Dandaniti (polity).[130] The *Matsya Purana,*[131] further, adds that the king should study politics, logic, philosophy and temporal science from those who are learned in these subjects. The *Agni Purana* says that humility is the mother of virtue and it springs from a perusal of the scriptural literature.[132] Thus it is clear that humility follows control of senses and the king who has acquired mastery over his passions and appetites is the fittest person to rule the world. The passions are compared to a mad elephant in our *Agni Purana,*[133] who is roaming uncontrolled in the forest and can be controlled only through the god of knowledge.

The *Agni Purana* further enumerates twenty-one qualities of the king such as noble-birth, character, age, ability, charity, celerity, non-interference in others' works, honesty, respect of the aged, gratefulness, divine favour, prudence capacity to keep feudatories under control, steadfastness, foresight and enthusiasm. Further, the king should be pure in character, humble, virtuous and a man of broad outlook.[134]

The Puranic literature not only mentions the positive qualifications of the king but also adds negative ones, from which the king is advised to keep himself away. The *Markandeya Purana* lays down that the king should abstain from hunting, gambling, sleeping during the day, calumny, concupiscence, dancing, singing, sporting, roaming, drinking, creating malice, ill will, deceit, cruelty and verifying others.[135] The same Purana further informs us that once the king Uttama was engaged in drinking with the courtesans who were adepts in dancing and singing, he offered a cup of wine to his beloved Bahula and she refused to take.[136] The *Agni Purana* further speaks in a similar tone and asks the king to give up sleep in the day time, roaming without purpose, using scurrilous language and keep himself aloof from all small talk and calumny.[137] He is also required to temper justice with mercy and never inflict inordinate punishments. It has been laid down that the king should not neglect the proper repairing of his forts which would affect mines and minerals resources of his country. He is further asked not to make gifts of money to unworthy persons who would create troubles.[138] The king is furthermore, required to refrain from other weaknesses such as passion of anger, covetousness, pride, arrogance, quarrel, boastfulness and use of harsh language which would spoil his work.[139] The *Markandeya Purana* states that the king Pandu was deprived of his life through lust, the king Anuhada was bereaved of his son through anger, Aila was detached of his life through covetousness and the king Vena was killed by the twice-born through his arrogance. Further, Anayus son, Vali was destroyed through his over-weening, self-conceit and Puranjaya was killed through excess of joy.[140] The same text further says that by conquering these high-souled the king Marutta subdued the entire earth.[141] It is said that control of the above-mentioned passions brings happiness to the king, and wins the allegiance of his own officers and the people of undertake the conquest of his external enemies,[141] which may be grouped into three heads viz., ancestral, racial and artificial. Elsewhere the *Visnudharmottara* and the *Agni* Puranas further suggest that the king should be free from the vices which consists of using of harsh and cruel words, infliction of cruel and inordinate punishments, spoilation of the sources of revenue, drinking, gambling, hunting, womanising, idleness, disinclination for all sorts of work and boastfulness.[142] The *Visnudharmottara,*[143] the *Matsya;*[144] the *Markandeya*[145] and the *Agni Puranas*[146] further instruct the king to imbibe the good qualities of even birds and animals. Accordingly the king should think of acquiring wealth with the eyes of the crane, valour of the lion, heel of the wolf, crookedness of the hare, firmness of the boar and variegated manners of the peacock, devotion of the dog, mellifluence of the cuckoo and suspicious nature of the crow. The *Markandeya Purana* further says that the king should spread like the scintillations of fire or like the seeds of cotton and govern the earth like the sun and the moon; he should learn wisdom from the prostitute, the lotus, the sarabha, the sulika, and the breast of a woman during pregnancy.[147] In other words the king should learn from the prostitute how to please many; like the lotus he should not only be beautiful but be accomplished also. The sarabha is a strong animal. Like Sulika he should entirely kill his enemy. As milk is formed in woman's breast for the future child, so the king should make provision for the future. Further as the milk-maid can make many things out of milk so the king should do many things.[148]

Daily Routine of the King

In ancient India the king was expected to direct his administration very ideally and to secure prosperity, to the people. Therefore, all ancient Indian political thinkers have prescribed a very sound time-table for the king, which hardly left any leisure to him. The Puranas, like other works on polity, prescribe the daily routine of the king which was to be methodically and regularly followed. The duties assigned to the king were to be performed by him in the following order daily:

1. Leaving his bed about an hour (two muhurtas-forty-eight minutes) before the break on dawn, with the songs of the court-panegyrists;[149]

   (i) audience with his spies before being seen by anybody.[150]

   (ii) hearing the report of his daily income and expenditure;[151]

   (iii) taking bath after cleaning his teeth;[152]

   (iv) performing daily rites of prayer, and worship of the god, Vasudeva;[153]

   (v) daily ablutions with making suitable gifts to the brahmanas;[154]

   (vi) wearing dress and ornaments, seeing auspicious things such as looking-glass, gold, clearified butter etc;[155]

   (vii) hearing the auspicious or the inauspicious nature of the day from his astrologer;[156]

(viii) taking medicines prescribed by royal physicians, and receiving blessings of his elders and superiors;[157]

(ix) attending his court and receiving brahmanas, ministers and high officials of the state, as also people in general presented by the usher of the court;[158]

(x) hearing the daily report of the works and determining the routine of business for the day;[159]

(xi) adjudication of law-suits;[160]

(xii) consultation with ministers on important matter of state policy;[161]

(xiii) practising gymnastics and physical exercises;[162]

(xiv) taking bath, worshipping and making gifts to the brahmanas;[163]

(xv) meal and rest after chewing betel-leaf;[164]

(xvi) study of theology of other religious scriptures;[165]

(xvii) inspection of treasury, army and stores;[166]

(xviii) evening prayer;[167]

(xix) assigning various duties to the spies and[168]

(xx) entering the harem and passing his night with music and song.[169]

Thus we find that the king was required to be engaged the whole day from the morning to night. The daily routine of the king has also been mentioned by other thinkers on polity.[170] Somedeva Suri says that the king should attend the urgent and the important works without any delay.[171] The king is further advised to look after the affairs relating to God, preceptor and religion personally.[172] The similar duties are assigned by Manu[173] and Yajnavalkya.[174] It is noticeable that the daily timetable of the king as suggested by our Puranic literature, is based on Kautilya's *Arthasastra*.[175]

Duties and Functions of the King

The office of the king was never regarded as sinecure in ancient India. His responsibilities were great and duties onerous, an idea of which can be formed from the schedule of his daily duties as prescribed by our Puranic records. The Puranas provide us with considerable information regarding the various duties assigned to and functions performed by the king.

The primary function of the king was to protect, with all efforts, his State both from external aggression and internal lawlessness adopting the policy of parents.[176] The *Agni Purana* advocates, at one place, that the Rastra (Territory) is the next in importance among all the seven constituents of the State and the king is asked to protect it by all means.[177] The *Matsya Purana*[178] further states that the protection of the state is as important as a nourished calf who becomes fit to carry loads, so the State which has been well-looked would be able to bear the weight of regality. Our Puranic literature[179] lays down that the seven limbs of the state are interdependent and it is duty of the king to protect them in order to ensure proper administration. The *Visnudharmottara*[180] and the *Matsya Puranas*[181] ordain to the king that if anyone causes rebellion, the king should take no time in destroying him. The *Agni Purana*[182] prescribes more deterrent punishment that any of our previous Puranas. It lays down immediate capital punishment for those who rebel against the seven factors of the government. The *Matsya* and the *Visnudharmottara* Puranas[183] further prescribe exile punishment to those who create disturbances in the proper working of the government. The *Agni Purana*[184] advises the king that in the event of revolt by the people, he should put it down with the help of the town people, but before resorting to these measures he should apply all diplomatic methods.

It is noticeable that the *Mastya*[185] and the *Agni Puranas*[186] declare two types of provocation (Kopa): *(i)* external and *(ii)* internal, and of these the internal faction is more dangerous than the external, because external wrath brings the ruin of the king. The revolt of the feudatories and other kings is regarded the external and that of the queen, crown prince, commander-in-chief, chief minister, prime minister is regarded the internal wrath and discontent by our *Matsya*[187] and the *Visnudharmottara*[188] Puranas. But the *Agni Purana*[189] does not include the queen, crown prince and commander-in-chief, in this list. It is significant to note that the *Matsya Purana*[190] advises the king to keep his vigilant eyes on internal defections because if the internal condition is satisfactory, the external sources of danger, howsoever great, can be easily dealt with by the king. This text further states that if the sovereign is surrounded with internal dangers he would perish although he may be powerful like Indra. Therefore, he should take a good deal of care against internal provocations.[191] The *Matsya Purana,*[192] elsewhere, advises the king that after providing against internal dangers he should suppress external foes. These external foes are of three kinds. Firstly, those who are equal to the king every respect; secondly, those who are below the king; and thirdly, accidental. The *Visnudharmottara Purana*[193] states that the king should protect himself and his state from external and internal troubles. It is advised that he should settle internal distrubances before marching against his enemies. The king is further asked to follow the policy of twelve-states (Mandala theory) for gaining the victory over his ememies.[194]

The other important duty of the king, as required by our Puranic literature, is to protect the people, who are to be nourished like his own begotten son.[195] In graphic language the *Visnudharmottara Purana*[196] states that the palace of the king whose people are well-protected is like heaven and the temple of the king whose subjects are not protected is hell. The same idea is discussed by other ancient authors on policy. Manu[197] states that the protection of the subjects is the highest dharma of the king. Kalidasa, too, alludes to the same dictum.[198]

Gautama[199] speaks that the protection of the subjects is the special duty of the king. Sukra[200], too, is of the same opinion and states that the highest dharma of the king is to protect the subjects and to put sown the wicked. The *Markandeya Purana* informs us that in the past the righteous king Alarka duly governed his subjects as his own sons, who were all filled with joy and established in the duties of their respective orders. He attained great joy by inflicting punishment upon the wicked and affording protection to the righteous. He gratified the deities with great sacrifices.[201] Somadeva Suri[202] even says that the protection of the subjects is king's sacrifice and he who does not protect his subjects is not a king. The *Visnudharmottara*[203] and the *Agni Purana*[204] lay down that the king receives one-sixth of the income of his subjects because he protects them. It further states that he acquires merits through providing protection and incurs sins by neglecting it. Thus it is eveident that like other literature on polity our Puranic literature[205] states that the king should sacrifice his own interests for the welfare and protection of his subjects as a pregnant woman sacrifices her own desires and pleasures, lest they should be harmful to the child to be born, so the king must sacrify his own conveniences inclinations and pleasures in order to be of the maximum help and service to his people. The *Markandeya Purana*[206] holds that the body of the king is not meant for the enjoyment of pleasures, it has to put up with great troubles and worries while carrying out the royal duty of protecting the subjects and fulfilling the *dharma*. The *Arthasastra*[207] and *Nitiprakasika*[208] are of the same opinion and lay much stress on the welfare of the people. It is significant to note that the *Markandeya Purana* quotes the duties of the king that have been instructed by the most excellent lady Madalsa to her son Alarka. According to the text Madalsa asks her son to be good to his friends and destructive of his enemies. She further says that he should atenttively gratify the brahmanas at every festival, satisfy the desires of this friends think of doing good to others and abstain from violating others' wives. By celebrating various sacrifices he should gratify the celestials and with plenty of wealth he should please the twice born and he should also satisfy the females with numberless articles of enjoyment and enemies with fight. He has also been asked to satisfy his friends in boyhood, to worship his relatives by obeying their commands in youth, to please the females having ornaments of noble ancestry in manhood. In the end she asks her son to gratify his friends, protect the virtuous, perform, sacrifices, destroy the wicked and enemies in battle on behalf of kin and brahmana during his reign.[209]

Protection consists in putting down internal dangers such as thieves, robbers, rebels etc. and in meeting external aggressions. The *Agni Purana*[210] states five dangers such as soldiers, thieves, and officers of the king, royal favourites and the cupidity of a foreign monarch. A similar view is found in the *Nitisara* of Kamandaka.[211] It is noteworthy that the *Markandeya Purana* lays down that a valiant and mighty king named Surath lost his royalty and all the treasure owing to his licentious ministers.[212] Elsewhere the *Visnudharmottara*[213] and the *Agni Puranas*[214] add the Subhagahvita, chata and Kayasthas in the list of internal dangers. Mitramisra[215] quotes the verses from the *Visnudharmottara Purana* and explains the term; Subhaga as 'as favoured wife' or ven harlot. Dr. B.B. Misra states taht it seems improbable that the queen tyrannized her subjects because, in our period or in the period gone by women possessed practically no say in the political or administrative affairs.[216] But we find that in ancient India there are numerous references to women taking active part in the administration and even ruling after the death of the husband. Prabhavati Gupta (daughter of Chandra Gupta II) for example, ruled at least for 13 years as a regent after the death of her husband Rudrasena II of Vakataka dynasty.[217] Hence, the suggestion made by Puranic record that subjects should be protected from the danger of the favourite queen is right because we find that under the Rastrakuta administration princess Chandrabeebha, a daughter of Amoghvarsha I was administering the Raichur

Doab in 837 A.D. Under the later Chalukays, the practice of appointing princesses to high government posts became very common, Mailadevi, one of the queens of Someswara I, Akhadevi, an elder sister of Jaysimha III and Lakshmidevi, the chief queen of Vikramaditya VI, were holding important administrative charges. Further we find that under Rastrakutas a crowned queen, Silabhattarika was making a land grant without permission of her husband Dhruva.[218] Thus it is quite probable that at times the queen may create troubles for her subjects, so our literature wanrs the king to protect his subjects from annoyance of his queen. The *Rajatarangini*[219] describes at great length the regime of the notorious queens Sugandha (904-906 A.D.) and Didda (980-81 A.D.) of Kasmira. The term Vita is translated as swindlers or robbers. But from the study of the *Agni Purana*[220] it appears that the compiler of this Purana has taken this term to mean Vaisyas whose main business was trade and commerce. It is just possible that like present days Vaisyas were extorting money from the common public by using false weights and measures, and by charging high rates for commodities. The above dictum is supported by Somadeva Suri[221] who is of the opinion that merchants are like thieves who rob the people in their very presence, and exploit them by resorting to false weights and balance and adulteration. They raise the price of a thing through competition. Thus the king is advised by the *Agni Purana* to protect his subjects against the tyranny of Vaisyas. The term *Chata* can be taken to mean soldiers. It is interesting to note that the *Visnudharmottara*[222] *Purana*, the *Abhilashitartha-Chintamani*[223] and the *Agni Purana*[224] reckon the Kayasthas as the greatest danger. We find references in the inscription of the Gupta period that the Kayasthas were appointed as scribes, whose work was to inscribe the royal writs and other important works relating to the state administration. Therefore, it is just possible for them to make alteration, commission and addition in the royal orders through which they may prove themselves dangerous for the subjects. The *Agni Purana*, therefore, prescribes highest punishment for such type of crimes. *Rajatarangini* informs us the tyranny of Kayasthas in Kasmira, when they appear as royal officers. Sivarath is described as a Kanvish Kayasthas. Soldiers, officers, robbers and thieves have been dagerous to the public from ancient times to be present day. Therefore, the king is advised by our Puranas to protect his subjects from the dangers mentioned above. The *Agni Purana* prescribes that the king should restore the value of an article stolen by a thief to the real owner and if the thief is not caught then the king should deduct the amount from the salary of the police officers.[225] This Purana further mentions the rule of Kartaviryarjuna, who was so powerful a king that thieves and robbers were afraid of him, if the things belonging to someone were left on the road, they were as safe as if they would have been kept in a strong room.[226] Megasthenes's account tells us that during the reign of Chandra Gupta Maurya, theft was of very rare occurrence, even though houses and property were as a rule, generally left unguarded.[227]

The king who is the protector of his subjects and state cannot protects them unless he himself is not protcted. Therefore our literature requires the protection of the king because he is root of the state.[228] The *Agni Purana*[229] further states that the king should appoint body-guards and spies for his protection and he should also consult this physician and astrologer for the appropriate medicine and the auspicious time as well as the ways of warding off planetry evils. The king is furthermore asked to take daily physical exercises and practices the handling of arms and weapons.[230] Thus it is evident that the king was considered to be an important factor. The *Visnudharmottara Purana*[231] lay down that in wartime the king should keep himself two miles away from the actual place of fighting and should not engage himself in the battlefield. The same idea is repeated in the *Agni Purana*.[232] Thus from the statements of our Puranic literature it appears that the death of the king would create grave danger for the people and the state. The king is, therefore, advised neither to sleep in the female apartment in the night nor to repose trust in the queens specially when they have sons.[233] The king is further asked to visit only those queens who are well-disclosed towards him and not to go those who are not loyal to him.[234] Thus our literature suggests the king that he should take such food, drinks, bed etc. which have been examined by trusted person. The king is further, ordained to take help from the animals and birds by which he may detuct the unhappening things. These animals and birds are required to be kept in the king's palace. The *Matsya Purana*[235] mentions an elaborate list of animals and birds to be kept in the royal princes. There are evidences in the history that the king Bimbisara of Magadha was troubled by his own son Ajatasatru who became the ruler after killing his father.[236] The Buddhist literature[237] records that Ajatashatru confessed the murder of his father before Gautama, the Buddha. Ancient authorities on polity, therefore, suggested that the king should keep himself away from the danger of his own princes. Kautilya[238] and Samadev Suri[239] compare the royal family containing a disaffected prince to a worm-eaten piece of wood, which crumbles down soon. The *Kathasaritasagara* compares the princes to the devils who are difficult to be controlled.[240] Therefore, the Puranic literature instrcts the king to protect his princes against greedy, angry and dishonoured people and to keep them engaged in the training of various branches of learning,[241] so that they may not foremost duties of a king.[247] The king is further required by the same Purana to protect the distressed, the infirm and the widows and to adjust the Varnasrma rules.[248]

Protection of cows is regarded as an important duty of the people from very early times. The *Agni Purana*[249] states that the highest duty of the king is to protect thelife of brahamanas and cows and he is responsible for their protection.[250] The same text furthermore, prescribes the amputation of hands and feet of the persons who is guilty of killing the cow, the elephant, the horse or the camel.[251]

Thus it appears that the Puranic literature follows the old Smriti tradition.

The most important duty of the king, according to our literature, is to impart justice in his daily routine. It is said that if the king imposes fines on innocent persons or brahmanas wrongly he is supposed to refund thirty times of the fine imposed to the person concerned. The king is further required to make arrangements for criminal and civil justice.

According to the *Agni Purana* the king should see that the different social orders of his kingdom are pursuing their proper and respective conations in the life.[252] The *Markandeya Purana* says that the king who protects the four orders attains happiness in the world and ranges with Indra in his own region.[253] Other authorities on polity like Kautilya, Manu and Somadeva Suri are of the same opinion and state that an important duty of the king is to uphold the Varnashrama. Somadeva Suri[254] states that the king should see that the rules of Vranasramadharma are being observed by the people and no one transgresses the prescribed code of conduct. He further states that kingdom is best where the Varnasramadharma is observed and where there is no mixed caste is to be found.

Religion also played an important in the duty of the king. Therefore, he was required to maintain religious places like temples etc. He is advised to establish images of Gods in the temples and to maintain the old temples and to build new ones. The Puranic literature reveals the construction of various types of temples, as of clay, wood, brick and stone. It has also been laid down that if the king constructs even the smallest temple, it confers prosperity on the king not only in this life but also in the next one. The *Agni Purana*[255] lays down five kinds of sacrifices for a king through which he should be expiable for all his sins. It further states that by performance of these five sacrifices, the king shall be free from public criticism and other weaknesses. The *Brhaddharma Purana*[256] says that the protection of the subjects by the king is equal to one thousand horse-sacrifices and if he rules according to law and order he obtains one-sixth of their spiritual merit. Similar ideas are discussed by Somadeva Suri.[257] Varahamihira states five important duties for the king which are equal to five sacrifices. These sacrifices are required to be performed by the king. These duties consist of punishment of the wicked, honour to the gentle, replenishment of the treasury in a just way, impartiality in judgement and protection of the kingdom.[258] Thus it is obvious that the king should perform his duties like sacrifices. The *Agni Purana*[259] says that the king should try to win the affection and loyalty of his subjects. The kingdom, territory and prosperity of the king arise from his popularity among his subject. The Agni Purana further enumerates that the strength of the king is the love of his subjects and that the word Raja is derived from the word Rajan (to please). Thus the king was the source of pleasure to the people[260] and the most important duty of the king was to please and to protect his subjects, and not to be an autocarat. From the study of the king's duties as enumerated in our Puranic literature it is evident that the king was required to protect his subjects from external and internal troubles and to preserve law and order so that the state may prosper in every respect. He was also required to fulfill political, economic, social, religious and moral obligations.

The Puranic record also stresses the development of economic prosperity. Undoubtedly agriculture had been the backbone of the state. The king is, therefore, asked by ancient Indian political thinkers to maintain agricultural production. It is interesting to note that the *Agni Purana*[261] suggests the king to maintain eight things—agriculture, trade-routes, forts, bridges and canals capturing of elephants, mines and minerals, imports of soldiers, and building of towns in uninhabited regions. These eight duties mentioned by the *Agni Purana* are also recommended by Manu,[262] Kautilya[263] and Kamandaka.[264] Thus the maintaining of agriculture, trade and commerce played a very important part in the king's duties and he is asked to ensure their growth. The king is required to acquire the wealth through just means and to save and spend for the right cause.[265] The king is further required to maintain relatives of those soldiers who are killed in the battlefield. But the Visnudharmottara Purana restricts this provision to the wives and other women who are issueless.[266]

The Puranic literature also ordains the king to protect his queen. The Agni Purana states that the king should study the science of erotic, perhaps to win the love of his queen.[267] At one place in the *Agni Purana,* Puskara says to Raja that the fair sex is governed by desire and women care much for pomp and pride. Hence the king is advised to collect gems for their satisfaction.[268] The Agni Purana further states that harm should be protected by the king because queens are source of powers, energy and religious purposes.[269] Somadeva Suri,[270] on the other hand, holds that queens are not meant for sexual enjoyment but they have to be protected to maintain the purity of the royal blood and toward off unfortunate events.

Divinity of the King

The Puranic literature contains references to the divinity of the king. The *Matsya*[271] and *Visnudharmottara* Puranas[272] state that the king was created by Brahma by taking portions of gods for wielding the power of punishment for the protection of all beings. The *Visnu Purana*[273] says that the gods Brahma, Visnu, Sambhu, Indra, Vayu, Sun, Fire, Varuna, Dhatta, Pusa, the earth, the moon, and all others who are capable of imprecating curses and conferring boons exist in the person of the king for the essense of a sovereign. The Markandeya,[274] the Visnudharmottara[275] and the Agni Puranas[276] further advocate that the king is like the sun, so no body could see him with naked eyes for his splendour, but he sheds a mellow light like the moon so that his subjects may be pleased from his sight. Further, the king is described as the wind-god, who roams all over the world in the person of his spies. He is also stated the God of Death (Yama) who rewards the virtuous and punishes the vicious. The king acts as the fire-god when he burns evil-doers and represents the god of wealth when he makes gifts to the Brahamanas. The king is, furthermore, the incarnation of the god of rain (Varuna) since he showers down wealth on the poor and he deserving people. The king is the primordial by hydra himself since this universe is poised his infinite forbearance. He is described as the god of Hari since he protects his subjects with the law and might force. Thus it is evident from our literature that as the king exercises the functions of the nine deities viz. The sun, the moon, Vayu, Yama, Varuna, Fire, Kubera, the earth and Visnu, he has the form of these. Other authors express similar views on polity. For example, Manu says "The creator created the king with the essential parts taken from Indra, the Wind-god, Yama, the Sun, Agni, Varuna, the Moon, and Kubera and lord of wealth and therefore, he surpasses all beings by his majesty".[277] The *Mahabharata*[278] and *Manavadharmasastra*[279] even speak that "one should not disrespect a boy-king with the thought 'he is human being, (like others)' for it is a great deity that stands (before people) in human form as a king".

The *Matsya Purana*[280] containing several interesting dicta, says taht the king in the form of Indra sustains his subjects as he pours rain for four months during the rains. The king receives revenue from his subjects as he sun draws the moisture by his rays for eight months. As air pervades through and then through all beings so the king moves about on earth through his spies. It has been further laid down in the same text that the king exercises he functions of eight deities viz., Indra, Sun, Vayu, Yama, Varuna, Moon, Fire and Prithvi, The *Markandeya Purana*[281] mentions that the king acts as Indra, Sun, Yama, moon and air. The *Vayu Purana*[282] further states that all the past and future universal emperors (Chakravartin) are born on the earth from the parts of Visnu. The *Matsya Purana*[283] mixes up the theory of creation of the king from the parts of gods with the lesser idea of his functions being similar to those of certain deities. The *Visnudharmottara*[284] and *Markandeya* Puranas[285] share similar ideas. The *Agni Purana*[286] describes the king of Yadu dynasty and informs us that the king Deva-Vridha was among men, equal to God. Elsewhere, the same Purana[287] discusses that the kings, princes and sages are incarnations or not. It is remarkable that the king is equated to the gods in Puranic literature, but Hari is certainly a new god with whom the king is identified. The *Visnudharmottara Purana*[288] states that the king is Indra; he rules with Visnu lustre and is the quintessence of all gods. Thus we find that the idea of the divinity of the king was very much popular in our Puranic period but it does not mean that the king was conceived of as the representative of God. Asoka is described as *Devanampiya* in his inscriptions. Even some rulers coming from foreign dynasties assumed high sounding epithets. Kanishka called himself "Son of God *(Devaputa)*". This tradition received wide acceptance during the Gupta epoch. In the Allahabad Pillar Inscription, Samudra Gupta is designated as "*Achinta Purusa*". He is also called *Loka Dhamodevasya*, i.e., the god dwelling on the earth and performing the human functions only to maintain Loka Maryada.[289] He has been further said to be equal to Kubera, Dhanda, Varuṇa, Indra and Yama.

The king is also equated with Chandra and Visnu in the first line of the Bihar Stone Pillar Inscription of Purugupta.[290] On the Gaya Copperplate Inscription of Samudra Gupta the monarch has been referred to "like the gods of Kubera, Varuna, Indra and Antaka in one". The coin legends, too, refer to these kings as conquering heaven by their good deeds after having conquered the earth.[291] Thus we find that kings were equated with the Gods and were invested with high sounding epithets. Dr. B.B. Misra is of the opinion that the practice of assuming high sounding epithetis did not always imply increasing power and Narasingh Gupta is the example who assumed the title of the rising sun (Baladitya) but a weak ruler.[292]

Undoubtedly, it is true but this type of references we find rarely. Generally the rulers of ancient India whose names were decorated with high sound epithets were really very brave and proved themselves worthy of those titles. It is noticeable that adopting high-sound divine titles was not confined in India but abroad too. Alexander the Great and Julius Caesar traced their descent to gods and goddesses. Alexander is deified during his lifetime by the Greek world.[293]

Royal Privileges

Stray references in our Puranic literature give us some idea of the privileges and the position of the king. The Agni Purana,[294] at one place, clearly lays down that a kingless state is not fit for inhabitation. The *Brihaddharma Purana*[295] in very graphic language compares a land without a king to a woman without her husband. This idea indicates the value of the king. The king is described in the *Agni Purana*[296] as the god Hari who protects his subjects with law and military force. Further, the king is to be supposed to be as good as an incarnation of God Visnu who protects and nourishes the gods according to the doctrine of the law.[297] Therefore, our literature asks the king to be virtuous towards his subjects and in return to expect the same devotion and loyalty from his subjects.[298] Narada is also of the same opinion and he says that the king is above criticism unless he diverges from the prescribed rules of conduct. Further, he states that the subjects should be loyal to their king. As a good wife is devoted even to a worthless husband so, too, the subjects should be loyal and obedient even to a worthless ruler. But it must have been noticed that the Puranic literature not only believes in principles but also asks theking to perform his function as the source of pleasure to his subjects.[299] Further he is also responsible for sins committed by his officers. Thus it appears that he was not absolutely above public criticism. The *Visnudharmottara Purana*,[300] at one place, states that the king should return the amount of theft to the victim if the thief is not arrested. The *Agni Purana* states that the king has to refund thirty times of the amount to the brahamanas if it is unjustly realized as a fine in a law court.[301] Thus it is evident that the king enjoyed the royal privileges with certain limitations.

According to our Puranas the King has extraordinary social privileges. Severe punishments were prescribed for adultery with the queen,[302] the misuse of seats and conveyance of the king,[303] sedition[304] and blasphemy,[305] hostility and disobedience and contravention of the royal orders.[306] Further regicide is declared to be the worst crime and that no impurity attaches to his relations[307] from the death of a man guilty of the king's murder.

The king is invested with personal prerogatives also. The *Agni Purana* state that no one was allowed to make claim on the king's property when in ordinary case every body was entitled to claim his legal right to movable and immovable property after ten or twenty years respective.[308] The king is, further, asked by the Visnudharmottara Purana[309] to keep unclaimed property in his custody for a period of three years and if the owner of the property fails to prove his ownershio if would go to the king's property. Similarly the property of the heirless persons also goes to the king.[310] The king is also asked by our literature[311] to act as the custodian of the property of an infant till he attains the age of discretion, and to manage the property of widows who are mothers of minor children or of those who have legitimate guardians or relations to protect them. The king is, further, asked to look after the property of those widows who had been faithful wives and those who are unable to manage their properties due to ill health.

The *Agni Purana,* further, enumerates that the king is entitled to get gems and precious stones acquired in war even by the ministers.[312] It has also been suggested by our Puranic literature that if the kings like gems, valuable stones, elephants, etc. are sold without the permission of the king on his prohibition, at a particular place, they are to be confiscated by him.[313]

The king, as the administrative head of the state, also enjoys royal prerogatives. The *Agni Purana*[314] lays down that the eyes of the man who does not obey, or contravenes, the orders of the king should be plucked out. The *Visnudharmottara Purana*[315] further enjoys punishment of the highest order for those who counterfeit weights and measures. The same verses are repeated in the *Agni Purana*.[316] The highest punishment is also suggested for those who declare base coins to be sterling and vice versa, and also for those who make alterations, omissions, additions, in the royal order.[317]

The subjects consider it is a great privilege to meet the king and they get pleasure in seeing him on auspicious occasions.[318] The *Agni Purana* fixes a time in the king's routine when the people may see him. Asoka, the great king of ancient India, actually put it into practice. In his rock edict VI he states that whether he be in the harem, the dining hall, the inner apartments, or even in the ranches or in the place of religious instruction, or in the parks, the officers have instructions to report the affairs of my people.[319] Thus we find that the royal privileges and prerogatives suggested by the Puranic literature were in practice in ancient India.

Crown Prince

Next to the king in importance in the administrative machinery in ancient India was the crown prince. So it was necessary that the *Yuvaraja* or crown prince should be well educated and trained so that he might be able to run the state administration with great efficiency after the death of the king. The ignorant king is to be considered more dangerous for the State because he would plunge the country headlong into dangerous circumstances, which would result in immense suffering to the people inhabiting the state. It was due to this that all political thinkers of ancient India stress that the Crown Prince should be well-versed in different branches of learning and it is the foremost duty of the king to train his princes for the future of the state-administration. Somadeva Suri,[320] a Jain thinker, prefers the anarchy of a kingless state to an illiterate king. He states that even the people do not like to install the king who is considered to be an unpolished gem.[321] He, further, stresses that the princes of the royal blood should be well versed. Fortunately, our Puranas devote a good deal of space to the education of the king and to his princes. The *Matsya,*[322] the *Visnudharmottara*[323] and the *Agni Puranas*[324] require that the princes should have received education in different branches of learning. It has been laid down in the *Matsya Purana* that princes should be brought up in the mould of austere educational discipline and both theoretical and practical training should be imparted to them by competent teachers. The same text further lays down that princes should be taught *Dharmasastra, Arthasastra,* science of erotic (*Kamasastra*), archery, the use of chariots, elephants, horses, arts and crafts and various other physical exercises.[325] It is furthermore, prescribes that a trustworthy teacher must be appointed to train them in the right direction.[326] Chief attention should be paid to instruct him in physical culture and to make his an able warrior. Instruction is given by the *Matsya Purana* that the prince need not rigorously speak the truth always, but may speak false words as if exigencies demanded.[327] It is rather difficult to realize the full implication of this aspect of instruction to a prince. Probably the exigencies of the state demanded it. If he is trained to speak nothing but the bare truth, sometimes such true words would be displeasing to others, and career would thereby being with the prejudice and ill-will of a discontented section otherwise this injunction neither is nor should be valid. The prince is further required not to mix himself with men of angry or avaricious disposition, or with persons who have been insulted and looked down upon.[328] He should also be kept away from the vices of drinking, hunting expeditions and gambling. The *Matsya*

Purana refers to many kings who, addiction to the above-mentioned vices, were ruined. Another healthy restriction provided for the royal princes is that they must be prevented from sleeping during daytime and also from going on tour with no specific purpose in view. As a prince, it is just possible that his mind may be poisoned by interesting persons with all sorts of temptations. So our *Matsya* and the *Visnudharmottara* Puranas advise the king to appoint personal guards for the princes, so that they would wean them away from beneficial and had influences. Much stress is laid down upon the environment of the princes and it is advised that they should be ever surrounded by good and virtuous persons, who by precept and example would make them tread on path of virtue and lead them away from passions during their 'Youth'.[329] In spite of such precautionary measuers, should a prince prove refractory and erring, he should be well-guarded is secret place, where all possible comforts should be provided.[320] It is ordained by the *Matsya Purana* that a prince devoid of politics and the virtue of humanity would not thrive. Therefore, it is obvious from the foregoing duscussion that the *Matsya* and the *Visnudharmottara* Puranas insist that the crown prince who would take up the reign of government in his hands, should be well trained in the science of state-administration as also in the different branches of learning. The foregoing examinations also show that the chapters of the *Matsya* and the *Visnudharmottara* Puranas dealing with the education and training of princes, except in certain details, closely resemble the Kautilyan polity. In the later part of the above-mentioned chapters of the Puranas it is said that there are seven constituents of the state viz. *Swami* or the king himself, *Amatya* (Ministers), *Janpada* (State), *Durga* (Fort), *Danda* (Army), *Kosa* (Treasury) and *Mitra* (friendly state). Among these component parts of an empire the king is the root of the state and the other six are like its branches and fruits, and it is the duty of the king to protect all these limbs.[331]

It is significant to note that the *Markandeya Purana* lays down that in the past, there was a very powerful king by name Shatrujit. His son Ritydhvaja became very mighty and capable of smiting his enemies, and his intelligence prowess and grace was equal to the preceptor Brhaspati, Sukra and Aswini.[332] The prince was always encircled by other princes of equal age, intelligence, energy, prowess and exertion. They sometimes used to engage themselves in scriptural discussions, sometimes in the criticiems of poems, dramas and music, sometimes in the pleasurable game at dice, sometimes in learning the use of arms and the art of warfare and sometimes in riding elephants and horses or in driving chariots.[333] The *Visnu Purana*[334] further informs us that Krishna and Balarama after initiation went to Sandipani who, though born in Kasi, resided at Awanti to study the science of polity. There, in the course of study, they had learnt the elements of military science, with the treatises on the use of arms and directions for the mystic incantations, which secure the art of supernatural weapons. Thus we find that the qualifications for princes required by our literature were in actual practice and the princes were well qualified in the different branches of learning and art. The *Markandeya Purana* further formulates that the prince should possess good character as well as the knowledge of scriptures and the prince whose friends speak highly of his qualities and enemies, of his prowess, should be considered a true prince.[335]

Besides, *Dharmasastra, Arthasastra, Kamasastra* and *Dhanurveda,* the princes are further required to be trained in the four traditional sujects—*Trayi, Dandaniti, Anvikshiki* and *Varta.*[336] Dandin[337] and Somedeva Suri[338] have stressed that these subjects should be studied by the king. It is noticable that Kautilya[339] and Kamandak[340] have discussed the relative importance of these subjects but our Puranas do not. According to them the school of Manava knows only three subjects and regards *Anvikshaki* as special branch of *Trayi,* but Brishaspati school considers *Danda-Niti* and

Varta to be the only essential subjects for temporal affairs, and Usanas school opines that *Dandaniti* is the only important subject for the study of the king as all other sciences originate from it. But Kuatilya is of the opinion that the king must be well versed in all the four scineces mentioned above. The subject *Trayi* includes theree Vedas, *Rik, Sama* and *Yajura*. But Kautilya[341] includes the *Atharvaveda, Itihasaveda* (Itihasa and Puranas) and *Vedangs* (six limbs of he Vedas) in it. According to him Itihasa deals with the Puranas, history, *(Itivrtta)*, tales *(akhyayika)* exemplification *(udaharana), Dharmasastra* and *Arthasastra*.[342] Kamandaka[343] and Somadeva Suri are of the same opinion, but they rule out the opinion of Kautilya and include Mimansa and Nyaya in place of Vedangas and they treat the *itihasa* and Puranas as a single subject. Our Puranas[344] like Kamandaka and Semadeva Suri provide a list of fourteen branches of learning. Thus it is evident from the Puranic records that the king and his princes must be well-versed in different branches of learning including Vedas and their allied subjects.

Study of Dandaniti was, by all ancient political thinkers, considered to be the most important subject for the king, as it helps the king in discriminating between the just and the unjust.[345] By the study of this subject the king would be able to protect his state and its people and punish the vicious. Our Puranic record lay down that he king should protect his state with best endeavours both from his own people and from outsiders, adopting policy of parents towards their sons.[346]

Anvikshiki has been interpreted by several ancient writers in different ways. Kautilya, for example, points out that it comprehends the philosophies of the Samkhya, yoga, and Lokayata schools. The *Amarkosa* takes it in the series of logic (Tarkaviddya). Kamandaka opines that Anvikshiki means metaphysics (Atmavidya), Ilakantha Bhatta is of the opinion that it includes logic and Vedanta. Our Puranic text[347] interprets these subjects to mean *arthavidya* (worldly affairs) and the *Visnudharmottara Purana* takes it in the sense of metaphysics.[348] Somadeva Suri, supporting our Puranas, states that by the study of this subject the king may pull out the thorn in State's side.[349]

The study of Varta stands for the expedients and obstacles in economic pursuits and it also deals with the knowledge of worldly affairs.[350] The *Visnu Purana* lays down that agriculture, commerce and tending of cattle come under the study of *Varta*. Agriculture is the subsistence of formers, buying and selling of traders, and kine of milkman.[351] In this respect our Puranas have followed Kautilya[352] Kamandaka and[353] and Somadeva Suri.[354] Somaeva Suri is of the opinion that if the Varta is prosperous then the king must be prosperous in his state which clarifies that the king should look after agriculture, weight and measure, price control, trade and industry, which nourish the state and its subjects.[355] Besides these subjects, the princes are required to study Dhanurveda, according to our Puranas. but it does not mean that princes of royal blood should study only archery, it includes various types of arms and weapons. Out Puranas have devoted separate chapters to this subject. The *Markandeya Purana* informs us that prince Maruta was educated in the Vedas, the science of archery and other scriptures by preceptors. After completing his education in the scriptures he took lessons in the swords, bow and other weapons. Having learnt the use of arms, mastered the Vedas and seen the other and of archery he became highly accomplished in all branches of learning.[356] It is noticeable that not only the princes but even the king is asked to practice various arms and physical exercises in his daily routine. It is significant to note that our Puranas advise the king to appoint Brahmanas as teachers for his princes. There is a clear reference that a Brahmana teacher should teach military science to the two higher castes.[357] Unfortunately our Puranas do not relate such elaborate methods of training as we find in the *Arthsastra* and the *Kadambari*. Kautilya, for example, advises the king that the princes should be associated with teachers of acknowledged authority, various heads of departments and theoretical and practical politicians, for specialized training in *Anvikshiki, Trayi, Varta* and *Dandaniti* respectively.[358] Somadeva Suri[359] is of the opinion that princes should be given training in the art of oration, various scripts. arithmetic, literature, logic, grammar, science of Government, science of erotic, gems the science of using various weapons, horses and elephants etc. by the royal priest. He further suggests that teachers of royal princes should be of noble family, good lineage, pure character and learning as the character of the teacher leaves a stamp on that of his pupil. The *Visnu Purana* like other thinkers on polity lays down the system had method of examination of the princes. The text of this Purana informs us that the prince Prahlada, the son of Hiranya Kasipu was being taught the science of polity, as essential to the adminstration of government by his Guru and after completing his education when his Guru saw him that he was at home in the state policy, and full of modesty, he told his father, "Now he is well-conversant with the rules of government as laid down by the descendant of Bhrigu, Prahlada knows it fundamentally." Hiranyakasipu, therefore, summoned the prince to his presence and asked, "how a king should conduct himself towards friends, foes, what measures he should adopt at the three periods (of advance, retrogresion or stagnation); how he should deal with his councilors,[360] his ministers, the officers of his government and of his household, his emissaries, his subjects, those of doubtful allegiance and his foes; with whom should he contract alliance, with whom engage war; what sort of fortress, he should construct; How forest and mountain tribes should be reduced; How internal grievances should be rooted out". Prahalda after hearing father's questions bowed affectionately and reverentially to thbe feet of the king and replied, "It is true to that I have been instructed in all these matters by my venerable preceptor, and I have learnt them, but I cannot in all approve them. It is said that conciliation, gifts, punishment and sowing dissension are the means of securing friends or overcoming foes."[361] Somesvaradeva advocated that the princes should be tested after their studies in scripture (Sruti), science of government (Niti) logic, literature (Kavya), grammar, military science (dhanurveda) some science relating to land (Bhumibala). Phonetics (svarsastra) arts, (Kala), different feats of archery (Chapavidya) the uses of various weapons and riding on horses and elephants. He further states that princes must be tested in *patavam* (experience) *bala* (strength), *prajna* (prudence) and *Kalakausala* (practical feasts).

Our Puranas advise[362] the king that princes should not be permitted to associate with those who are greedy or disrespected persons and should be guarded by the persons whose cruelty watch the movements of princes. Our record[363] further informs that if princes are incapable of learning they should be kept in a prison of pleasure, and those who are obedient and submissive should be appointed as the superintendents of various departments of the state so that they may learn the art of administration before anointment as a king. Details regarding the education of the prince Chandrapida is found in Bana's *Kadambari*.[364] We are told that prince Chandrapida was only six years of age when he was sent to school for his education, which was situated outside the village. There, he received his education for ten yars under very learned teachers. Prince Chandrapida received proficiency in grammar, mimamsa, logic, science of laws, various branches of political science, the use of different weapons, instrumental music, various scripts and dialectsof country, all mechanical arts, the vedas, and in many different branches of learning: thus it is evident that the curriculum of education prescribed for princes by our Puranic record is very much similar to that in Bana's *Kadambari*. Dandin, too, has suggested similar subjects but it is strange that he states that gambling, thieving and other similar crooked arts should also be learned by princes.[365]

Though it is difficult to say that all the kings and

princes of ancient India received the education prescribed by our Puranas and other works on polity, yet there are epigraphic as well as literary references which show that generally the kings of ancient India were well-versed in different branches of learning. The Allahabad Pillar Inscription informs us that the king, Samudra Gupta, was well-versed in proficiency in scripture (Prasama-Sastravakyyodaya), Valour (bhuja-Vikkrama) and liberality and generosity (Pradana). He was equally efficient in the field of diplomacy and war. It was on account of the merits of Samudra Gupta that Chandra Gupta I, who was not only the first Maharajadhiraja of Gupta dynasty but also one who had laid the foundation of the Gupta splendour, declared Samudra Gupta as the noblest and the best prince before the couuncil of minsters and in the presence of princes themselves. Likewise Skanda Gupta was not only the champion or hero of the Gupta age but also the saviour of the fortune of the Gupta family. We are further told from Hathigumpha Inscription[366] that Kharavela learnt Lekha (official correspondence), Rupa (currency), Ganana (accountancy) and administration of justice and also Gandharva veda (music) when he was only crown-prince. The Junagarha inscriptionof Rudradamana rcords that Mahasatrapa was famous for his deep study, retention and actual practice of grammar, Artha (Lexicography or politics), music, logic and other branches of knowledge. He was expert in riding horses, elephants and chariots and was a great adept in wielding the sword and shield and in wrestling.[367] King Harsa is famous for his knowledge of literature his three extant dramas, viz. The *Ratnavali*, *Priyadarsika* and *Naganand*. The other kings, too, are renowned for their scholarship in different branches of learning.

Checks of the King

The political thinkers of ancient India regarded the king only as ideal, whose life was dedicated for enjoyment of pleasure but it had to put great troubles while carrying out the royal duties of protecting the subjects and fulfilling his Dharma. They opined that the king was not to act as he pleased high office as a sacred trust and was put advised to take whole counsel with the ministers who were required to control and supervise the state administration. It is laid dawn in the Puranic literature that the ministers of the king who share in the multifarious activities of the state administration should be the citizen of the state, born of good and well placed family, of high and noble blood, well-versed in arts and science, foresighted, intelligent, eloquent etc.[368] These above mentioned qualifications signify that ministers of the kings were well-qualified persons and they had the control over the king. Naturally the king had to work in cooperation with the ministers because all the authorities are opposed to one-men rule. It is interesting to note that like other authorities on law codes the Puranic literature asks the king to perform his duties according to rules and regulations prescribed in the law books.[369] It is said in the Puranic text[370] that if a king levied an unjust fine he was to reufund thirty times that amount to the person concerned. Further, the *Visnudharmottara*[371] *Purana* lays down that if the king gives his judgement with anger and attachment he is required to return thirty times amount to the brahmanas. The *Agni Purana*[372] very pertinently advises the king to try to win the affection and loyalty of his subjects. The state, the territory and prosperity of the king arised from his popularity among his subjects. He has to function as the source of pleasure to his subjuects.[373] It is further said that the king who oppresses the people is soon destroyed and lives in hell for an indefinite period. Obviously this threat is held to check the autocracy of the king. It is significant to note that the Puranic[374] literature does not allow the king to increase the taxes according to his own discretion. He has to follow the rules laid down by the Dharmasastras. The *Markandeya Purana,*[375] at one place, designated a king as a thief who wrongfully received excess taxes from his subjects. Thus it appears that the king was under the law and not above the law. A healthy check on the autocracy of the king is provided by the *Agni Purana*[376] that the king should be free form the use of harsh and cruel words, infliction of cruel punishments, exploitation of the sources of revenue, drinking, gambling and hunting, idleness, disinclination for all sorts of works and boastfulness. Thus it is obvious that these limitations were prescribed so that the king may not lead to the encouragement of anarchy.

Relations Between the King and the People

The Puranic literature like other works on polity throws the light on the relation between the king and his subjects. On the one hand we find that the subjects should obey the orders of the king and on the other hand we find that it was the primary duty of the king to protect his subjects like his own begotten son.[377] It is further said that the king should protect his subjects both from external aggression and internal lawlessness adopting the policy of parents. Thus, we find that relation between the king and his subjects were cordial. The *Visnudharmottara Purana,*[378] at one place, pertinently remarks that the palaces of the king whose people are well protected is like the heaven and the temple of the king whose subjects are not protected is the hell. The *Agni Purana*[379] also says that the king should try to win the affenction and loyalty of his subjects. The kingdom, the territory and the prosperity of the king arise from his popularity among his subjects. It is further said that the strength of the king is the love of his subjects and the word Raja is derived from the word Rajan (to please). Thus, the king was the source of pleasure to the people.[380]

The Puranic literature prescribes that the taxation is meant for providing protection to the people against natural calamities as well as external and internal troubles. The *Visnudharmottara Purana*[381] specifically lays down that a king is entitled to receive taxes from his subjects in return for the protencton he offers to them like a pregnant woman who sacrifices her own desires and pleasures for the protection of her child. It is further said in the *Agni Purana* that if the king does not protect his subjects and gives troubles to them he well be destroyed soon and will have a long sojourn in the hell.[382] The text of the same Purana,[383] at one place, asks the king to a virtuous towards the subjects and in return to expect the same devotion and loyalty form his subjects. Further the king is also responsible for sins committed by his offiecers.

The Puranic literature[384] also lays down that the king should punish the wrong doers and if he does not punish them he would go in the hell. It is said that the king receives taxes in the form of his livelihood in the same way as the sun who receives taxes in the form of his livelihood in the same way as the sun who receives a portion of all the waters on the earth and return in the form of rain. Thus we find that the king was entitled to receive that taxes in lieu of protection that he offered to his subjects. The *Visnudharmottara Purana*[385] informs us that when the people are protected they contribute gold, crops, clothes, conveyance and other material to the king. The *Matsya Purana,*[386] the infirm and the widows and to provide them with boarding and lodging and endowments and adust the Varnasrama rules. The *Agni Purana*[387] furtehr advises the king to banish, form the country, the officer found guilty of extorting money the subjects. Thus we find that there were cordial relations between the king and his subjects.

Ministers

In the masterly arduous task of state administration the need of proper council from the ministers is vital and necessary for the king. His office requires constant counsel with the ministers. Therefore, the political thinkers of ancient India hold that the Ministry or the Council of advisers is the most important wheel of the administrative machinery. Hence, the ministers have been invariably assigned the second place amongst the Prakritis[388] of the state and their importance has been emphasized in graphic language by several ancient writers. Manu, for example, lays down that even a task, however, very easy and simple, cannot be accomplished by a person single-handed. How then, he questions, can the work of the king, which involves great issues, be accomplished without the assistance of others?[389] The *Mahabharata* also advocates that a king cannot rule his kingdom, without the assistance of his ministers, even for three days.[390] It further set forth that a king is as vitally dependent upon his ministers as animals depend upon clouds, Brahmanas on the Vedas and women on their husbands.[391] Great thinker like Kautilya, Sukra, Kamandaka etc., also stress the need of good council of ministers for the help and guidance of a king in the day-to-day discharge of his royal duties. Kautilya holds that kingship is possible only with (the aid of) assistants: A single wheel can never move (a carriage), therefore, the King should appoint ministers and listen tc their opinions.[392] Sukra is more clear on this point and his dictum is that a king should not decide political issues without consulting his ministers, however, proficient he might be in the practical polity and other sciences, otherwise he would plunge the state into misery and himself into unpopularity.[393] Kamandaka, who attaches greater importance to the power of counsel (Mantra-Sakti) than to the power of arms, compares a king without the ministers to a bird whose wings have been clipped.[394]

Like other works on polity the Puranas also embody the views as have been expressed by other authorities. the *Matsya Purana* clearly lays down that even a smallest work cannot be successfully performed by a single man who has nobody to help. Now then can a state be well administered without the assistance of competent ministers.[395] To put it in other words, a state cannot properly function without the aid and cooperation of suitable council of ministers. It further advocates that a king truly interested in the welfare of his state, ought to look forward simultaneously with his coronation to the appointment of competent persons to form his council of ministers where the kingdom may find its stability.[396] The *Visnudharmottara Purana*[397] also asserts the foregoing view. The *Agni Purana*[398] enjoins upon a king that he should, soon after his assuming the kingship, appoint the royal priest, astrologer, ministers, his chief consort, and also probably the high functionaries of the state. Further, it lays down that if a king dies before electing his council of ministers, no time should be lost in providing with his sucessor and in slection of the ministers.[399] The *Markandeya Purana*[400] while subscribing to the above view, explains that as man would meet his doom (in eight ways) from the strong wheels of a car (chariot) it would bring about a king's destruction where he was dispense with the adveceof his ministers. Therefore, a king by keeping his counsels may protect hemself against his enemies. The *Visnupurana* also lays down that the king should consult his ministers before starting his state work.[401]

Illuminating the importance of the ministers, Somadeva Suri, a Jain political thinker of 10th century A.D., writes that the king in spite of his being equipped with four-fold strategy cannot reign without his ministers[402] and he goes on to say that as fire needs the help of wind to flare, in the same way even powerful and efficient ruler cannot rule without the assistance of his ministers.[403] Katyayana is of the view that a king should not decide any case on his own accord but seek suggestions form his ministers. The *Nitivakyamrita,* at another place, observes that a king who does not appoint the ministers and rules arbitrarily annihilates his kingdom.[404] The *Panchatantra* describes the ministers as the pillars of the state.[405]

The result of the studies of these giants of political thinking leads but to an undisputed fact that a king i.e. who rules over his subjects must have a well-formed council of ministers drawn from the best talents amongst his followers, for the proper and efficient functioning of the multifarious affairs of his state. Hence the need of a royal council consisting of ministers becomes indispensable for the proper working of the government. Therefore, every king in ancient India had council of ministers to advise him in political and administrative matters since the very day of his consecration. The Puranas are no exception to this rule.

The English word 'minister' has been denoted in a number of words in the Puranas. the *Agni Purana* contains *Mantri, Dhisachiva, Amatya, Mahamatra* and *Pradhana* synonymously.[406] While *Mahamatya*[407] also occurs there. In the *Markandeya Purana* such words as Mantrin,[408] Amatya[409] and Sachiva[410] stand for ministers. But the technical interpretation of each one of these terms is not clear form our text. It is rather difficult to make a distinction between technical interpretation of these words in the context of their political and legal status. However, in the *Agni Purana* we come across the words Amatya and Mantrin, which would seem to indicate that there is distinction between these two, perhaps to denote the respective position of these two functionaries. It is, however, observed that in case the terms Amatya and Mantrin were intended to mean a single functionary, there was hardly any need to mention at different places these terms as synonymous. The *Ramayana*[411] and the *Arthasastara*[412] also seem to draw a distinction between Amatyas and Mantrins on the basis of their qualifications. Somadeva Suri also described Amatyas and Mantrins separately, covering two chapters in his *Nitivakyamrita*.[413] On the other hand the *Rajanitiprakasa*,[414] for example, states that Amatyas are styled Mantrins. In the *Ramayana*[415] we actually find that Sumantra has been designated with both the titles. The Deogradha Inscription of Chandella King Kirtivarman records that a minister is styled both as Amatya and Mantridhara. But from the study of the Puranic records it appear that in later period when the Puranas were compiled Mantrins were considered to be of a higher rank than the Amatyas.

The difference between Amatyas and Sachivas is also made clear in the *Agni Purana*. It states that after coronation ceremony the Pratihara comes with Amatyas and Sachivas to introduce them to the newly consecrated king.[416] The same text further enjoins upon a king to weigh in proper scales the merits and the demerits of his of his councils, Amatyas and Sachivas which have been separately dealt with is this context. Though in the *Manusmrti* Sachiva has been equated with Amatya, this does not seem to be true in the Puranic period. It is noticeable that the *Agni Purana* used the terms *Amatyasachivadimscha*,[417] *Mantramatyatmajadikah*[418] and *Amatyamantrinastatha*[419] whereby one might conclude that Sachiva ranks after Amatya and not the Mantrin leaving it to any body to guess what was the relative status of these functionaries amongst themselves. The text of the *Agni Purana* further differentiates the Amatyas and Sachivas on the basis of their qualifications. The *Nitiprakasika*[420] seems to draw a distiction between the Amatyas and the Sachivas on the basis of their qualifications and it, further, states that the king should appoint seven or eight Sachivas while appointment of only two or three Mantrins is laid down. The *Abhilasitarthachintamani*[421] also uses their terms—*Amatya, Sachiva* and *Mantrin* side by side. It prescribes that these functionaries should take their respective seats in the court allotted to them by the king. They are also advised to occupy their respective residence in the different quarters of the capital. Thus it is clear that during the puranic period there were some states in which Sachivas were equated with Amatyas while there were other. kingdoms where Amatyas, Sachivas and Mantrins had different status. The term Mahamatya is probably used for the Prime Minister in the *Agni Purana*[422] and the facility of residence of other officials into light. Rajasekhara[423] also uses the term *Mahamatya* for the Prime Minister. The term *Pradhana* of the *Agni Purana* is probably stands for the Prime Minister. (Sivaji styled his Prime Minister as *Astapradhana*).

Strength of Ministers

As regard the strength of ministry, there is divergence of opinion among ancient Indian political thinkers. The *Agni Purana* merely informs us that the king Dasratha had eight ministers,[424] and Ravana seven.[425] This description is based on the *Ramayana*. Manu recommends that the ministry should consist of seven or eight ministers[426] but he has given freedom to fix the number according to the needs of the state business. The above mentioned number of ministers has been favoured, among others, by the *Ramayana*,[427] the *Mahabharata*,[428] and the *Sukraniti*.[429] From the *Arthasastra*,[430] which quotes different opinions on this subject, we learn that Manu, Brihaspati and Usanas schools vavoured a ministry of 12, 16 and 20 members respectively. Sukra favours a ministry of 10 but he also suggest a smaller body of 7 or 8 persons. A western Chalukya King Somesvara seems to have followed the tradition of Smrtis in constituting his council of ministers. He advises the king to keep seven or eight ministers in his council.[431] However, Somadeva Suri, a Jain writer, advises the king not to be content with only one minister. He points out that where there is a single minister, there is grave danger of such a person tending to autocracy. Moreover, the concentration of administration in the hands of a single minister tends tomake him behave like a rival of the king himself. He therefore, suggests that the king should never take the risk of appointing a single minister, because vesting of absolute power in him will return his had and he will always try to supplant the king. For the same reason, he further recommends that the king should not appoint two persons a minister,[432] lest they should conspire against the king and be on the lookout for an opportune moment to raise the standard of revolt. The way for internal disruption will be clear and open. They will conspire and try to overthrow the king. On the other hand Somadeva disfavours a very large number of ministers as he thinks that such ministry might prove harmful to the efficient running of the government on account of jealousy and other human weaknesses. Therefore, he advises the king to keep a cabinet of three, five or seven ministers.[433]

As against this some ancient treatises suggest that the king should keep a fairly large ministry with a small inner cabinet. The *Mahabharata,*[434] for example, recommend that the king should have thirty-seven *Amatyas.* It gives a detailed information regarding the number of ministers selected form the different castes of the society. According to it, there should be four members from the Brahman caste, eight from the *ksatriya,* twenty-one from the Vaisya and three from the Sudra and one from the Sutas. But this treatise further adds that the king should discuss the state business with ministers and decide his policies in the midst of eight mantrins.[435] Likewise the *Ramayana* and *Arthasastra* record that the king should take counsel from three or four ministers. Kautilya clearly lays down that there is an extra-ordinary matter, the Mantrin and the Mantrin Parishad should be called together and informed.[436] It is thus clear that there were two kinds of ministers viz., those who were of cabinet rank and those not so privileged. The Puranas do not mention the exact number of ministers, but from the study of the *Visnudharmottara*[437] the *Matsya,*[438] the *Agni*[439] and other Puranas, it could be surmised that the numerical strength of the ministry was left to the king who was to decide their number according to the requirements of his state. The Puranas advise a king to consult neither one nor many ministers on his state business. The text of the *Visnudharmattara,*[440] the *Matsya,* and the *Agni* Puranas[440] lays down that the king should consult his ministers separately, so that the ministers may not be jealous of each other and may not be able to tamper with the king's policy to suit their purpose. Thus it appears that the Puranic literature advises the king to consult his ministry, which should not be consist of either one single minister or too many ministers.

Qualifications of the Ministers

Ministers being vitally necessary for a king to enable him to run his administration efficiently it was of greatest importance that they should be the persons of high caliber and distinguished versatility. Their education, character and personality must be of a very high order. The various qualifications of a minister are broadly discussed in Kautilya's *Arthasastra, Manusmrti, Yajnavalkyasmrti* and *Kamandakiya Nitisasra* etc. There are different texts but almost all are unanimous on the requisite qualifications of a minister. According to Kautilya a minister must be a native of the country, born in high family, influential, well trained in arts, possessed of foresight, wise, strong in memory, bold, eloquent, vigilant, intelligent, possessed of enthusiasm, dignity and endurance, pure in character, affable, affectionate, firm in loyal devotion endowed with character, strength health and bravery, free from procrastination and ficklemindedness, affectionate and free from such defects as excite hatred and enmity.[441] In actual practice all the qualifications could not be found in all ministers but an effort was made to make the selection in the light of the aforesaid ideals. This was the case in every administration in ancient India and the Puranas are no exception to it. From the text of the Puranas, we learn that the ministers were well qualified in different branches of knowledge. The *Matsya Purana*[442] clearly points out that the king should select his ministers from the men of respectable families and they must be valiant, strong, imposing, capable of bearing hardship, ambitious, handsome, having Satvaguṅa and forbearance, good, virtuous sweet-spoken, able to give friendly advices, loyal to the king, knowing to act in the proper time and place and eager for a good name. The *Visnudharmottara Purana*[443] too, devoted a full chapter on the qualifications of the ministers separately. According to it the minister should be versatile, Brahmana, well-versed in the knowledge of the Vedas, polite, of pleasing personality, firm in decision, devoted to the king, courageous, sweet spoken, proficient in the polity of Brihaspati and Sukra, free from anger and indolence, dauntless form a public slander, capable of bearing hardship, endowed with character, well versed inthe secret counsel, intelligent, devotee to the duty, proficient in reasoning, brave, neither haughty nor arrogant, competent in the art of spy-system, knower of the six-fold policy, expert in devises, eloquent, clever in state work, same in dealing with state servants, virtual, understanding of time and task, grateful, lovding to all, observer of official works, expert in state policy etc. The *Agni Purana*[444] further, advises the king to appoint the minister who possesses necessary qualifications. It is provided with the text that a minister should be man of eloquence, condidence, strong in physique and possessing a good retentive memory. He should be ingenuous and well versed in the code of laws and different branches of the fine arts. He is also required to bc courageous, able to bear the public censure for the good and welfare of his country and capable to removing evils of the state. He should keep a vigilant eye upon the affairs of his neighbouring states. He should also be well versed in the principles of war and treaty. He should be capable of reading the secret counsels of the foreign courts and executing his work at the opportunate time and place. Further, he should never allow private considerations to mould his decision in the council of state and should be free from all pride, hunter, fickleness and bragging. He was supposed talent, character, noble paranta, energy, influence and promptness. His zeal for work, patience during distress, watchfulness, gallantness, unostentatious, gravity, amiability, purity, integrity and honesty were also required for him. He should be truthful, patient, wise, experienced, and above all suspicious. Perseverance and closeness of counsel are the essential qualifications of a minister for a state.[445] This Purana, further, recommends the king to appoint ministers after ascertaining their qualifications. It is provided that the king should examine, if necessary, their watchfulness and proficiency in fine arts with the help of spies, lineage, social status and influence from their friends and relations thoroughly. The king should judge their efficiency in service, knowledge and power of endurance, as well as their amiability and general ingenuity. Their eloquence and truthfulness in speech should be examined through conversation. Likewise, their energy, prowess, power of enduring distresses, attachment, comprehension, purity, devotion, friendliness and calmness shoud be examined from their past record. Their strength, character physique, gravity of disposition and calumnies are to be ascertained from their companions and colleagues. In addition to these tests the king is advised to examine their dumb-foundedness, fickleness, meanness and gentleness of his ministers in their presence.[446] But actions of ministers are to be scrutinized privately. Hence, the *Agni Purana* specifies the positive and negative qualifications of minsters as well as the method of examination. In this sontext the purania text has followed the view of Kautilya[447] in several respects. Elsewhere the Purana[448] advises the king to appoint pious men in the religious department, brave in the army, intelligent persons in the finance, eunuchs in the harem and ruffians in the difficult work and virtuous people in the department of revenue. The *Agni Purana*, prescribes that the king should appoint a person to a job suited to his nature and aptitude. The king is, furthermore, advesed to make the appointement of persons after testing their fidelity.[449] Thus, we learn that the state functionaries should be given assignments to match their qualifications. On this point the *Arthasastra* of Kautilya and the *Agni Purana* agree to each other. While Kautilya has laid down a detailed process for test of the qualifications of ministers, there are, however, no such details in the *Agni Purana*. It is, thus, clear form the Puranic records that, firstly, the ministers shouldbe endowed with such personal qualities as noble birth, eloquence, honesty, modesty, truthfulness etc. so that they may command obedience and respect of all sections of the society. Secondly, the ministers should be the citizens of the state, should also bear allegiance to the king and the country and be of firm mind and determination. Thirdly, the ministers should be able to execute state affairs and be proficient in the science of polity. They should be well versed in the diferent branches of arts and learning, ablė in the arts of strategy, war and peace. They are required to keep themselves well informed of what is going on in the neighbouring countries for the purpose of internal security and defence from aggression and foreign attack. Finally, the ministers should not allow themselves to fits of anger, greed; fear and untruthfulness should not touch them.

It is, however that the aforesaid qualifications of a minister as mentioned in the *Agni Purana* are verbatim extracts from the *Nitisara* of Kamandaka,[450] with the difference that what has been said for the king in the *Nitisara* has been made applicable to ministers in the *Agni Purana.* After important verses of the *Nitisara* do not find place in the *Agni Purana,* perhaps, due to ingorance of the compiler. This variation probably points out the growing importance of the ministers in the times of *Agni Purana.*

It is worth mentioning that the *Agni Purana* lays down the qualifications of ministers at two different places,[451] the second list is merely being reproduction of the first, except that the minister should be the resident of the country. Both these lists are found in the *Nitisara,* but probably they have been borrowed form the *Arthsastra* as well as from the old *smrtis.*

This importace of qualifications required for aminister could not escae the attention of other ancient Indian political thinkers too. For examle, Manu[452] recommends that the ministers should be scions of noble families, well versed in the Sastras; men of heroic temperament and experienced in state business. He gives preference to the hereditary ministers, subject to the condition that a minister should be appionted only after their passing the tests required of them. Likewise Yajnavalkya also suggests that ministers should be wise, brave, pure and born in high family.[453]

Brahaspati[454] is also of the same opinion.

The above-mentioned qualifications of the minsters have engaged the attention of other authorities too, including Valmiki[455] Bhisma,[456] Kamandka,[457] Sukra,[458] Somadeva[459] and Somesvara[460] etc. These authorities advise that the minister should be the citizen of the state, born of good and well placed family of high and noble blood versed in arts and sciences. Foresight, intelligent, enthusiastic, eloquent, heroic, pure and devoted to the king. They were also required to be proficient in the principles of Dharma and to be free form anger, greed, fear, arrogance, and fickleness. The epigraphic records of different ages belonging to different dynasties of ancient India have proved that above mentioned qualifications were not merely cherished as an ideal but were in actual practice.

It is interesting to note that the Jain political thinder Somadeva Suri has not prescribed only the positive qualifications of ministers but negative as well. Thus, Somadeva Suri advises the king not to appoint the ministers who are foreigners[456] sensuous, haughty,[457] powerful,[458] obstinate,[459] extravagant,[460] miser,[461] coward[462] and born in low caste,[463] because probably he was aware that a foreigner might be led by the sentiments and feelings of his own country, and when his country's interest runs counter to the country he is serving, there are chances of his betraying and working as the enemy agent. Therefore, he does not allow the appointment of a foreigner for this august office. A sensuous person stands every chance of being led astray by the enemies of the state. Thus, he cannot be trusted to be placed on the keypost. The person who is of haughty nature cannot be realistic and sober in any situation and he is always allergic to sudden outburst of temper that will completely nor the efficiency of the action that he is going to take. Such a person will also be a complete failure if he is called upon to being negotiations with some foreign power. Nobody knows what action he might take when he is in the grip of frenzy and anger.

The powerful man may also standup against the king and overthrow him. If such a person is appointed by the king as minister, the court will soon become an arena of party politics and the king will not be an arbitrator in his own administration. An obstinate person should also be excluded from the appointment as minister. He will never be able to understand the point of view of others and his obstinate nature will only aggravate the situation, which is upsetting the state and its administration. An extravagant person should also be not taken into consideration when the king has to make appointment to the office of a minister. The finance has always been the backbone of the country. A bankrupt state always invites insurrection of the masses within and foreign invasion outside. An extravagant minister will run out the state treasury without proper check on its resources. A miser person too does not find favour with political thinker. He is placed on the list of those who should in no case be taken into consideration when the king appoints his ministers. A minister who is miser by nature, will always put money above the welfare of the state, and is not therefore a fit person for assignment. A coward is not to be entrusted to any job, much less important than the responisble office of a minister. A coward if elevated to the post of a minister, will bring about the ruin of the state, chiefly in two ways. Firstly, he would be unable to govern and control undesirable elements in the internal affairs of the state, and secondly such minister would be an utter failure in resisting and beating back a foreign threat, aggression and attack. Somadeva Suri has not favoured the appointment of the persons of low caste probably because such persons were classified to serve the high-caste people. Besides he holds that Brahmanas, Ksatriyas, relatives, friends and class fellows of the king should not be appointed to the post of ministers. In supprt of what Somadeva Suri says against the appointment of Brahmanas, Ksatriyas to the post of the ministers he gives his views about the characteristics of these people making them unsuitable for the assignment. If a brahmana is appointed as a minister, due to his trait he will not return the money if he gets the opportunity of grabbing it. The exclusion by Somadeva Suri of a Brahmana from the post of a minister, is not to be construed to mean his prejudice to that class; he is equally opposed to Ksatriyas in this respect. A Ksatriya minister may prove to think in terms of violent actions. He may resort to the means, which might suppress the rising and crush the conspiracy. His rash actions might well prove more harmful than beneficial to the various interests of the state. But our Puranic records do not lay down any caste qualification for ministership with the exception that they have advised the king to appoint a Brahmana or a Ksatriya as the Commander-in-Chief of the army, which is the most important post among the ministers of the state. The *Agni Purana* reveals that at the time of a King's coronation, the ceremony was to proceed in the presence of ministers belonging to all the four castes. We are not quite sure that Somadeva's advice was actually followed by the kings of ancient India. All that we know is that our Puranas make it clear that great care should be taken in the selection of a person to the post of a minister.

The Theory of Heredity

The theory of hereditary ministership propounded by the thinkers[464] of ancient India was vividly followed by the compilers of the Puranas. The *Matsya Purana* specifically mentions that the ministers and other officers of the state should be appointed on hereditary principle without any hard and fast test.[465] The *Visnudharmottara*[466] and the *Agni Puranas,*[467] too contain the same rule and suggest the king to appoint the state officer whose father and grand-father had been serving the state from the times of the grand-father and father of the king. Our literature[468] further adds very sensible remark that such hereditary ministers should not be allowed to dispose of the cases of their agnates *(dayadas).* Thus it appears that the Puranas have followed the view of the Smrti writers that the sons or relations of a minister should, if possible, be selected while making new appointments in the ministry, though *Rajanitiprakasa*[469] clearly lays down that the principle of hereditary ministership did not apply to those cases where the son or the grandson of a former minister did not possess the requisite qualifications. It is noticeable that our literature informs us that sometimes ministers were selected from the members of the royal blood. The *Matsya Purana*[470] clearly lays down that where the relations of the king are not placed, the friends of the king may be appointed which shows that the preference was given to the members of the royal blood in the appointment of the ministers. The epigraphic evidence, however, records that the premier of the Chahmana ruler Visaladeva was his own son Salkakshanapala.[471] Harsha of Kashmira had also appinted two sons of a former ruler as his ministers.[472] The hereditary character is borne out by many inscriptions of ancient India. For example, in the Allahabad pillar inscription of king Samudra Gupta dynasty we find that Harisena himself was Mahadandanayaka and his father Dhruvabhuti was also Mahadeandanayaka. Similarly in the undated Udayagiri cave inscription[474] of Chandra Gupta II, Virasena is described as Anvayapraptasachivya i.e. one who hereditarily obtained the post of Sachiva. The Karadanda[475] stone inscription refers that Prithavisena was the minister of Kumara Gupta I and his father Sikharaswami was the minister of his father Chandra Gupta II. Thus we find that the appointment of ministers on the hereditary principle proposed by the Puranic record, was widely followed in actual practice in ancient India.

Caste of Ministers

Let us now consider the question of the caste of ministers. Authorities on ancient polity have different opinions on this subject. The Puranas have adviced the king to appoint Brahamanas and Ksatriyas as his ministers. The *Matsya Purana*,[476] at one place, clearly observes that minister for the army should be appointed either from the Brahmana or the Ksatriya caste. The *Visnudharmottara*[477] and the *Agni*

Puranas,[478] too, are of the same view. The compiler of the Agni Purana favours the appointment of a Ksatriya as the minister of justice.[479] It further lays down that the minister should be able to execute and recite the laws of justice or *Dandaniti*.[480] It seems that our Puranic literature has followed the view of Bahmical sources[481] and also of the Arthasastra.[482] Thus it appears that the compilers of the Puranas did not allow the Vaisyas and Sudṛas to be the ministers of the King's council. On the other hand we find that the *Mahbharata*[483] prescribes a ministerial council representative of all castes, including Sudras and Sutas. Birhaspati enjoins that in the absence of qualified Brahmanas, Ksatriyas and Vaishyas may be recruited as Ministers but he rules out Sudra.[484] The same view is taken up by Sukra.[485] The Jain writer Somadeva,[486] at one place, recommends the three higher castes for the post of ministers but at another place he does not favour the appoiṅtment of Brahmanas,[487] and Ksatriyas[488] as ministers of the king's council. The exclusion of Brahmanas and Ksatriayas form the appointment of ministers clerly shows that the Jain political thinker was not led by caste prejudice. It also makes clear that only Vaisyas are to be appointed as Ministers though nowhere do we get categorical answer to this problem of appointment of ministes. It is not clear why a clear-cut reply has not been given.

Duties and Functions of the Minister

The primary duty of the ministers, according to our literature, was to advise the king but they were also administrative heads of hte department.[489] The other functions of the ministers may be inferred from their qualifications laid down in the literature. They are asked to be well-versed in the policy of war and peace and keep vigilant eyes upon the affairs and preparations being carried on in the neighbouring states. Information regarding the secret counsels of foreign courts should also be known to the ministers. These informations must be preserved by the ministers through espionage system which was organised by the ministers through espionage system which was organised by the minister concerned. The minister for peace and war *(Sandhivigrahika)* was supposed to conduct the foreign policy of the state. They were further required to win the loyalty of the enemies of the king to their master and to make them obedient to him, as a tame elephant helps to bring the wild ones under control.[490]

Our Puranic literature also asks the ministers to look after financial matters,[491] because the treasury is the backbone of the country. The *Agni Purana*[492] lays down that a treasury nearly drained or not filled up with daily shortage or not kept with a proper account should be deemed as defective, so it was the duty of the minister to lookafter it properly. Further, according to the same text[493] the ministers are required: *(i)* to deliberate the measures of the state to the king; *(ii)* to take steps for successful implementation of the schemes; *(iii)* to put into effect all decided plans or policies, *(iv)* to supervise the income and the expenditure of the state, *(v)* to draft civil and criminal laws for the state, *(vi)* to sheck the encroachement of a foreign enemy, *(vii)* to remove affections of the state and finally *(viii)* to protect the king and his kingdom.

It is thus obvious that the ministers were required to advice the king on all important matters and execute them in the day-to-day administration. It is also laid down that if ministers fails to perform the duties assigned to them would spoil the treasure of their master along with clothes, foodgrain and vehicle etc.[494] Therefore, the king is asked to take interview of the ministers daily, presented by the usher of the court,[495] so that the king and the ministers may get the opportuninty to discuss the state-policies by mutual consultations and to execute the schemes framed by the king and his functionaries.

The ministers were also required to look after the income and the expenditure of the state. In other words, they were supposed to see the business of revenue-collection and expenditure. It was the duty of the minister concerned to observe that the money which had been collected through revenue should be spent on useful and productive purposes. It is noticeable that other writers on polity too have laid down similar duties of the state officials. For example, Somadeva Suri asserts the four-fold duties of the ministers including the supervision of the finances. He suggests that the minister should enter the reserve fund in the Register and should audit it properly.

During the Puranic period, probably the political condition of the country was not sound and healthy. The kings were encountering among themselves. The *Agni Purana,* therefore, suggests that the king, newly enthroned, should, wage the war with his minister against his enemies.[496] So it was the foremost duty of the minister to protect the king in the battle-field. The *Visnu Purana* informs us that Banasura was accompanied by his ministers in the battlefield.[497] The contemporary literature and the epigraphs inform us the growing military power of the ministers. The undated Udayagiri cave inscription[498] of Chandra Gupta II clearly states that his foreign minister *(Sandhi-Vigrahika)* Virasena was with him in the battle-field of Malava. According to *Nitisara* of Kamandaka[499] the ministers constitute an integral part of the Skandhavara (war camp). Somesvaradeva[500] provides a reward of ten thousand for him who kills a Sachiva or Amatya. the *Visnudharmottara*[501] and the *Agni* Puranas[502] instruct the king not to go to the actual fighting-place and keep himself two miles away from the battlefield. It suggests that during our Puranic period the military power was shifted to the war minister and it was the duty of the minister concerned to go to the batlefield and to conduct the war according to the directions given by the king.

The most important duty of the ministers was to look after the justice of the state. Consequently it appears that is was the responsibility of the ministers to help the king in the matter of judicial administration. In actual practice the minster for justice was the highest court of Appeal in the absence of the king. The *Agni Purana,*[503] therefore, instructs that the officer who is found guilty for extorting money from the subjects of the king and those who have been found disloyal to their duties should be banished from the ocuntry and all his estates should be escheated to the king. It further states that the ministers (Amatyah) and Justice (Pradavivaka) found betraying their duties, assingned by the king, should be exiled from the realm and their property should be confiscated.[504] To lookafter the revenue, expenditure, protection of the royal family and the department of army by the ministers are also required by Somadevasuri.[505] He further says that a good minister is one who is liked by the army and allies and who properly looks after the treasury and kingdom and is devoted to the king. Besides they are required to audit accounts, to look-after registration, food and agriculture, manufacture and salt.[506]

The king is advised by our Puranas to control and supervise state-administration with the help of his ministers and high officers, by which he may win his enemies and expand his empire.[507] The king is further advised to detect the weaknesses of his state-officers through his ministers and superintendents of the various department. It has also been provided that the king should only consult those ministers who are loyal to him just as a tame elephant is employed to catch the wild animals.[508]

Other writers on the polity of ancient India, too, are of the same opinion regarding the power and functions of the minsters. For instance Bharadvaja speculates the following duties to the minister "deliberating in council, accomplishment of the works, the business of revenue collection and expenditure, recruiting the army, the driving out of the enemy and the wild tribes, the protection of the kingdom, taking remedial measure against calamities, the protection of the heir-apparent and the installation of the princes".[509] Kautilya[510] is of the same opinion and states that "all activities proceed from the minister; activities such as the successful accomplishment of the works of the people, security of person and property from internal and external enemies, remedial measures against calamities, colonization and improvement of wild tract of land, recruiting the army, collection of revenue and bestowal of favour." Kamandaka[511] and Somadeva Suri[512] have followed the policy of Kautilya. It is thus evident that the powers, functions and duties of the ministers assigned by our Puranas follow the views of Kautilya and Bharadvaja.

It is significant that our Puranas state the defects of the minsters. There are the use of harsh and cruel words, infliction of cruel and inordinate punishment, spoliation of the sources of revenues, drinking, over-fondness for female company, hunting and gumbling, idleness, disinclination for all sorts of works, boastfulness, irresolution and stupidity."[512] Somadeva Suri adds that "eating away the state revenue in the treasury and monetary transactions" are the defects of the ministers. It is thus evident that such defects should be omitted from ministers who hold very important posts in the state administrations. Thus in fact the scope of work on the ministers intended to the entire administration and they helped the king whenever knotty problems confronted him. As ministers were often learned and capable persons, the kings very much depended on their advice and held them in high regard. The efficiency of the administration was very much dependent on their mutual co-operation.

The Puranas like other ancient treatises recommend that the minsters should be consulted by the king on all-important afairs of the state-adminstration individually as well as collectively. Kautilya[513] emphasizes the importance of Mantri in an arrow discharged by an archer may kill one man or none at all, but a (well-considered) scheme put into operation by wise man may destroy even those who are only conceived. The *Matsya Purana* specifically lays own that the king should consult his ministers individually and separately but the advice of one minister should not be signified to others. It is further suggested that the king should not take full confidence of each counseller. He is also advised by our text that after taking advice from his ministers he should reconsider the whole matter by himself before enforcing his policy.[514] The *Visnu Purana* informs us that Khandikya consulted his Purohita and minister in lonely place on the subject of state policy.[515] The *Visnudharmottara Purana*, too, advises the king to consult the ministers individually.[516] But it is said that the minister should not disclose the secrets otherwise the king would spoil his policies and the state.[517] The *Agni Purana*[518] concisely puts the same by saying that the king should consult his ministers neither with one on or too many nor of ignorant and untrustworthy. But if it be necessary to take advice from many ministers, the king is asked to seek their advice separately and also see that none of his ministers should disclose his secret. He is further asked not to trust in one and the same minster in all matters at all times. He should counsel with many counselors but may follow the decision of a single minister. Thus it is clear that the king is advised to frame his state policies through his wise and learned ministers but to keep them secret in such a way that people may not know them till the result of his undertaking manifest themselves, because there is always the risk of leaking out when the matter is in the hands of unreliable persons. The Puranic literature records that there were many kings who were ruined owing to bad advises from their ministers and unsoundness of their policies. Therefore the king is asked to take council from competent and trustworthy ministers. It is laid down in the *Matsya Purana*[519] that if the policy of the sovereign is not known to any one until it is accomplished the king may conquer the whole world. The other ancient political thinkers are of the same opinion. Manu,[520] for example, advises the king to consult his ministers individually and collectively. It was a wholesome proposition. A minister might have good reason for not giving out his mind in the presence of his colleagues. For example Medhatithi says that "some people are shy in assemblies, but bold in private, while others are more fit in the assemblies. On the other hand Kautilya[521] is of he opinion that minsters should speak "boldly and sensibly and with no fear of contradiction form the cabinet (Parishada)". But Sukra feels that ministers might prefer to "go dumb" through extraneaous consideration. Therefore, he desires the king to invite their opinions in writing.[522] Normally, however, there was no king in ancient India who would mock the advice of his minsters. Kamandaka[523] rightly observed in one place that "the king who accrosses his ministers is himself crossed by his enemies."

Our Puranas also mention the time place for consultations with ministers. The *Visnudharmottara* and the *Agni* Puranas[524] state that in his daily routine, the king is required to take counsel with his ministers and follows his adjudication of civil and criminal cases before his meals. But it is not known from our text whether consultations were made in the night as *Abhilasitarthachintamani*[525] informs us that the king should consult his ministers at noon after meals and in the latter part of the night when he is refreshed by sleep. Unfortunately this practice is not discussed in our Puranic record.

We are frequently referred by the *Agni Purana*[526] that the king should deliberate with his ministers on the following five-fold divisions of consultations. These are:-

(1) the preliminaries to an undertaking *(Sanayah)*

(2) the provision of necesary means *(Sadhanopaya)*

(3) fixing up the right place *(Desavibhaga)*

(4) determination of the right time *(Kalavibhaga)*

(5) anticipation of the difficulties that might be encountered and provision of remedies against them *(Gipatteschapratikarah)*. The *Agni Purana*[527] further informs us that advice should be tendered to the king on these aspects of a subject. The ministers are supposed:

(i) to posses the knowledge of things which are not

known, so that they might plan for future;

(ii) to decide upon the ways and means of achieving the plan in future;

(iii) to remove doubts and ambiguities on matter of policies and finally;

(iv) to see the success of the plan.

Like the *Nitisara* of Kamandaka,[528] the *Agni Purana*[529] speaks that the plan of the kings cannot be successful in their aims if the counselors are not attentive, cheerful, faithful, cooperating and having ingenuity and energy. From the Puranic records it is obvious that ministers should be consulted on every matter of state-policy including king's coronation. The *Markandeya Purana* informs us hat the king Karandhama consulted his ministers, who were well versed in the science of polity, on the question of the marriage of his son Avikshita.[530] From the *Agni Purana,*[531] we learn that Dasaratha, the king of Ayodhya, consulted his ministers about the proposed consecration of Ramachandara as the crown prince. Sometimes, it is found that skilled ministers selected the kings. The *Agni Purana,* further informs us that after Dasratha's death Vasistha and other ministers including Sumanta brought Bharata from the place of his maternal uncle and requested him to be the king. We are also told that after the death of king Grahavarman, the son of Maukhari king Avantivarman of Kanauj, the ministers at the suggestion of their chief Poni, as stated by Hiuen Tsang, persuaded the king Harsha-Vardhan of Thaneswara to accept the responsibility of the administration of Kanauj and after some hesitation, Harsha accepted the offer and finally the capital was shifted from Thaneswara to Kanauj.[532] We further find Gopala, the founder of Pala dynasty, being elected as the king by ministers (Prakritis). But from the study of our Puranic record it is not clear whether the collective responsibility of the ministers was in force. Further, this also is not evident whether ministers were required to tender their advice was maintained. As the Puranic record relates the individual consultation of minister the question of collective responsibility does not arise. Thus it is distinct that the ministers were very high functionaries in the state administration but they were in office as long as they enjoyed the confidence of the king.

Sandhivigrahika (Minister for Peace and War)

Sandhivigrahika was the minister for peace and war or foreign affairs. Therefore, he was required to be well versed in the King's foreign policy. The requisite qualifications mentioned by the Puranic texts are that he should be expert in the six-fold policy of the state such as the Sandhi (alliances) Vigraha-- war, Yana (March or expedition), Asana (halt), Asraya (seeking shelter).[533] In addition to these qualifications the *Visnudharmottara*[534] and the *Matsya* Puranas[535] further require that the minister for Peace and War should possess the knowledge of different countries and their languages and be proficient in the art of administration and should be loyal to the king. Somesvara provides a still longer list of the qualifications of this functionary than our Puranas do. He opines that he should be well versed in various scripts and languages, and be knowing the priciples of war and peace. Further, he should be loyal, learned, wise, proficient and able to read and write fluently. He should also know the income and expenditure of the country and be ready to protect the state-treasury.[536] Somadeva Suri adds that the Minister for peace and war should know grammar and logic, various languages and their scripts, the laws of Varnasrama and be proficient in reading and writing frequently.[537] The qualifications mentioned by the Puranas and other literature lead us to think that his chief duty was to make advice to the king in making treaties and declaring wars. From the *Rajatarangini*[538] we are informed that Mitrasarma, the minister for peace and was of king Lalitaditya of Kasmira was present at the time of he drafting of the treaty betwen Lalitadiya and Yasovarma; a king of Kanauj. The name of

Yasovarman was recorded first in the treaty. Numerous inscriptions of our period show that he was also incharge of drafting the copper plate charters, granting lands and villages to Brahmanas, temples and monasteries.[539] All this shows that he was the most important functionary among the members of the king's council.

Relations with the King

The political thinkers of ancient India were altogether opposed to one-man rule. Hence the ministers have been always regarded as a very vital organ of the body politic. Sukra is of the opinion that the relations between the king and his ministers should be very cordial. In very graphic language he further remarks: "How can the state be brought to prosperity by those ministers whom the king is not afraid of offend?" "Such ministers, according to him were not better than ladies decked in finery."[540] Kautilya asserts that it was the duty of the ministers to avert the calamity in which the king was involved.[541] So does Kamandaka: "When a monarch blinded by passions, pride and arrogance falls into the snare set by his enemies, it is the exertions of his ministers alone that can extricate him"[542] No wonder, therefore, that he asks the king to attach the same importance to their advice as to that of his spiritual guide.[543] They were truly *raja-rastra-bhrita*.[544]

The king was required not only to consult his ministers even on emergent occasions[545]—but to abide by their advice. Sukra regards a ruler who did not listen to the advice of his ministers as a thief—a minister of the people's wealth, and likewise, he brands the ministers who militate against their king as secret thieves.[547] The Mantriparishada could discuss the suggestions of the king. It could even countermand his orders. The Radhagupta ministry refused compliance with the orders of Asoka to make certain gifts to the Buddhist Sangha.[548] Rudradaman proposal to repair the Sudersan lake was also opposed by his ministers and, he had to finance to project from the privy purse.[549] Manu advices the king to repose full confidence in his Prime Minister and to entrust to him all the business of the state. Kamandaka says; "Finding that he councilors are unanimous in their decision, their minds uninfluenced by any misgiving and finding that their decision is approved by men of quality and good counsel", the king should adopt it unhesitatingly.[550]

Like other works on polity the *Matsya Purana* says that a king truly interested in the welfare of his state ought to look forward simultaneously with his coronation to the appontment of competent pesons to form his council of ministers where the kingdom may find its stability.[551] The *Agni Purana* further lays down that if a king dies before electing his council of ministers, no time should be lost in providing with his successor and in selection of his ministers,[552] which shows that without the ministers the king was not in a position to rule his kingdom. It is laid down in the *Agni Purana* that if the ministers fail to perform the duties assigned to them would spoil the treasury of their master along with clothes, food, grain and vehicle etc.[553] Therefore, the king is asked to interview the ministers daily.[554] The king is further advised by the Puranas to control and supervose the state adminstration with the help of his ministers, by ehich he may win his enemy and expand his empire. From the above-mentioned facts it is clear that normally the king had high regard for his ministers and the latter were loyal to him. They also regarded themselves as trustees of the interests of the people. Ministers were the pillars of the state and generally the kings used to accept their advice, though the ultimate responsibility rested with the king. There are references in the history of ancient India to show that minsters were held high regard by the kings and their advice was followed by them. For example, Marayana, the foreign minister of the Rastrakuta king, Krishna III, is described as his right hand.[555] A record of the Yadav king Krishna compares his prime minister to his own tongue and right hand.[556] Thus we find that the relations between the king and his ministers were very cordial.

REFERENCES

1. *Ait. Br.* I, 14.
2. MDS. VII. 3.
3. *Ibid.*, VII, 4-5 & 8.
4. NS. I, 32-33.
5. 220.30, VDP. II, 65.21.
6. 225.11; 233-12 & 239.1.
7. *Ait. Br.* I. 14.
8. Chapt. 59, 67.
9. MDS. 7.3-4.
10. *Arth.* I. 13.
11. VP. Chapt. VIII, VSP. B.K. 1. Chapt. VI, MKP. Chapt. 46. MP. Chapt.
12. X.
13. *Ibid;* 8.46; MKP. 46 13, 15.
14. *Ibid;* 8.47,48,49,52,62,65. MKP. 46. 14-18.
15. *Ibid;* 8.60.
16. *Ibid;* 8.57-60.
17. 8.80.
18. 46.51,61.
19. 8.135; MKP. 46.51.
20. *Ibid;* 8.234.
21. *Ibid;* 8.155-158.
22. *Ibid;* 8.160.
23. 8.161-163.
24. VP. Chapt. 57.55
25. *Ibid;* 57.55-56. MKP. 47. 14-15
26. *Ibid;* 57.56-57.
27. *Ibid;* 57-58.
28. *Ibid;* 57.41.
29. BK. 1, Chapter 13.
30. VSP. BK. 1, Chapt. 13.13-14.
31. *Ibid;* BK. 1, Chapt. 13.16-17.
32. *Ibid;* BK. 1, Chapt. 13, 29.

33. Chapt. 62.
34. Chapt. 10.
35. I. 108-109.
36. Chapt. 18.
37. MKP. 24.5, 11.14. VDP. II, 34.37.
38. *Ibid;* 24.9; VDP. II, 4.9. and 20; MP 215.88.
39. *Ibid;* 24.10; ;;69.20. 113.15. VDP. II, 2.76; 4.21; 6.12; 24.36 & 46.
40. VDP. II. 7.9.
41. *Ibid;* II. 2.14; 5.14; 24.7.
42. MKP. 113.32.
43. *Ibid;* 113.28.
44. VDP. II. 5.-11.24.28.
45. MKP.24.19.
46. VSP. Bk. I. 13. 56; AP. 366.2.
47. AP. 18.15; VSP. BK. 13.13,15.
48. MKP. 113.22; VSP.BK. 13.13,15.
49. *Ibid;* 113.22.
50. AP. 225.12.
51. *Ibid;* 66.9.
52. *Ibid;* 366.1
53. *Ibid;* 366.1-2.
54. *Ibid;* 360-76.
55. *Ibid;* 211.27.
56. AP. 211.66.
57. *Rajanitiprakasa,* pp. 42-114; *Nitimayukha* pp. 1-13.
58. *Rajadharmakanda,* II. pp. 6-10.
59. II. 18.2.
60. 218.5.
61. 366.1.
62. Ch. 5-11.
63. Ch. 12-15.
64. AP. 6.3.
65. *Ibid;* 6.24-25.
66. Sircar, D.C. *Select Inscriptions,* 1965, p. 263.
67. Radhanpur Plates, E.I. IV pp. 242
68. *The Struggle for Empire,* 1957, p. 236.

69. CII. IV p. 294.
70. AP 14.27.
71. V. 23.5.
72. II. 18.2
73. 218.5.
74. 6.49.
75. Raychaudhuri, H. *Political History of Ancient India,* 6th Ed. Calcutta.
76. 1953, p. 417.
77. *The Classical Age,* 1954, p. 180.
78. *The Age of Imperial Kanauj,* 1964, p. 8-9.
79. GOS. p. 33.
80. Arth. 5-6.
81. VDP II. 18.2-3.
82. Ibid; II. 18.4; AP. 218. 5-6.
83. AP. 218.4; English Translation Vol. II, p. 780.
84. Ibid; 218.3-4.
85. Ibid; 360.76.
86. II. 7.1-7.
87. VDP. III. 7.4-7.
88. III. 323.22; MDS. VII. 77.
89. II. 12. 1-2.
90. VDP. II. 12. 3-5.
91. II. 12.6.
92. II. 13.1.
93. III. 16.
94. AP. 218.5.
95. Ibid; 218.6.
96. Ibid; 218.6.
97. VDP. II. 18.4.
98. VDP. II. 19.1; AP. 218.7.
99. Ibid; 19.; AP. 218.8.
100. VDP. II. 19. 2-5; AP. 218.8.
101. Ibid; II, 21. 2-6;; AP. 218. 12-17.
102. Ibid; II. 21.7; Ap. 218. 17.
103. Ibid; II. 21.8-10; AP. 218. 18-20.
104. Ibid; II. 21.10-11; AP. 218.20-21.

105. Ibid; II. . p;. 218. 22.
106. Ibid; II. 21.14.
107. VDP. II. 21.15; AP. 218.24.
108. Ibid; 21.15-17; AP. 218. 24-25.
109. Ibid; II. 21. 19; AP. 218. 26.
110. Ibid; II. 21. 19-21.
111. Ibid; II. 21.23; AP. 218.27.
112. Ibid; II. 21.28; AP, 218:28.
113. Ibid; II. 21-27-28; AP. 218.28.
114. Ibid; II. 21-29, AP. 218.28.
115. Ibid; II. 21.31 and 35, AP. 218. 29 and 31.
116. VDP. II. 21.33; AP. 218.29.
117. Ibid; II. 21.33; AP. 218.30.
118. Ibid; II. 21.26; AP. 218.31.
119. Ibid; II. 21.38-39; AP. 218-32.
120 Ibid; II. 21.42-43; AP. 218. 33.
121. Ibid; II. 21.44; AP. 218. 34.
122. Ibid; II. 21. 45-46; AP. 218. 34.
123. Ibid; II. 22. 1-182; AP. 219. 1-72.
124. VDP. II. 18. 14.
125. AP. 218.26, VDP. II. 21. 18-24.
126. 218. 14.
127. Arth. 2.36.
128. Mookerji, R.K.; ASOLS, Delhi 1955, p. 181.,
129. 19.20.
130. 18.15.
131. II. 3. 1-7.
132. I. 13. 61-63.
133. 238. 4-5.
134. 18.19-20.
135. AP. 238.10.
136. Ibid; 238. 11-12.
137. 66. 3-5.
138. AP. 238. 8.
139. 215. 53-54.
140. 238.3.
141. 238.7.

142. 238. 2-5.
143. 24. 6, M.N. Dutt, Tr. FN. p. 126.
144. 66. 14-16.
145. 225.5.
146. MKP. 24.6, M.N. Dutt, Tr. F.N. p. 126.
147. Ibid; 24.24; AP. 225.8, 15-16.
148. 24. 15-16.
149. Ibid; 4.17.
150. MP. 219.14-16; VDP. II. 65. 15-17; AP. 225. 8-9.
151. VDP. III. 323.5; AP. 241. 25-26.
152. II. 65. 61-64.
153. 215. 69-71.
154. 24.20.
155. AP. 225.27-30.
156. 24. 20-21.
157. Dutt, M. N., Tr. p. 127.
158. VDP. II. 151.2; AP. 235. 1-2.
159. VDP. II. 151. 3; AP. 235.2.
160. Ibid; II. 151.4; AP. 235.3.
161. Ibid; II. 151.5; AP. 235. 3-4.
162. Ibid; II. 151.8; AP. 235.4.
163. Ibid; II. 151.10; AP. 235.5.
164. Ibid; II. 151.10; AP. 235.6.
165. Ibid; II. 151.14; AP. 235.6.
166. A. 235.7.
167. VDP. II. 151. 16-17 AP. 235.8.
168. VDP. II. 151. 17-18; AP. 235.9.
169. Ibid; II. 151. 17-18; AP. 23.9.
170. Ibid; II. 151.20-27; AP. 235. 9-12.
171. Ibid; II. 151.31; AP. 235. 13.
172. Ibid; II. 151.32; AP. 235.14.
173. Ibid; II. 151.36; A. 125.15.
174. Ibid II. 151.37; AP. 235.16.
175. Ibid; II. 151.37; AP. 235.16.
176. Ibid; II. 151.38; AP. 235.16.
177. Ibid; II. 151.38; AP. 235.16.
178. Ibid; II. 151.39; AP. 235.17.

179. Mbh. Santi Chapts. 57, 9, 65; MDS. 7. 145-146, 222-246; Arth.;
180. BK. I chapt. XIX; NVM. chapt. 25, SN. I. 78-91; Yaj. 2.327-333.
181. NVM. 25. 70-71.
182. Ibid; 25-76.
183. MDS. 7. 145-146, 222-225.
184. Yaj. 1.327-333.
185. 1.19.
186. MP. 220-44.
187. 230-2.
188. 220.41-42.
189. VDP. II. 65.21-22; MP. 220. 20-21; A. 239.1.
190. II. 65.23.
191. 220.22.
192. 225.11; 12, 233.12-13.
193. VDP. II. 145. 3-4.
194. 223.7.
195. 226.11.
196. 223.8-9.
197. II. 65.8-9.
198. 223.10.
199. MP. 223.11.
200. Ibid; 220.16.
201. II. 68. 7-12; AP. 226.11.
202. AP. 224. 13.26.
203. Ibid; 223.32; 225.24.
204. II. 61.24—35; AP. 223.9-10.
205. VII. 144.
206. *Raghuvamsa* 14.67.
207. X. 7.8.
208. SN. 1. 117.
209. 34. 1-2.
210. NVM. 7.21.
211. II. 61. 25-26.
212. 223. 10-11.
213. VDP. II. 61. 22-23; AP. 223.8.
214. 126.33-34.

215. 1.19.
216. 8.2.
217. 23.55-62.
218. 239.46.
219. 5.82.
220. 78.7.
221. II. 61. 28-29.
222. 223. 11-12.
223. *Rajnitiprakasa*, p. 256.
224. *Pollity in the Agni Purana*, 1965 Calcutta, p. 64.
225. Altekar, A.S. *State and Government in Ancient India*, 1958, p. 357-358.
226. *The Classical Age*, 1962, p. 180.
227. V. 249 and VI. 332.
228. Dutta. M.N. Eng. Tr of Agni Purana. Vol. II. 167, p. 797.
229. AP. 152.1; 157.4.
230. NVM. 8. 14, 17-19.
231. II. 61.29.
232. 1.2, 58.
233. 223.12.
234. 227. 63-64.
235. 8. 2383.
236. 223. 21-22.
237. 275.7.
238. Majumdar, *The Age of Imperial Unity*, Bombay, 1968, p. 69.
239. AP. 225.12.
240. Ibid; 220.4; 220.20, 235.7, 335.12.
241. AP. 235.13.
242. II. 177.23-24.
243. 236.33.
244. AP. 224.42; NVM. 24.31.
245. Ibid; 224.10.
246. Chapt. 219. Raychaudhuri, H. *Political History of Ancient India*, 1953.
247. P. 209.
248. *Dighanikaya*, II. 72.
249. Arth. 1.17.
250. NVM. 24. 72.

251. VI. 2. 152 and 155.
252. AP. 225.2-3, VDP. II. 65. 2-3.
253. Ibid; 223.30-32; VDP. II. 61.65-67.
254. II. 61. 63-64.
255. 223.29.31.
256. VDP. II. 61. 65-66, AP. 223.31.
257. Ibid; II. 32.17; AP. 222.18.
258. 215.58.61.
259. Ibid; 215, 61-62; AP. 225.25-26.
260. 173.7.
261. 292.1.
262. 227.32.
263. 225.26.
264. 24.34.
265. NVM. 7.2., 5.5.
266. 222.11-16; 2255.23.
267. II. 32.7; AP. 222.15-16.
268. AP. 223.9.
269. 223.9.
270. III. 323. 25-26.
271. III. 3. 10-11.
272. NVM. 26.66.
273. *Yogayatra* 2.23.
274. 225.33.
275. 220.24.
276. 239.44-45.
277. MDS. 7.154.
278. 7.1.
279. KNS. 5.78-79.
280. AP. 238, KNS. 1.18.
281. II. 177.91.
282. 224.3.
283. 224.3.
284. 224.1.
285. 24.15.
286. 226.1.
287. II. 71. 4-10.

288. BK. I. 13. 21-22.
289. 24. 23-28.
290. II. 71.1-10.
291. 226. 17-20.
292. MDS. VII. 4-5.
293. Santi. 68.40.
294. Manu. VII. 8.
295. 226. 1-11.
296. 24.27.
297. 57.72.
298. 226. 1-11.
299. II. 2-9.
300. 25. 23-28.
301. 275. 23-26.
302. 276.25.
303. II. 2.9. and II. 71. 11-12.
304. Sircar, D.C., *Select Inscriptions,* 1965, p. 266, 267.
305. Ibid; p. 325.
306. Asvamedha Type gold coins of Samudra Gupta, Sircar, D.C. Select.
307. Inscription 1965, p. 275.
308. *Polity in the Agni Purana,* 1965, p. 34.
309. *The Cambridge History of India,* Vol. VI. p. 433.
310. 155.24.
311. III. 4. 33-34.
312. 226.20.
313. AP. 276. 24-25.
314. Ibid; 151.5.
315. VSP. I. 13.48; AP. 220.24; 225. 14,33.
316. II. 61.49.
317. 258.82.
318. AP. 227. 63; 258.78.
319. Ibid; 227.64, 258.78.
320. Ibid; 258.8.
321. Ibid; 155.29; 258.78.
322. Ibid; 258.80.
323. Ibid; 258.80

324. AP. 253.54.
325. II. 61. 42-43.
326. AP. 223. 16-17.
327. VDP. II. 61. 46-48; AP. 223. 18-20.
328. 236. 62.65.
329. AP. 258.51.
330. 258.80.
331. II. 72. 183.
332. 227. 60-61; 258.34.
333. AP. 221.42-43; 127.18.
334. VDP. II. 72.186; AP. 227.63; 258.74.
335. Mookerji, R.K. *Asoka*, Delhi, 1955, p. 143-145.
336. NVM. 5.37.
337. Ibid; 5.38.
338. 220. 1-12.
339. II. 65. 1-14.
340. 225. 1-7.
341. 220. 2-3; VDP. II. 65. 204.
342. 220.1; VDP. II. 65.3.
343. MP. 220.3., VDP. II. 65.4.
344. MP. 220.4; VDP. II. 65.5; AP. 225.3.
345. Ibid; 220.8; VDP. II. 65. 9-10; AP. 225.4.
346. Ibid; 220.9; VDP. II. 65. 11; AP. 225.5.
347. Ibid; 220.4; VDP. II. 65.6.
348. Ibid; 220.6; VDP. II. 65.7.
349. MP. 220. 19-20; VDP. II. 65.20-22; Ap. 225. 11-12.
350. 18. 1-3.
351. MKP. 183-6.
352. V. 21. 18-24.
353. 18.25.
354. VSP. V. 10.27-28; VDP. II. 65.46; AP. 225.21-22, 233.8.; MDS. VII.
355. 43; Santi. 59.33; Arth. 1.2; Yaj. 1. 211; Kamandaka II. 1. *Sukraniti*.
356. 152.
357. *Dasakumarcharita*, VIII. Para I, p. 202.
358. NVM. 5.55.

359. Arth. 1.2.
360. KNS. 2.3-6.
361. Arth. 1.3.
362. Ibid; 1.5.
363. KNS. 2.13.
364. NVM. 7.1.
365. VDP. I. 22. 129-133; AP. 219. 59-56.
366. AP. 238.9.
367. MP. 220.44. VDP. II. 65-73.
368. II. 65.46.
369. NVM. 6. 32-33.
339. VDP. II. 65.46, AP. 225.22.
340. V. 10. 28-29.
341. Arth. 1.4.
342. KNS. 2.14.
343. NVM. 8.1.
344. NVM. 8.2.
345. 125. 12-15.
346. VDP. II. 178.10; AP. 249.7.
347. Arth. 1-5.
348. NVM. II. 4-5.65 and 5.70.
349. VSP. I. 19.26-35.
350. MP. 220.4; VDP. II. 65.5-6, AP. 225.3.
351. MP. 220. 6-7, VDP. II. 65. 7-8, AP. 225. 3-4.
352. Para 71 pp. 167-169.
353. *Dasakumarcharita* NSP. 1951, pp. 23-24.
354. E.I. Vol. XX. p. 79, II 2. and 5.
355. E.I. Vol. XX. p. 79, II. 2 and 5.
356. VDP. II. Chapt. 6; AP. 239.6-11.
357. VSP. I. 13.48; AP. 220.24, 225.14.33.
358. VDP. III. 324.10-11.
359. III. 324. 10-11.
360. 225.33.
361. AP. 220.24.
362. VDP. II. 61.31; AP. 223.13.
363. 16.125.
364. AP. 241.25-26.

365. Ibid; 223-33.
366. II. 61. 24-25.
367. 225.33.
368. AP. 220.24.
369. II. 61. 22-24.
370. 225.33; VDP. II. 61.21.
371. AP. 151.5.
372. AP. 226.14.
373. II. 61.25, AP, 223. 10.
374. 241.18-19.
375. 215. 62-64.
376. 227.47.
377. Mbh. Santiparvan, 69. 64-65; DS. IX. 249; Arth VI. 1; KNS. 4.1.
378. MKP. 24.11; MP. 220.19; VDP. II. 65. 20-21 & III. 323. II; AP. 225. 11.
379. *Manasollasa* Index, 20.
380. MDS. VII. 55.
381. Mbh. XII. 106. 11.
382. Ibid; V. 37-38.
383. Arth. I. 7. 15.
384. SN. II. 1-4.
385. KNS. XIII. 25.
386. 215.3.
387. 215.2.
388. II. 24. 2-3.
389. 218.3-4.
390. Ibid; 218.5.
391. 24. 7-8.
392. VI. 6.26-27.
393. NVM. 18.1.
394. Ibid; 18.4.
395. *Viramitrodaya*, p. 4.
396. NVM. X, 142.
397. 1. 126.
398. 366.2.
399. Ibid; 106.11.

400. 24.11 & 126.28.
401. 24.7.
402. 126.32.
403. II. 112. 17.
404. I. 8. 33.
405. KNS. Chapts. 4 & 12.
406. NVM. Chapts X (Mantri—Samuddesa) & XVIII (Amataya
407. Samuddesa)
408. P. 178.
409. 1.7.3. and 1.8.4.
410. I.A., XVIII. 238.V. 5.
411. II. 65.39; 151.20.
412. 215.48.
413. 225.19.
414. XII. 85. 7.9.
415. XII. 85.11.
416. Arth. 1.15.
417. II. 65.39; 40. 151.20.
418. 220.37.
419. 225.19.
420. *Manasollasa*. II. 2.57.
421. NVM. X. 66-67.
422. Ibid; X. 67-68; cf. Arth. 1.15.
423. NVM. X. 71.
424. 239.15-16; 239.10-15.
425. *Viddhasalabhanjika*, p. 143.
426. 6.3.
427. 9. 17.
428. MDS. VII. 54.
429. 1.7. 2-3.
430. II. 72.
431. 1.15; KNS. 11.67.
432. 218.31.
433. Manu. VII. 54, 60.
434. 218.31.
435. 226.11.
436. 235.8.cf. VDP II. 151.16.

437. 8.18-19.
438. III-II. 1260 & III. II. 1297.
439. III-II. 1260 & III. II. 1297.
440. 215. 4-6.
441. II. Chapt. 6.
442. 239.6.11.
443. AP. 239.12-16.
444. Ibid; 239.18-23.
445. Arth. 1. 9.
446. AP. 220.12-13.
447. AP; 220.14.
448. KNS. 4. 6-20.
449. 239. 6-11 & 239. 12-16.
450. MDS. VII. 54; also Mbh. XII. 118.2-4.
451. Yajnavalkya, I. 312.
452. Brihaspati, I. 171.
453. *Ramayana*, I, 7.7-14; II. 100-4, 25, 28-31, etc.
454. Mbh. XII. Chapts 80, 83 and 118.
455. KNS. IV. 5-26, 28-31, 34-40.
456. SN. II. 52-64.
457. NVM, X. 5.
458. *Manasollasa*. II. 2.52-59.
459. NVM. 10.6.
460. Ibid; 18-13.
461. Ibid; 18-15.
462. Manu, VII. 54; Yaj I. 312; *Ramayana* II. 100.26. Mbh. Sabhaparva 5.43.
463. 215.84.
464. II. 24. 55-56.
465. 220.16.
466. MP. 215.83-84; VDP. 24, 55-56. AP. 220. 16-17.
467. P. 176.
468. 215.85.
469. I.A. XIX. p. 218.
470. VIII. 874.
471. Sircar, D.C., *Select Ins*. 1965; p. 268.
472. Ibid., 9.280.

473. Ibid., 9.290.
474. 215.10.
475. II. 24.11.
476. 220.1.
477. 293.33.
478. Ibid; 239.12.
479. Manu. 7.58, Yaj I, 312.
480. I. 9.
481. XII. 85. 7-9.
482. I. 1.78.
483. II. 418.419.
484. NVM. X. 5.
485. Ibid; XVIII. 22-23.
486. Ibid; XVIII. 24.
487. AP. 239.8.
488. Ibid; 220.15.
489. VSP. VI. 6.47.
490. 241.29.
491. 241.16-17.
492. AP. 241. 18.
493. Ibid; 235.8.
494. A.P. 20.1.
495. V. 33. 8-9.
496. Sircar, D.C. *Select. Ins*. 1965, p. 280.
497. 16.38.39.
498. *Abhilas*. I. 2.1164.
499. II. 177.23-24.
500. 236.33.
501. 227.47.
502. AP. 227.49.
503. 18.6.12.
504. *Manasollasa* 18.66, 18.69, 18.71.
505. A.P. 220.1, 11.
506. Ibid; 220.15.
507. Ibid; 220.15.
508. Ibid; VIII. 23-24, Trans. p. 354.
509. KNS. 13.23-24.

510. NVM. XVIII. 5.
511. AP. 241. 26-27.
512. *Arth.* X. 6.
513. MP. 215. 47.49.
514. VI. 6.26.27.
515. II. 151. 19-20.
516. Ibid; II. 151. 20-22.
517. 225. 17.21, 235. 10-11.
518. VII. 57-59.
519. Arth. V. 4.
520. SN. II.
521. KNS. II. 52.
522. II. 151. 19-20.
523. 235. 9-12.
524. I. 2.704.
525. 241.4, *Arth.* I. 15; I.15; KNS. XI. 56; *Panchatantra* I, p. 85.
526. 241.3.
527. XI. 62.
528. 241.5.
529. 122. 11.14.
530. AP. Chapt. 6.
531. *The Classical Age,* 1962, p. 101.
532. A.P. 220.3.
533. II. 24.16.
534. 215.16.
535. *Manasollasa* II. 2. 127-130.
536. NVM. 32.3.
537. 4. 137.138.
538. Altẹkar, A.S., *State and Government in Ancient India*, 1958. p. 171.
540. SN, II. 81.
551. Arth. V. 6; VIII. 1.
552. KNS. IV. 48.
553. Ibid; IV. 44.
554. SN. II. 74.
555. Arth. I. 15.
556. SN. II. 80.

557. Ibid. II. 247-49.
558. R.S. VI of Asoka.
559. *Divyavadana*. p. 430.
560. E.I. VIII. p. 44. II. 16-17.
561. KNS. XI. 59-61.
562. 215.2.
563. 218.5.
564. AP. 241.18.
565. Ibid. 235.8.
566. Ibid; 220. 1-11.
567. S.I. IV. p. 60.
568. Ibid; IX. p. 254.

4

Public Service and Administrative Division

The political thinkers of ancient India realised that the adminstration was beyond the capacity of one-man rule, howsoever, qualified he might be and hence they have advised the king to appoint qualified persons to run the state administration. An analysis of the duties and functions of the king and his officials discussed in the Puranic literature shows that they were brain centr of the government. But just as the brain cannot function through instrumentality and co-operation of a number of senses and organs so also the king requires the assistance of a central secretariat and heads of number of departments. The strength of high functionaries and holders have been different at different times. Sukra,[1] for example, enumerates ten principal high functionaries of the king viz. *Purohita, Pratinidhi, Pradhana, Sachiva, Mantri, Pradvivaka, Pandita, Sumantra, Amatya* and *Duta*. The *Rajatarangini*[2] also informs us that in the former times there were only seven departments, that later on they became eighteen and that five more were added to these eighteen.[3] The Puranas contain a long list of high functionaries of the central secretariat who assisted the king in the day-to-day functioning of the state business.

Purohita

The king is asked by the *Agni Purana to* appoint the royal priest before he is properly crowned.[4] The *Visnudharmottara Purana* has devoted one full chapter on the qualification of this official. According to it he should be healthy, well-disposed, sweet-spoken, well-versed in *Artharvaveda* and *Yajurveda*, handsome, having good knowledge of astrology and Puranas, intelligent, dispassionate, and should be well-versed in *Panchakalpa* and *Panchayajya*. The king is suggested to appoint that person as his Purohita who possesses these qualities, but should not dismiss him from his services otherwise he would destroy his state and would go in the hell for three generations.[5] It is, further, said that Purohita is equal to mother and father who obliterates oppressions by his deeds.[6] Furthermore, Purohita is expected to be well-versed both in the three Vedas (*Rigveda, Samaveda* and *Atharvaveda*) and political science (*Dandaniti*) and is also required to know the procedures of religious ceremonies and sacrifices laid down in the *Atharvaveda* for the welfare of the king. Virtue, knowledge and integrity of character are also required by the *Agni Purana.*[7] The Jain political thinker, Somedava Suri, states that the priest should be well-versed in the Vedas with their six-fold branches, of noble birth, cheerful, and having sterling character. He is, further, required to be able to face divine calamities, omens and portents.[8] The royal priest is placed after the mantrin and the astrologer in the hierarchy of ministers in the *Agni Purana*, which shows his importance in the administrative machinery. The coronation ceremony was celebrated under his supervision.[9] The daily sacrifices and worship of God Vasudeva were performed under his guidaence.[10] All this shows that the royal priest must have wielded considerable influence among the state officials.

The chief duty of the royal priest was to put an end

to the divine calamities and aggrandize the king's prosperity through the rituals described in the *Artharvaveda*.[12] The *Visnudharmottara*[13] and the *Agni* Puranas devote four chapters to the rituals of the four vedas. Our *Agni* Purana[14] like *Nitisara*[15] divides calamitiles into two sections-- divine and human. The divine calamities include fire, flood, famine, disease and pestilence. These natural or divine calamities can be abrogated through human efforts coupled with propitiatory rituals. The propitiatory rituals are specified in great detail in the *Visnudharmottara*,[16] the Matsya[17] and the *Agni* Puranas.[18] Unfortunately the human calamities are not mentioned in our Puranas but it is suggested that they can be checked though successful execution of state policies. It is noticeable that these rituals mentioned in our literature are mostly based on *Yajnvalkya Smrti*, which are to be performed by or under the supervision of the royal priest. He was also required to perform the rituals for the victory of the king in the battlefield.[19] In this way he protects the nation by counteracting the magical charms of the enemy and ensuring its prosperity by performing the requisite rituals (purohiti karmas) recommended in the *Arthavaveda*.[20] He is further required to remove the king's wickedness and conduct his work according to astrology.[21]

The *Mitaksara* and the *Viramitrodaya*[22] suggest the king to follow up the deliberations with other ministers by consultations with Purohita on all religious and secular matters.[23] They quote Katyayana[24] and speak that the priest was the member of the judicial court with Pradvivaka, the Amatya, the Brahmana etc. But our Puranas do not throw light on this particular function of the priest and it is not known whether the priest was required to participate in the administration of justice. Sukra places Purohita at the head of the ministry.[25] The Chandradeva and Copperplate grant[26] of Gahadavala king Chandradeva and Madanpala of A.D 1090 indicates that the royal priest occupied the fourth place among the royal functionaries. The first three are—the chief queen, the crown prince and the Mantri (probably chief minister). From other inscription of the Gahadavala dynasty it is evident that the royal priest was very much honoured by the members of the royal family. We are told that Jagusarman who was the royal priest of Govindachandra secured a large number of tax-free villages.[27] Sometimes the royal priest acted as the preceptor of the king. Praharajasarman, son of Jagusarman, was not only the royal Priest of the king Jayachandradeva but was also his preceptor.[28] The grants of lands, houses and villages as suggested by the *Visnudharmottara*[29] and the *Agni* Puranas[30] were actually made during the period.

Astrologer

In addition to the appointment of the royal priest the Visnudharmottara Purana also speaks about the astrologer. The text of this Purana lays down that the king should appoint only that person as the astrologer who is versatile, polite, of pleasing personality, handsome, well-dressed, magmificent, grave devoted to dharma, self-controlled, destitute of corporal form, well-versed in the Vedas and their branches, proficient in sixty four grandeur's, clever in reasoning, knower of the present, the past and the future, expert in mathematics.[31] It is remarkable that the astrologer is descrinbed as the father and mother of the king. He is further designated as the king's Guru, which shows the importance of this official in the day-to-day state administration. The main function of the astrologer was to lookafter the auspicious and inasuspicious eccasions for the king. The king is further asked by the Purana to consult his astrologer every time before starting his work.

The *Visnudharmottara,*[32] the *Matsya*[33] and the *Agni* Puranas[34] further provide a long list of other important officers if the central government.

They are as follows:

Pratihara (Royal Chamberlain)

The Pratihara is the next important member of the king's council in our literature and is placed next to the Commander-in-chief. From the epigraphy and literary sources[35] it is evident that he played a very important role in the state administration from the Gupta period onwards. The Puranas[36] state that the Chamberlain should be of a noble family, having tall stature, handsome, humble, honey-tongued and able to influence others. Besides having these qualificaions, he was expected to be well-versed in political science (Nitisara) and in sixfold policies. These qualifications are also required by other writers on polity. The Visvarupacharya[37] specifically, mentions that besides possessing nobility, braveness, loyalty, immunity from disaffection and knowledge of infantry, the royal chamberlain is also required to have military qualities. The Puranas do not throw much light on the duties of this official. The *Visnudharmottara*[38] and the *Agni* Puranas[39] ask the royal chamberlain to introduce the Amatyas and Sachivas to the newly consecrated king and to manage the interview of Brahmanas, ministers and officers of the court as also the rich and the illustrious persons with the king. Thus the function of the chamberlain was very much similar to that of the Senapati indicates the imoportance this official in the administrative set up. There are references to prove the importance of this official in the administration of ancient India. We find that Pratihara, Ratnavardhana, secured the throne for the prince, Sankaravarman in A.D. 883.[40] Further, the Mau Inscription of Chandella King Madanavarman informs us that the illustrious Gadadhara who was well-versed in the military science and having efficiently managed the departments of Kosa and Danda was promoted from the rank of Pratihara to the post of the Chief minister *(mantrimukhya)* by Prthvi-varman owing to his brilliant success in the battle of Antarvedi.[41] The Gahadavala inscriptions,[42] too, refer to the importance of this official and he is given fifth place in order of precedence. It is notable that he is placed even above the

Commander-in-chief. Thus we find from the foregoing discussion of the duties and functions of the pratihar, that he was a powerful functionary in the administrative machinery and his chief duties were to take part in the King's Coronation ceremony and to introduce ministers and other officers to the newly consecrated king and other persons in the King's court.[43]

Duta (Ambasador)

The ambassador is a highly important official in the matter of foreign affairs. He represents the king or the country in foreign courts. Therefore, our Puranas require very high qualifications for this functionary. According to the *Visnudharmottara*[44] and the *Matsya* Puranas[45] the king should appoint those persons as his ambassadors who possess knowledge of different languages of various countries as well as the language so their own country (Desa-Bhasavidsaradah) and are able to speak frequently and to bear distress. He is further required by our literature to state the pacts in toto and to tender advice about Niti at proper time to the king. Accorinding to the *Garuda Purana*[46] the ambassador should be intelligent, able to understand the feelings of others, cruel and able to submit true and accurate reports. The *Agni Purana*[47] further lays down that an ambassador should be a man of sharp memory, ingenious, dexterous in warfare and scriptures and eloquent. It further adds that he must be honey-tongued, brave and influential. From about the first century A.D. we are informed that the institution of embassies had become very important and that they were exchanged between distant countries, e.g. between India and the Roman empire, or between India and Iran, between India and China, or between India and Ceylon, for all which we have some historical references. Exchange of ambassadors was considered to be part of the system of politiacl alliances, e.g. the embassy, sent by the king of Ceylon to the court of Samudra Gupta or by Bhaskaravarman to the court of Harsavardhana.[48] The office of the ambassador was very important in ancient India, so that almost all ancient Indian political thinkers[49] and their contemporary literature[50] stress the qualifications of an ambassador and they demand that he must be a man of noble blood, proficient in making peace and war and in the knowledge of the topography of the country, competent to judge the time and place, proficient in tautology, allegiance and integrity. It is worth mentioning that the *Mahabharata* and *Nitivakyamrta* lay down the weaknesses of an ambassador. According to the Udyogaparva of the *Mahabharata*,[51] the Duta should not be stiff-necked, nor timid, nor dilatory and liable to bribed but instead, kind, amiable, free from diseases, and endowed with a fine mode of speech. The *Nitivakyamrt* states that personal weaknesss and foolishness are disqualifications of the envoy. But such disqualifications are not mentioned in our Puranic text.

The ambassaders are divided by the *Agni Purana*[52] into three categories on the basis of old classification made by ancient Indian political thinkers.[53] They are, *(i)* Nisristartha *(ii)* Mitartha and *(iii)* Sasanaharaka. Mr. M. N. Dutta[54] is of the opinion that Nisristartha is that ambassador who is entrusted with the management of an affair according to his own light and discretion; Mitartha is that ambassador who discharged with the execution of a mission according to the direction received from his sovereign; and Sasanaharaka is the ambassador whose duty is to delivet the decision of his master on a particular question. On the other hand Mitaksara on the *Yajnvalkya Smrti* is probably the earliest authority who states that Nisristarthas are those who enjoy full powers to plead the case of their king considering the time and place according to their abilities. Mitarthas are those who possess limited powers, and they are authorized to speak what has been allotted by the king; and Sasanaharakas are those who are only required to carry letters and messages of the king to the courts of other kings. Our Puranas give more importance to this office than to others. It is said that each preceding class is less limited in authority than the one immediately following it.[53] The *Agni Purana*[54] states that an ambassador is required to keep secrecy in foreign affairs.

Though our Puranic literature does not mention the caste of the ambassador, Somadeva Suri, a Jain political thinker is of the opinion that even a barber may be appointed as an ambassador.[55] Chandesvara[56] even suggests that even a *mlechchha* can be appointed on this responsible post. But preference should be given to the Brahmanas, Somadeva Suri opines that lady ambassador should be appointed in dealings with women.[57]

The *Agni Puraṇa*, further, recommeds that the ambassadot should mor enter the enemy's country without proper verification. The ambassador is further required to ascertain the weakness of the king in general and the treasury in particular. He should also notice the condition of his enemy's and allies army, and personal likes and dislikes of the king.[58] The same text further affirms that an ambassador, while going to the enemy's country, he is advised to seek assistance from his spies.[59] Our Purana does not mention the four methods, but Kamandaka explains the four methods through which an ambassador may please the king. The methods are comparing with the ambassador's master in respect of his high lineage, his fame, and his commendable deeds.[60] It is, thus, evident that the most important function of the ambassador was to gather secret informations of the country to which he was appointed and to pass them on to his king so that the future policies of hes country could be framed accordingly. The epigraphic records, too, tell us that at least in the time of Jivit Gupta[61] and the king's of Pala[62] dynasty, the ambassador seems to be permanent officer.

Dhanadhyaksha (King's Treasurer)

The finance Department is the very root of the government, therefore, it must be looked-after properly. The treasurer was thus required to be wise, dexterous, clear-headed, free from laziness and avarice and able to evaluate things. The chief articles that went into the treasury were iron, deer-skin, cloth and jewels. The king's treasurer had a number of assistants. There was an officer-in-charge of disbursement and his status was equal to that of the treasurer. The accountants of the treasury department were required to write nearly and legibly. They were educated and clever enough to use short phrases pregnant with meaning. Further, the department was required to see that the money be spent on useful purposes.[63] The treasury, undoubtedly, was a very important official in ancient India. We find that even in 1044 A.D., Anatadeva, the ruler of Silahara dynasty had a ministry of three officials and the treasurer was one of them. The *Mahabharata,*[64] the *Arthasastra,*[65] the *Kamandaka Nitisara*[66] and the *Nitivakyamrta*[67] express that the treasurv is the root of the state and therfore, the king is asked to look after it properly. The treasurer also figures invariably in the Gahadwala copper plates.

Sthapati (Engineer)

Our Puranas[68] state that the engineer of the king should be proficient in the art of architecture *(Vastuviddyavidhanagya)* and also be able to prepare the state plans, hardy, energetic and nimble fingered. He is further required to be industrious and keep foresight.

Dharmadhikarana (Incharge of the Judicial Department)

Dharmadhikarana or *Dharmadhyaksha* was incharge of the judicial department in which persons well-versed in law-codes *(Dharmasastra Visardah)* were appointed. The *Visnudharmottara*[69] and the *Matsya* Puranas[70] recommend that the Chief Justice should be well-versed in the code of laws (Dharmasastras), of noble birth and equal in dealing with friends and foes. The *Garuda*[71] Purana further suggests that *Dharmadhyaksha* should be proficient in the laws of Smrtis, learned, virtuous, courageous, and valiant. The work of the Chief Justice was heavy and exacting. Therefore, it may be inferred that there were several Judges who were working under the Chief Justice. It was the duty of the Chief Justice to look after the efficiency of all the branches of the Judicial Department. It should be noted here that the Judges of the Judicial Department could be only those brahmanas who possessed the specific qualifications in addition to that they must possess the knowledge of human heart and should be bountiful.[72] Somesvaradeva[73] states that the Chief Justice must be proficient in the smrti laws, free from greed, covetousness and bold. It is also specified that he should be brahmana by caste and able to punish the culprit according to penology and also always drastic and investigation. Thus, it is evident that the Chief Justice presided over the highest court of appeal in the absence of the king.

Lekhaka (Scribe)

According to the Puranic text the scribes were required to be well-versed in all Sastras and able to write neatly and legibly. They were further required to be educated and clever enough to use short phrases full of sense and secretive.

Desaarakshita

This is a new term that has been found in our Puranic literature and which is most probably use for provincial governor. Dr. V. S. Agrawal is of the opinion that this term is probably corresponding to a Gupta or one who was incharge of revenue officers.[74] The Puranas advice the king to appoint that person to this office who possesses the ability of knowing the merits and demerits of his subordinate officers, the income and the expenditure.[75]

The Puranic text contains scattered references to some other officers who are not mentioned in the consolidated list mentioned above. They are as follows:

(i) *Tulasasanakarta* (Officer of the weights and measures)[76]

(ii) The officer of promulgating the price policy of the king[77]

(iii) *Dandanatha* (Chief Police Officer)[78]

(iv) *Atavika* (Forest Officer)[79]

(v) *Samantachari* (Superintendent of the gold)[81]

(vi) *Kanakadhyaksha* (General Superintendent)[82]

Unfortunately the qualifications and the functions of the above-mentioned officers are not known to us from our Puranic period. These functionaries were in all probablity appointed by the king and they were members of the central government.

In addition to above-mentioned officers of the state the Puranic literature informs us about personal servants of the king. They are as follows:

Tambuladhari (The Royal Betel-Bearer)

This is a new term, which has been found probably for the first time in our literature in the list of high functionaries. The Puranas[83] prescribe that the betel-bearer of the king should be free from avarice and immune from the influence of the others. The Agni Purana requires that in addition to these qualifications, he should be sweet-spoken and having the capacity of allaying the fatigue of the king by his services. It is very much interesting to note that the Puranas state this official as being either a man to a women. Dr. V.S. Agrawal is of the opinion that he seems to have been of the grade of a Pratihara appointed for the court and the palace.[84] It is worth noting that the betel leaf, was known in the Gupta and the post Gupta period. It was so popular that Indian scholars have mentioned it in their works and we find the references of betel in the *Panchatantra, Kamasutra, Harsacharit* and

Kadambari. The betel-bearer was called *Tambulavahaka*,[85] *Tambuladhara*[86] and *Tambulavahini*.[87] The Muslim historian, Alberuni, too, mentions that the practice of chewing the betel-leaf was prevalent in India[88]. The *Agni Purana*[89] attaches greater importance and suggests the king to chew the betel leaf after meals. Kamandaka is also of the same opinion.[90] The other works on polity like *Abhilasistrhachintamani* *Rajanitipraksa*[91] and *Rajhadharmakanda*[92] also mention the post of the betel-bearer. We are further told from the Rewa stone inscription of Vijayasingh of A.D. 1193 that Jagatasingh, a man of ministerial rank was appointed as the distributor of betels.[93] From the *Naisadhiyacharitam*[94] it is evident that the court of Gurjara Pratihara kings honour the scholars with two betel and a seat. The above discussion shows the importance of the betel-bearer and hence the distributor of the betels acquired importance and his power and position was enhanced in the king's court and the post was created in the office of the central government. The most important duty of this official was to please the king.

Sarathi (Charioteer)

It appears from the *Agni Purana* that the charïoteer of the king should be skilled in calculating the strength of the hostile army and able to deduct its weak points.[95] The *Matsya* and the *Visnudharmottara Puranas*, further, suggest that the royal charioteer should possess the knowledge of the principles of omens, well-versed in the training of horses and their treatment, divison of the country and the power of warriors. These Puranas further state that he should be firm in sight, gentle in speech, brave, learned and proficient in the different branches of knowledge regarding warfare.[96] Not it is clear that *Sarathi*, *Khadgadhari* and *Dhanurdhari* were the personal servants and guards of the king in the battle-field, in the journey and other places where the king used to go out of the palace.

Somesvara states that the Charioteer of the king should be expert in the treatment of horses and their training. He is further required to be honey-tongued, brave, learned, showing love to all and having the knowledge of omens.[97]

Sudadhyaksha (Superintendent of the Royal Kitchen)

Our Puranas[98] provide the appointment of Sudadhyaksha in the royal palace, whose most important duty was to live in the royal kitchen and look after food prepared for the king. Therefore, the Puranic literature required that this official should be handsome and proficient in the science of medicine and cookery. It has also been suggested that he should be a man of strong character so that no outsider could influence him. The Puranic literature asks the king to appoint only those person in the kitchen who particular in clipping their finger-nails and also generous. The *Garuda Purana* informs us that the king is required to appoint those persons whose father and grand father were in the same service and who is proficient in cooking, truthful, incontaminate and rigid. Thus it appears that the superintendent of kitchen was required to be skilled in the culinary art.

Vaidya (Royal Physician)

The royal physician is, undoubtedly, a very important official in the administrative machinery. In the real sense he is indeed the protector of the king's life. Our Puranas have suggested the king to follow the advice of his physician so that he may enjoy the fruits of his future life. Therefore, the royal physician is required by the literature to be well-versed in the eight-fold medical science. Further he should belong to a noble family, whom nobody could influence. He is also expected to be free from avarice and be virtuous. Mostly he was a hereditary officer. The *Garuda Purana*, especially, lays down that he should be well-versed in treatment, handsome and good nature.[99]

Antahpuradhyaksha (Office-in-Charge of the Female Apartment of the Royal Palace)

The Puranic Records expect that the officer-in charge of the female apartment should be a man of advance age, of noble birth, sweet-spoken, devoted to his ancestors, virtuous, meek and modest, so that he might maintain the efficiency of female department where the queens and princesses used to live.[100] Our records further show that both the sexes to be appointed in the harem. If he is male, then he should be over seventy years of age and if a female, then she should be over fifty. The *Agni Purana* suggests that he or she should be allowed to move every where without any restriction.[101] It is noticeable that our Puranic literature asks the king that eunuchs should be employed in the harem for day-to-day work. Kamandaka,[102] too, states the same qualifications with the difference that the age—qualification is eighty years instead of seventy.

Khadgadhari (Sword-Bearer)

Sword-bearers are included in the personal servants of the king. They are required by our literature,[103] to be tall young, brave, hardy and loyal to the king. They should also be of noble blood. The *Agni Purana*[104] suggests that sword-bearers, who protect the life of the king, should be armed with swords.

Dhanurdhari (The Bow-Wielder)

The bow-wielder, according to the Puranas,[105] should be proficient in the art of riding elephants, horses and chariots. The Puranic text further suggests that *Dhanurdharis* should be well-versed in archery, powerful and able to bear all sorts of distress.

Dauvarika (Gate-Keeper)

The gate-keeper of the king was required to be of noble family, equal in dealing with friends and foes and also munificent.[106] His most important duty was to make the contact of the king with outsiders. An indication of his duties and importance is given by the description of Bana in the *Harsacharita* and in the *Kadambari*.[107]

Narmasachiva

The *Agni Purana*[108] mentions a new type of official named *Narmasachiva* who, according to the literature, was incharge of the king's dress and merriment. The *Narmasachiva* is referred for the first time by Kamandaka.[109] For proper understanding of the duties and position of this functionary we should try to know its meaning. Sir Monier Williams has translated this word as amusement.[110] Sri V.S. Apte also translated the word *Narman* to mean pas-time.[111] The term *Narmasachiva* is broken into *Narmas-usachiva* in the Vachaspatyam[112] and *Narman-sachiva* in the St. Petersburg dictionary. Vachaspatyam designs the *Narmasachiva* as *Parihasasahaya*. The *Sabdakalpadrum*[113] uses the term *Narma* meaning *Parihasah*. In *Kathasaritsagara* the word *Narmasuhrid* is used in the similar tone when it introduces *Narmasuhrid* Vasantak[114] as one of the three important ministers of Udayana the legendry king of Vatsa. The same text further informs us that Vasantaka's son Tapantaka was also appointed as *Kridasachiva* of Narvahanadatta.[115] The post of Vasantaka was hereditary.[116] We are further told that Vasantaka, the *Narmasuhrid* of Udayana secretely organised the marriage of his lord with a princess named Manjulika who was sent by his brother-in law Gopalaka.[117] From this text it is clear that his most important duty was to amuse the king and his queen. In *Sisupalabadha*, Magha tells that the moon acted as the *Narmasachiva* of Ravana.[118] From *Yasastilka Champu*[119] it is evident that king Maridatta is surrounded by sons of *narmasachiva* at the time of amusements such as drinking and hunting. The commentator of the *Yasastilka*, Srutadeva Suri,[120] states the Narmasachiva as a jester or *bhanda*. Rajsekhara in his drama *Viddhasalabhanjika*[121] mentions an important *narmasachiva* Charayana along with the king of Kuntala.

The commentator Jivanand has translated this word as rahasya-sahaya[122] or the minister incharge of private or personal affairs of the king. Probably Rudrabhata[123] is that first man who mentions the qualifications of the *Narmasachiva*. According to him the *Narmasachiva* should be a man of pure character, loyal to the king, able to keep secrets and to amuse and eloquent. The epigraphic sources, too, record *rahasyadhikkrta,*[124] *rahasya*[125] or *rahasadhikata*[126] were officials and their chief duty was to look after the king's private affairs.

Conduct of Government Servants

In the *Visnudharmottara,*[127] the *Matsya*[128] and the *Agni* Puranas.[129] There are excellent chapters on the conduct of the government servants. According to these Puranas a government servant must be loyal, faithful and true to his lord. In the public he must speak words agreeeable to the in manner, prejudicial to his own-being then he must seek audience in private and speak to him what he felt with regard to that particular matter.[130] The servants are required to avoid two things always-- over work and misappropriation. Further, the servants are suggested not to try to imitate the king in his dress or in his speech or any other action. They should also avoid unpleasant things and should show respect to whatever honours confer by the sovereign. They must not enter the harem and other departments intended for royal ladies.[131] They should not be allowed to associate with the spies of the enemy.[132] Further, one should volunteer to do service in the interests of administration but always within the limits of prescribed hours of business. In the assembly it is ordained that the government-servants are asked to listen the king's utterance and should not interrupt him.[134] A personal request to the king for some favour should never be made directly but through some friend or well-wisher.[135] He should not disclose the king's secret before anybody,[136] able or irreprochable would not also be disclosed to any one. The servants are further asked not to repeat repeatedly the favourite things of the king before him but should always remain modest and never knit their eyebrows in his presence or laugh too much before him. They are further required not to talk much nor remain silent in the presence of the king. They should not be careless and proud.[137] Furthermore it is the duty of the government servants that they should not yawn or show signs of weariness or cough or assume, angry, demeanour or rest himself against anything or knit his eyes or vomit and belch in the presence of his sovereign.[138] They should not praise themselves but get others to do it for them.[139]

It has also been suggested that during the course of gambling and at the game of dice the government servants may show their skill to the king but latter on the opportunity of success should be given to him so that he may be declared to the winner. Our Puranas further state that the government servant should not speak the caluminating deeds of the king. They should also accept the garments, weapons and ornaments presented to by the king. They are furthermore suggested that the presentations presented to by the king in the momentous occasions should not be handed over to any other person.[140] They are further required not to sleep before the king or to meet him at an improper place.[141] The princess, friends and councillors of the king should be saluted by the government servant every day.[142] The servants should not speak anything without the permission of the king and if it is necessary to speak that the servants should not speak anything, which is unpleasant to him. The king should have no faith in his ministers.[143] Some similar state-rules for a government servant by which he becomes approved for service. Lastly it is said that the servants who adore the king in spite of his being ignorant, go to the domain of Indra that is inhabited by the Devas.[144]

Administrative Divisions

The Puranic literature supplies us a very dim and

fragmentary picture of the local administration. The whole kingdom, according to the *Visnudharmottara* and the *Agni* Puranas, was divided into many smaller administrative units such as Rastra,[145] Janapada,[146] Desa,[147] Visaya[148] and Mandala.[149] These Puranas further inform group of ten, hundred, and even more villages, and for a Visaya.[150] Besides these administrative units there were towns (Nagara) Khetakas (half of the town) and Kharvatas (mountainous).[151]

Before we consider the provincial district and the village administration, it is necessary to understand the territorial divisions mentioned in our Puranas. The Janapada is most probably mentioned in the sense of kingdom itself. There are numerous references in our record where the genealogies of the past and the territorial divisions of the country are referred, lay down various janapadas such as Kalinga, Matsya, Malla, Magadha, Asmaka, Gandhara, Keral, Chola, Pandya, Anga, Vanga, Pundra, Chedi and so on.[152] Some of these Janapadas were fomous even in the sixth century B.C. and others were small kingdoms of south India. Moreover, in our Puranas the Janapada is described as one of the seventh constituents of the state at several places.[153] Thus it is clear that janapada stands for the kingdom as a whole.

The other territorial division, Rastra, too, is described in the sense of territory at certain places. But it appears from the study of the Puranic literature that our Puranas are influenced by the *Manavadharmasastra*[154] and the *Mahabharata*[155] regarding the territorial divisions of the kingdom. We learn from these two literary sources that the whole kingdom was proposed to be divided into two parts -- Pura or Durga and Rastra. Pura is described as the King's capital and the rest of the kingdom, as Rastra: we are further informed that the whole Rastra was divided into a village, a groups of ten, twenty, hundred and even thousand villages. The *Visnudharmottara*[156] and the *Agni* Puranas[157] also follow the same principle with some modification. Fruther, these Puranas refer to one, a group of ten and hundred villages which indicate that our literature adopted the theory of decimal fraction. Moreover, the *Matsya Purana* informs us that Pura is used for king's capital and vivid description is found for its construction. The *Visnudharmottara Purana*[158] further mentions the Rastradhipati, the officer-in-charge of the Rastra like the Rastrapala of the *Arthasastra*[159] and Rastrpati or the Rastrakuta of the Rastrakuta administration.[160] From the study of these literary sources, it appears that the whole kingdom was divided into Pura (capital) and Rastra. Pura was directly administered by the king himself and the rest part of the kingdom was administered by the officers appointed by him. During the Puranic period, the provinces were called Rastra and its administering officer was known as Rastradhipati, who was helped by a council of ministers called Rastrapalika.[161] Unfortunately, the strength of its members, powers and jurisdiction and not known to us from our record. But from the study of contemporary literary and epigraphic sources we are told that the heads of the provincial administration were officers of the high ramk. Generally, the princes of royal blood were appointed to this responsible post. We are informed from the *Divyavadana*[162] that under the Mauryas, Bindusara, Asoka and Kunala served as provincial governors in different provinces of the empire. Under the Sunga rule the crown prince Agnimitra was the viceroy of Malava.[163] Likewise Damodar copper plate Inscription of 224.G.E. and Vaisali seals of prince Ghatotkacha tell us that Maharajaputra Devabhaṭṭaraka Ghatotkacha Gupta and Govinda Gupta served as Viceroys in the Punduvaṛdhan that the king was asked to kill the head of the Rastra if he committed some sinful act.

The next administrative unit in the Puranic text is Desa which was roughly corresponding to the size of a commissioner's division of the modern times. The head of the Desa was known Desaswami, Desesvara or Desapala,[164] who corresponded to the modern divisional commissioners.

For administarative purposes the Desas were divided into Visayas which usually corresponded with the district of the modern administration. The head of the Visaya was called the Visayesvara in the Puranic literature.[165] The Puranic text further states that the king should appoint the head of a single, ten, a hundred and even more villages, besides the officer-in-charge of a visaya, (district) which leads us to think that all heads of the administrative units from Rastra to village were appointed by the king himself. Furthermore, it is laid down that in case of emergency, the village headman should try to meet the situation but if he fails, he has to report to the head of the ten villages who has to report to the head of hundred villages if he is not able to meet the problem and further more if the head of the hundred villages does not maintain the position he will have to report the matter to the head of the Visaya[166] and finally to the king. The *Agni Purana*[167] speaks that the protection of the district contributes to the financial prosperity of the king. Thus, it appears that like the modern district magistrates they were responsible for maintaining the law and order in their districts as well as to assess and sends taxes to the king.

Between the village and the district the *Agni Purana* states that there was some administrative division known as Mandala[168] which would roughly be corresponding to the modern Tehsil. The nature and dimension of the Mandalas mentioned in the Puranic text are not known to us. The officer-in-charge of such mandalas was known *Mandaladhipati*[169] who corresponds to the modern Tehsildar.

Like the *Manavadharmasastra*[170] and the *Mahabharata,*[171] our Puranic literature recommends those ten villages form one administrative unit and ten of latter should constitue bigger one consisting of one hundred villages, which would roughly correspond to modern Paragana. The officer-in-charge of one hundred villages was called *Satagramadhipati*[172] corresponding to the modern Paraganadhish of Uttar Pradesh. The Officer-in-charge of ten villages was known as *Dasagramadhipati*[173] roughly corresponding to modern Chaukidar.

Unfortunately, we have very little information about the administration of the cities in the Puranic literature. A town was called *pura, nagara, sakhanagara* (Suburban town) *pattana* (post town), *putabhedana* etc.[174] As the area of the town is concerned our literature informs us that the town should be four hundred arrows and the Kaharvata of two hundred arrows. The officer-in-charge of the Pura was known as Puraswami.[175] It has also been laid down that a town should to be protected bya wall which must be so high that it (the town) could not be seen by the camel. How the Kharvata was administered is not known to us.

The last and the most important link in the administration was the village which had been very important unit of social life and administration in India since very early times. It is, undoubtedly, contributed a great deal to the peace and prosperity of Indian people in the preservation of their freedom through all the storms and stresses which were frequently occurring in India. In the word of Sir Charles Metcalf "The village communities of ancient India were little repbulics having nearly everything they can want within themselves and almost independent of any foreign relations. They seem to last where nothing lasts. Dynasties after dynasties tumble down, revolution succeeds to revolution......but village communities remain the same".[176] Unfortunately, Puranic literature does not give us adequate information regarding the working of these republics but some stray references throw light on the subject. In the *Agni Purana* we have some information regarding the functioning of the village administration but it is not sufficient enough to give us its clear picture. We are informed that the village administration was carried on under the supervision and the direction of the village headman who was variously called *gramadhipati,*[177] *gramapala,*[178] *gramesa,*[179] *gramani,*[180] and *grambharta.*[181] He was appointed by the king like other heads of the territorial divisions. It is noticeable that each village possesses the crown land and common pasturage land.[182] Most probably this land was looked after by the village headman. The *Agni Purana,* at one place, states that the village headman *(grambharta)* was responsible for acts of rapine and murder committed within his territorial jurisdiction. However, he was also responsible for theft and if the stolen amount was not recovered from the thief, the provision was made, that it should be realised from the Office concerned.[183] The *Agni Purana* further informs us that if the criminal escapes from the village and runs away to another place, it was the duty of he village headman to search him out from the place where he took shelter. Furthermore, the *Visnudharmottara Purana* lays down that in the case of a theft of horse or an elephant, the five or ten successive villages within the radius of two miles where the theft occurred were held responsible to the crime.[184] Thus it seems that the village headman was the most important and influential person in the village. Sukra[185] observes, at one place, that he was like the father and the mother to the villager. Therefore, it appears that the protection of life and property, maintaining peace and order, proper management of public and crown property situated in the village were some of the most important functions of the village headman. The *Agni Purana* lays down that the position of the village headman was very honourable.[186] Probably the village head man was assisted by a village council. The text of the *Agni Purana,* at one place, discusses the Yoga philosophy and draws similitude between working of the doby are compared to the five house-holders (Kutumbas) of the village council. It is headed by the soul, which is distinguished by all like the *Mahattras* of the village. It shows that they were enjoying the powerful position. Thus most probably the village administration was to be run by *Mahattras* like mahattras of the Pallava,[187] the Vakataka[188] and the·Gahadawala[189] dynasties from C 250-550 A.D. with the help of five members. In the Gupta period we find that the village council consisted of five members only which is expressly designated *punchamandali* in the

Gupta inscripation.[190] It is noticeable that in the *Harsacharita*, Bana not only compares the five great senses of the body to the Panchakula but also lays down its duties which include judicial as well as general administration of the village. It appears that the village administration was carried on by village headman with the help of the members of the village council called Panchakulas. Unfortunately, our Puranic literature does not give us adequate information as to how and by whom the member of the village council were elected and how it was constituted. In the Gupta period we find that municipal council was constituted by the chief merchant (Sarthavaha), the chief scribe (prathama Kayastha), the chief artisan (prathama Kulika) and the president of the guild (nagarasresthi).[191] Similarly, Sukra[192] asks the king to appoint six functionaries in every village - *(i)* head of hte village (gramaneta), *(ii)* collector of the land revenue (bhagahara) *(iii)* collector of the customs duties (sulkgraha), *(iv)* magistrate (sahasadhipati), *(v)* scribe (lekhaka) and *(vi)* the guard of the village headman was helped by certain officers mentioned in our Puranic text. They are Charuraraksadhikari,[193] Raksathakhikrita[194] Saulika,[195] Dandika[196] and the Lekhaka or Kayastha.[197] It also appears from the study of contemporary sources that the defence of the village was the most important duty of the village headman. Certain references have been found relating to the village headmen that they had lost their lives in defending their villages. The collection of the Government revenue was the next important duty of this functionary.

The *Agni Purana* records an officer named *Sthanapala* whose duties are described to keep the lost or stolen property recovered by him in his custody for a year and after that if the rightful owner did not make his claim it should be restored to the state treasury. This officer is also mentioned in the *Ramayana,* the *Harscharita* and the *Rajtarangini*. It shows that most probably he was officer of the police department. Dr. V.S. Agrawal takes this officer as the head of military garrison. Dr. D.C. Sircar thinks that he was the watchman or policeman.

From the study of the Puranic sources it is evident that all officers form the province to the village level were appointed by the king and were responsible to him. The central government exercised a general supervision over all administrative units and if some officer had been found misusing his power and neglecting his duties he was punished by the king. The daily report of these functionaries was received by the king through his spies.[199] The Puranic literature, unfortunately, does not inform us about the salary, allowances and other emoluments of these functionaries as had been laid down by the other authorities like the *Manusmrti*,[200] the *Mahabharata*,[201] and the *Minipradasika*[202] etc. But these functionaries certainly played an important and creditable part in defending the interests of the whole kingdom and in promoting the happiness of the people in general.

It is interesting to note that the *Agni Purana* sates that the functions of the feudatories cannot be performed if they are disaffected.[203] It is further said that their revolt is considered to be external danger as against the internal danger posed by the disaffection of the prince, ministers, high functionaries and such other persons.[204] Apprehending the danger posed by them, the *Agni Purana*[205] instructs the king to destroy a rebellious and disloyal feudatory. The text of the same Purana further informs us the duties of the feudatories. They were required to appease public feeling, to help the paramount sovereign in times of war, to collect allies and auxiliaries and to distinguinsh friends from disguised enemies.[206] It is further said that a king surrounded by rebellious or discontented vassals could never extort such services from. Thus all this shows that feudatories were thought to be sufficiently important by the Puranic period.

REFERENCES

1. SN. II. 69-70.

2. I. 120.
3. IV. 141-42 and 512. Quoted in the *History of Dharmasastra*. Vol. II. p. 213.
4. 218.3.
5. VDP. II. 5.1-14; Arth. 1.9; SN. 2,77-79.
6. Ibid; II. 5.10.
7. VDP. 239. 16-17. Arth. 1.3' *Manasollasa*, II. 2.60.
8. NVM. II. 1.
9. VDP. II. 21. 1-44; AP. 218.5-6.
10. AP. 235.4-5 and 14.
11. VDP. II. 55.5.
12. II Chapt. 124-127.
13. Chapt. 259-262.
14. 241. 14-16.
15. 13. 20-21.
16. II. Chapt. 124-127.
17. Chapts. 259.262.
18. AP. Chapts. 133-135; 137-236.
19. Altekar, A.S., *State and Government in Ancient India*, 1958. p. 168.
20. VDP. II. 5.1.14.
21. The *Viramittrodaya* and the *Mitaksara* on Yajnavalkya, I. 353.
22. Mit. On Yaj. 312-13.
23. Ibid; On Yaj, 2.2. pp. 390-391.
24. SN. II. 69-70.
25. EI IX, p. 305.
26. Ibid; IV. pp. 101-103.
27. *The History of Gahadavala Dynasty*, p. 170.
28. II. 21.38.
29. 218.32.
30. II. 4.1.18.
31. II. Chapt. 24.
32. Chapt. 215.
33. Chapt. 220.
34. *The Classical Age* 1954, p. 343, Bhita seal No. 52, refs. to the Pratihara; Basarh Seal Nos. 16, 18 in Bloch's list refers to the Mahaparatihara.
35. VDP. II. 24. ii-12; on Yaj. 1.307.

36. II. 151. 16.17.
37. 235.8.
38. Ray. H.C. *Dynastic History of Northern India*, Vol. I, 1931. p. 117.
39. EI.I. pp. 200-206.
40. IA XVIII. pp. 19-20; JASB, XLII. pp. 324-28.
41. VDP. II. 24.16.17; M.P. 215-16. A.P. 220.3.
42. II. 24. 12-14.
43. 215. 12-13.
44. 112.8.220.2.241.7.
45. Agrawal V.S. *Matsya Purana—A Study*, p. 293.
46. Smti. 85.28. Manu. 7. 65-68; Arth. 1.16; KNS 12.2.
47. Visvaricharya on Yaj. 128. NVM. 13.2; Yasas, III. 111.
48. 37.27.13.2.
49. AP. 241.18.
50. Arth. I. 16, KNS. 12.3.
51. *Agni Purana* (Tr) Vol. II. 1967, p. 863-64.
52. 241.8.
53. 241.12.
54. NVM. 13.19.
55. Yasas. III. 111.
56. NVM 24.26.
57. 242. 9-10.
58. AP. 241.11.
59. KNS. 12. 11.
60. Deo. Barnark Ins. of Jivita Gupta. II.
61. *The Age of Imperial Kanauj*, 1964. p. 242.
62. Ibid; 106.11.
63. 24.11 & 126.28.
64. 24.7.
65. 126.32.
66. II. 112. 17.
67. I. 8. 33.
68. KNS. Chapts. 4 & 12.
69. NVM. Chapts X (Mantri—Samuddesa) & XVIII (Amataya
70. Samuddesa)
71. P. 178.

72. 1.7.3. and 1.8.4.
73. I.A., XVIII. 238.V. 5.
74. II. 65.39; 151.20.
75. 215.48.
76. 225.19.
77. XII. 85. 7-9.
78. XII. 85.11.
79. Arth. 1.15.
80. II. 65.39; 40. 151.20.
81. 220.37.
82. 225.19.
83. Manasollasa. II. 2.57.
84. NVM. X 66.67.
85. Ibid; X. 67.
86. 68; cf.
87. Arth. 1.15.
88. NVM. X. 71.
89. 239.15-16.
90. 239.10.15.
91. Arth., p. 143.
92. 6.3.
93. 9. 17.
94. MDS. VII.
95. 54.
96. 1.7. 2-3.
97. II. 65.39; 40.
98. 151.20.
99. 220.37.
100. 225.19.
101. *Manasollasa.*
102. II. 2.57.
103. NVM. X. 66.
104. 67.
105. Ibid; X. 67.
106. 68; cf.
107. Arth. 1.15.
108. NVM. X. 71.

109. 239.15-16.
110. 239.10-15.
111. MDS., p. 143.
112. 6.3.
113. 9. 17.
114. MDS. VII.
115. Ibid., XI, 68.
116. AP. 224.42; NVM. 24.31.
117. Ibid; 224.10.
118. Chapt. 219. Raychaudhuri, H. *Political History of Ancient India.*
119. 1953, p. 209.
120. *Dighanikaya,* II. 72.
121. Arth. 1.17.
122. NVM. 24. 72.
123. VI. 2. 152 and 155.
124. AP. 225.2-3, VDP. II. 65. 2-3.
125. Ibid; 223.30-32; VDP. II. 61.65-67.
126. II. 61. 63-64.
127. 223.29.31.
128. VDP. II. 61. 6566, AP. 223.31.
129. Ibid; II. 32.17; AP. 222.18.
130. 215.58.61.
131. Ibid; 215, 61-62; AP. 225.25-26.
132. 173.7.
133. 292.1.
134. 227.32.
135. 225.26.
136. 24.34.
137. NVM. 7.2., 5.5.
138. 222.11-16; 2255.23.
139. II. 32.7; AP. 222.15-16.
140. AP. 223.9.
141. 223.9.
142. III. 323.25-26.
143. III. 3-10-11.
144, NVM. 26.66.
145. *Yogayatra* 2, 23.

146. 225.33.
147. 241.12.
148. NVM. 13.19.
149. Yasas. III. 111.
140. NVM 24.26.
141. 242. 9-10.
142. AP. 241.11.
143. KNS. 12. 11.
144. Deo. Barnark Ins. of Jivita Gupta. II.
145. *The Age of Imperial Kanauj*, 1964. p. 242.
146. Ibid; 106.11.
147. 24.11 & 126.28.
148. 24.7.
149. 126.32.
150. II. 112. 17.
151. I. 8. 33.
152. KNS. Chapts. 4 & 12.
153. NVM. Chapts X (Mantri—Samuddesa) & XVIII (Amataya
154. Samuddesa)
155. P. 178.
156. 1.7.3. and 1.8.4.
157. I.A., XVIII. 238. V. 5.
158. II. 65.39; 151.20.
159. 215.48.
160. 225.19.
161. XII. 85. 7-9.
162. XII. 85.11.
163. Arth. 1.15.
164. II. 65.39; 40. 151.20.
165. 220.37.
166. 225.19.
167. *Manasollasa*. II. 2.57.
168. II. 151. 19-20.
169. 235. 9-12.
170. I. 2.704.
171. 241.4, Arth. I.15; I.15; KNS. XI.56; *Panchatantra* I, p. 85.
172. 241.3.

173. XI. 62.
174. 241.5.
175. 122. 11.14.
176. AP. Chapt. 6.
177. *The Classical Age*, 1962, p. 101.
178. A.P. 220.3.
179. II. 24.16.
180. 215.16.
181. *Manasollasa* II. 2. 127-130.
182. NVM. 32.2.
183. 4. 137.138.
184. Altekar, A.S., *State and Government in Ancient India*, 1958, p. 171.
185. SN, II. 81.
186. Arth. V. 6, VIII. 1.
187. KNS. IV. 48.
188. Ibid; IV. 44.
189. SN. II. 74.
190. Arth. I. 15.
191. SN. II. 80.
192. Ibid. II. 247-49.
193. R.S. VI of Asoka.
193. *Divyavadana*. p. 430.
194. E.I. VIII. p. 44. II. 16-17.
195. KNS. XI. 59-61.
196. 215.2.
197. Ibid. III, 248-250.
198. II. 112. 17.
199. I. 8. 33.
200. KNS. Chapts. 4 & 12.
201. NVM. Chapts X (Mantri—Samuddesa) & XVIII (Amataya
202. Samuddesa)
203. P. 178.
204. 1.7.3. and 1.8.4.
205. I.A., XVIII. 238.V. 5.

5

Fiscal Administration

Stability and strength of the state and success of its government depend mainly upon sound finances. Ancient Indian Political thinkers had realised the importance of this proposition. Hence, they had included rich treasury *(Kosa)* among the seven constituents of the state. The Puranas also paid due importance to this aspect of the administration as they realinsed that any negligence on their part in this direction would sap the very foundation of the state. The Puranic literature, threfore, took very great care in suggesting the king that his treasure should always remain full, so that security and efficiency of the state might be assured. The *Visnudharmottara Purana*, at one place, specifically states that *Kosa* (treasury) is the root of the tree of the State.[1] Similar dictum is also recommended by the *Agni Purana*.[2]

From the study of ancient Indian literature we find that this idea was continued from very early period and was commended by the sastras. It has often been described as the very root the state.[3] Manu[4] lays down that the treasury.... (is) dependent upon the king, and Kulluka, commenting upon it, writes that the treasury "should not be made over to the charge of any other person. The king should look after it himself." Kautilya is of the same opinion and remarks, very aptly, that all undertakings of the government depend upon *Kosa*. Therefore, the king must pay the first attention to it.[5] The Jain writer, Somadeva Suri, beautifully remarked in this work *Nitivakyamrta* that it is the treasury and not the life of the king which keeps him alive. He further states that treasury constitutes sovereignty and not body of the king.[7] Our *Visnudharmottara*[8] and the *Agni* Puranas[9] compare the poor with degraded person and remark that a poor man is unable to control even his own wife. They further add that all efforts without finance are fruitless like small river in summer.[10] Thus it is evident that the Puranas like most of authorities have advocated the maintenance of full treasure. Kamandaka desires that the king's Kosa should be full of all desired kinds of wealth.... rich in pearls, gold and jewels... (and capable of bearing great strains of expenditure).[11] Somesvaradeva, likewise states that it should be always full of gold in the form of bars or coins-silver, jewels, ornaments and costly cloths.[12] Sukra makes the almost impossible suggestion that the treasury should contain so much of wealth as would suffice to maintain the national army for a period of twenty years, even without receipt of taxes. Not only was the king required to maintain gold and silver reserves, he was also asked to maintain stocks of grain. These, according to same authority, should be for three years' consumption in the country.[13] Thus we find that the treasury occupies an important place in the body politic of the state and king is required to maintain it with all means, because an empty treasury always contributes to the downfall of the state and the ruling dynasty.

It is significant to note that some important principles of taxation which have been enunciated by Epics, Dharmasastras and the *Arthasastra* are discussed in our Puranas. The first and the most important principle, as has been laid down in somewhat poetical and picturesque language, according to the Puranic literature, is that taxes should be reasonable and equitable neither too excessive to be felt as an oppressive burden by the people nor too little to affect the stability of the state itself. The *Garuda Purana*[14] advises the king that as a gardener strings a garland of flowers by culling one from each plant in the garden, so the king shall raise his revenue by imposing a light tax on his individual subject, without inflicting hardship on any one. In short, the king is advised to act like the maker of charcoals, who fell down all the trees in the garden and reduce them to cinders. It further states that "draw the milk but do not bury the udders".[15] In the *Mahabharata*[16] we find a very lovely discussion between Bhisma and Yudhisthira on this principle. Bhisma told Yudhisthira "If the calf be permitted to suck it grows strong and bears heavy burdens. On the other hand, if the cow is over milked the calf becomes lean and fails to do much service to the owner. Similarly, it the people are over-taxed they fail to perform great tasks." Manu,[17] too, undoubtedly very rightly advises the king neither to cut off his own roots by not realising taxes and duties, nor to cut off the roots of people through excessive greed.

Secondly, the Puranic literature prescribes that taxation is meant for providing protection to the people against natural calamities as well as external and internal troubles. The *Visnudharmottara Purana* is of the view that a king is entitled to receive taxes from his subjects in return for the protection he offers to them like a pregnant woman who sacrifices her own desires and pleasures for the protection of her child.[18] The king is warned by the *Agni Purana*[19] that if he does not protect his subjects and gives troubles to his people, he will be destroyed soon and will have a long sojourn in the hell. Manu[20] has very rightly observed that the king who receives only the just dues from his people thrives both in this world and the next, whereas by taking what ought not to be taken, he proclaims his own weakness and suffers both here and hereafter. His dictum is that the king should collect the taxes for the protection of his subjects. The *Markandeya Purana*,[21] at one place, designated a king as a thief who, wrongfully, received excess taxes from his subjects. Epigraphic evidence shows that this principle was usually followed by the kings in ancient India. We have historical examples that owing to overtax the powerful Nandas became unpopular and it was the most potent cause of their downfall.

Thirdly, the king is not allowed by the Puranic literature to increase the taxes according to his own discretion. He has to follow the rules laid down by the Dharmasastras.[22] This principle has been enunciated by all the ancient political thinkers.[23]

Fourthly, we are informed that taxes should be recovered at the proper time and place.[24] Kautilya,[25] at one place, says that "Just as fruits are gathered from a garden as often as they become ripe, so revenue should be collected as often as its becomes ripe. Collection of revenue or of fruits when ripe shall never be carried on, lest their source may be. Kamandaka[26] is also of the same opinion and states that a monarch . . . . . should in proper season in gather his subjects . . . Just as cows are at one time tended and at other times milked, so are the subjects to be at one time and at other time to be levied taxes upon them. Both tend and sprinkle water on his plants and flowers from them. Thus it is evident that rates prescribed by the Dharmasastras were not followed in rigid sense perhaps to meet the natural calamities and external revolts and internal troubles.

Fifthly, the Puranic literature allowed the king to receive taxes from every earning members of the society. Agriculturists, cattle-rearers, merchants and manufacturers have to pay a certain percentage of their income to the government. The *Agni Purana* lays down that the king receives taxes in order to give back to him in the form of his livelihood in the same way as the sun who receivers of all the waters on the earth and return it in the form of rain.[27] The same expression is found in the *Manusmrti*[28] that even a very poor man who maintains by following some should be asked to contribute every year in the.[29] Finally, our Puranas state that the king should receive taxes even from persons who sell merchandise of little importance such as roots, fruits, leaves, pot-herbs, hays, bamboos, hydes wicker-works, earthen-pots, stone vessels, honey etc.[30]

However, certain categories of the people were exempted from the payment of taxes. According to the *Visnudharmottara Purana*[31] ambassadors, spies, brahmanas, women, srotriyas and ascetics (brahmanas learned in the Vedas) should be exempted from taxes. The *Agni Purana*[32] also expresses the same dictum. Thus, it is clear that our Puranic literature repeats the ideas of ancient Indian political thinkers like Manu[33] and Bhisma[34] that the brahmanas should be exempted from taxation. The *Visnudharmottara Purana*[35] advocates that the king is like dead in whose realm a learned brahmana (Srotriya) well-versed in the Vedas famishes for food. It has been further suggested by the same text that it is the foremost duty of the king to ascertain acquirements and occupation of each brahmana residing in his country and he should also provide him a decent annuity and feed and protect him like his own begotten son.[36] It is said that the merits of religious ceremonies performed by brahmanas give long life to the king and improve the condition of his subjects.[37] Hence the *Visnudharmottara Purana* says that only learned brahmanas should be exempted from taxes. The whole of the brahmana class, however, is exempted by the *Agni Purana*[38] but Manu[39] on the other hand, recommends that only learned brahmanas should be exempted. There are divergent opinions on this point. The *Mahabharata*,[40] for example, declares that the brahmanas who are holding lucrative appointments in the government service or those who are following the money-making professions like trade, agriculture and cattle-rearing, are to be charged usual taxes and cusses at their full rates. Narada[41] is of the same opinion and says that limited taxation even from the learned brahmanas should be received and he further advocates that the commodities owned by brahmanas and intended for trade should be taxed. Likewise Parasara[42] says that the brahmanas should pay one-sixth of the land produce to the king if they engage themselves in the agriculture. It is noticeable that the *Mahabharata*,[43] at one place, lays down the levy of taxes and carvee from such brahmanas who are not learned and do not perform sacrifices. It further recommends that during the time of shortage of money the king should collect taxes from all brahamanas except from those who are Brahmasama and Devasama. Further more, the king is advised by Somadeva Suri to take only so much from the brahmanas and traders and remains in their hands after deducting the amount incurred on religious persons, and for keeping up the family. He is also allowed to levy taxation on the property of rich people, childless couples, widows, religious heads, village officials, prostitutes and the ruffians.[44] In spite of this we find occasional references that the entire brahmana class was exempted from certain taxes. A record of the king Somasimhadeva of the Paramara dynasty[45] tells us that brahmanas were exempted from the taxes. Thus we find that exemption of taxes seems to have been enjoyed by brahmanas and were excluded only on rare occasions. As a general rule all brahmanas had to pay taxes, excepting those who were learned and poor and had received no state patronage.[46]

The property belonging to the temples was exempted from the taxation. The *Agni Purana*[47] states that the king who appropriates the temple's property and the property of brahmanas goes in hell for a long period.

Let us now consider the sources of revenue. The Puranic record recommends an important source of revenue is Bhoga which has been explained in the sense of periodical supply of fruits, firewood, flowers to the king. Unfortunately, our Puranas do not mentioned the rate of the Bhoga tax. But with the help of epigraphic and literary sources we are informed that the Bhoga tax was paid to the king and his officers by the villagers. Dr. Altekar[48] is of the opinion that this tax was paid by villagers when the king used to go on pleasure trip. The articles which were paid were betel leaves, fruits and vegetables etc. This tax was received daily by local officers. He further states that this was extra tax, which was not included in land tax. The *Visnudharmottara*[49] and the *Agni* Puranas[50] like Manu lay down the appointment of heads of one; ten, and hundred villages and the lord of Visyas. These Puranas further recommend that the share of these officers in Bhoga will be in accordance with their work. Manu speaks in the same tone and states that the daily supply of cereals, firewood, etc., should be made by the villagers to the village headman. Thus it appears that this was extra tax, which was paid by villagers to the officers of the state as was prevalent in northern India before Independence. The *Matsya Purana,*[51] at one people, employs the word Bali in the sense of the 6th part of produce of land that the king levied as a tax.

Customs duties were also known to the puranas, but they varied according to the commodities as is prevalent in the present times. The duties were levied on the products of one's own country and also on imported goods. The Visnudharmottara Purana[52] recommends ten percent duty on products on king's own territory and five percent on imported and exported goods from foreign countries. Elsewhere the same literature[53] lays down that the tax on foreign trade should be determined according to the actual cost of their manufacture, the wear and tear and the actual profit derived by the merchant. It further adds that if the merchant does not pay the tax king is entitled to charge five percent as the penalty. This is notable fact that the *Agni* Purana states that this custom duty on imported goods from foreign country should not exceed more than five percent on the net profit.[54] It is remarkable that our Puranic literature is very much liberal in fixing the customs duties. For example, Kautilya is of the opinion that 20 percent of value should be charged as import duty.[55] Similarly Visnu[56] ordains the king to take 10 percent of the net profit. The *Visnudharmottara Purana*[57] ordains the king to take 10 percent of the net profit. The *Visnudharmottara Purana*[57] further informs us that the import and export duties should be accepted in cash and particularly it should not be accepted in different coins, which leads us to think that the different types of coins were flourishing in the country; but there was some standard type of coin which was prescribed for the custom duties due to lack of foreign exchange.

Alongwith the customs duty, we find ferry tax *(Tarasulka)*[58] which was probably paid for passengers, goods, cattle and carts. The *Visnudharmottara Purana* state that this tax was not allowed to collect from spies, brahmanas, state officials, women and wandering mendicants.[59]

In addition to the ferry tax, the Puranic literature enjoins the king to levy one-sixth and one-eighth on *sukadhanya* (autumn) crops and *simbidhana* (rain crops) respectively.[60] But the *Agni Purana* recommends that the rates may be varied according to the time and place.[61] Similar tenet is recommended by the *Visnudharmottara Purana*[62] and it state sthat the king is allowed to change one-sixth of rain crops, one-eighth of autumn crops and one-tenth on the crops grown land that was fallow for many years as share in the land produce. Cattle-breeding, perfumery, medicinal herbs, gold, liquids, flowers, roots and fruit-leaves, vegetables, grass, bamboo, things made of bamboo and hide, wicker-works, earthen and stone vessels, honey, meat and clarified butter were another important sources of revenue.[63] The *Agni Purana*[64] ordains the king to receive one-fifth share on animals and one-sixth on the rest articles. The *Visnudharmottara Purana*,[65] too, recommends the same principles as advocated by the *Agni Purana*. Manu, too, is of the same opinion and recommends one-sixth on fuel, meat, honey, ghee, scents, medicines, flowers, vegetables, earthen pots and leather-goods.[66] Further it is said that five percent tax should be charged from envoys and labourers.[67] The *Markandeya Purana* informs us that the king was entitled to receive one-twelth from merchants and one-sixth from cow-herbs and cultivators as a tax.[68]

Another source of income to the state was for crown-land tax. Generally, the ownership of the cultivated land in ancient India vested not in the state but in private individual. The state, of course, had the right to realise tax from such lands but it could not claim possession over them. Sometimes, however, the ownership of a piece of land was transferred to the state on account of the absence of its rightful claimant or on account to non-payment of the land tax. State acquired ownership only in such pieces of land. In most of villages such pieces of land existed which belonged to the state. Besides, the state also had ownership over unsettled or fallow land. Thus there were two types of land in the state one belonging to the king or the state and other belonging to private individuals. Kautilya[69] clearly differentiates between the crown land and private crown land and private land in his *Arthasastra* and so also other lawyers like Katyayana, Mitramisra, Narada etc. The *Agni Purana*[70] advises the king to set apart a piece of crown-land as the common pasture of the villages. It includes the crown-land and the property of the king in the list of objects of which ownership is not lost by adverse encroachment for long.[71] Thus, it is evident that the king was expected to hold crown-land in various parts of his kingdom. Hiuen Tsang[72] speaks that the people used to pay one-sixth part of the land produce to the king who were cultivating the crown land. Yajnvalkya[73] and Somesvaradeva[74] also state that the king should provide the pastured land to the villagers. Thus we find that most probably one-sixth was common tax for cultivated crown-land as had been recorded by Hiuen Tsang.

The hidden treasure was another source of income. The *Visnudharmottara Purana* speaks that if who latent property is found by a brahmana, he should pay nothing to the king, while a Ksatriya, a Vaisya and a Sudra recover it, they are liable to pay one-sixteenth, one-eighth and one-fourth respectively to the king's treasure.[75] It is noticeable that the *Visnudharmottara Purana*,[76] further like Manu,[77] and Yajnavalkya[78] recommends that the occult property discovered by the king himself should be distributed 50 percent to the brahmanas and rest to his own treasure.

The state should also utilise its right on unclaimed property and discovered treasure. The Agni Purana states that a property of merchant being in a foreign land should go to his relatives, and in their absence to the king.[79] In the same Purana it has been stated that the king is authorised to commend his power over such water reservoirs (setu) which are boilt by one on the land of others and are without rightful claimants.[80] Manu,[81] Gautama,[82] Yajnavalkya[83] and Narada[84] are of the same opinion and lay down that the king is fully empowered to utilise the unclaimed property. The *Visnudharmottara*[85] and the *Agni Purana*[86] like Manu[87] further state that the king should keep unclaimed property in his custody for the period of three years and if no body claims it as rightful claimant it would go int the king's treasure. The Agni Purana, furthermore, suggests the king that any lost or stolen property, discovered either by the police officer (Sthanapala) or the customs Officers, should be kept in the state treasury for one year, and if no rightful owner of that property is found it should go to the king's treasury.[88] Kautilya, too, prescribes the same rule but opines that articles should be kept in the custom-house only three fort-nights.[89] Moreover, the kings is authorised by the Angi Purana[90] to claim 5 percent of the abandoned goods. It is noticeable that Somadeva Suri, on the other hand, is of the opinion that the king should not use judicial fines, money recovered in gambling, lost or heirless property, things seized from thieves, women's property and property left for public danger. But our Puranic literature does not lay such type of rule. Thus it is evident that unclaimed property and discovered treasure belong to the state in which they are found. The citizens who informed the state about the discovery of treasure and troves were undoubtedly, honoured and the property of the people, dying without legal heirs belonged to the crown.

Force or unpaid labour was common in ancient days. The people, who were unable to pay their regular taxes, were forced to pay something to the state in return for their protection they get from it. Generally, those people used to pay their taxes by offering their free services. The *Visnudharmottara Purana*[91] and the *Agni Purana*[92] like Gautama,[93] Manu,[94] Vasistha,[95] speak that artisans were required to work one day every month and manual labours had to work for the king as they were fed. The *Visnudharmottara Purana,* further, adds that the carpenters, artisans and Sudras should do one day manual labour in every month.[96] Manu even says that a very poor man who maintains himself by following some occupation should be asked to contribute every year something in the nature of tax, while workers (like cooks), artisans (like blacksmith) sudras who subsist by manual labour (like porters) should be worked to contribute one day's work to the king in the month.[97] It, therefore, shows that it was traditional labour-tax which was prevalent in our Puranic period.

According to the Puranic literature,[98] the Upahara or tribnutes and spoils of war also added to the state income. This amount, however, was uncertain and weak rulers, feudatories and villagers were used to pay the presents and tributes as token of submission to the powerful king. The Allahabad pillar inscription, for example, informs us that Samudra Gupta had extended his influcne and power by means of Digvijaya. Therefore, wealth received by those compaigns enriched the state treasury. The tributes received from the vassal king and some independent ribes and gifts also added considerably to the income of the state.[99]

The *Agni Purana*[100] like Kamandaka,[101] advocates that the king should negotiate the treaties of friendship with some gifts. This Purana, further, suggests the king to distribute spoils of war among his soldiers and the gems, precious stones to himself. On the other hand the *Visnudharmottara Purana* extends the royal right to shields, weapons and conveyances.[102]

Our Puranic literature[103] lays down that the king was authorised to dispossess the virgin land from its owner who is unable to cultivate it or not being cultivated by another. The king is further asked to settle such virgin land with another person for its cultivation. It leads us to think that the virgin land was the king's property. It is just possible that during the settlement of this type of land between the king and other person some payment of amount was fixed which unfortunately is not mentioned in our record.

The interest on loans was another source of king's income. The *Agni Purana* lays down that the king may advance loans on interests to private persons. It further advises the king to lend his money in accordance with Dharmasastras. Furthermore, it opines that when debt is repaid by various creditors, the brahmanas are entitled to receive back their money first and the king next.[104] It is noticeable that the Agni Purana ordains the king to protect and maintain the eight sources of revenue agriculture, trade routes, capital town or the fort (durga), dams and bridges, captured elephants, mines and minerals levy or import of army and settlement of vacant land.But unfortunately, this Purana does not mention the method through which these sources enrich the king's treasury.

Fines were naturally another source of revenue because the fines were very common and were imposed by the kings for petty offences. Heavy fines were imposed in case of grave offences. Fortunately our Puranic literature throws a flood of light on this subject, which has already been descussed in the chapter of judiciary. The *Visnudharmottara Purana*[105] states that every thing dug up from mines belonged to the king. The *Manasollasa* asks the king to guard mines of gems, gold and silver over all wealth and specially over what is inside the earth.[106]

The Puranas have also discussed the justificatin for realisation of the taxes from the people. They are off the opinion that the king was entitled to receive the taxes in lieu of protection that he offered to his subjects. The Agni Purana[107] ordains the king to increase his treasury when he finds his kingdom is well protected. It has also been laid down by the *Visnudharmottara*[108] and the *Agni* Puranas[109] that the king receives one-sixth of the good and bad deeds performed by his subjects. The *Agni Purana*[110] further informs that when the people are protected they contribute gold *(Hiranya),* crops *(Dhanya),* clothes, conveyances and other various materials to the state. Thus, it is evident that the king receives taxes from his subjects in lieu of giving protection to them. Manu[111] also says that a ruler it thief who receives taxes but does not perform his duties. The *Markandeya Purana*[112] speaks that if the people pay one-sixth as their revenue but are not protected by the king, he certainly goes to hall. It is further said that if the king does not protect his subjects he is sharer of sin. This Purana further regards the one-sixth tax as king's wages[113] *(Vetana).* If he fails to protect his subjects he becomes thief.

Let us now consider the items of expenditure in the state budget. Unfortunately, we do not get any reliable information on this subject from our Puranic literature. Our Puranas neither define expenditure nor provide systematic treatment of the percentage of the state income which was spend each item of expenditure. The king is asked by the Purana[114] to spend his money on maintenance of the poor, the destitute the old, the widows and women in general.[115] He is further, required to provide pensions to the relatives of soldiers.[116] It is noticeable that our *Visnudharmmottara Purana*[117] does not allow the king to give the protection to the women who are issue-less.

The king, according to the Purana, was expected to spend a good deal of income on the defence of the kingdom. Our literature informs us that a large amoutn of the king's income was spent on the prepartion and execution of war effort on bribes to create dissension in the rank and file of the enemy, and on presents to the inimical as well as friendly monarchs.[118] The *Visnudharmottara Purana*[119] states that monetary allurements may be offered to the adversaries and it has been made as one of the constituents of the state. So huge amount was expected to be spent on the military force.

The king is further asked to provide decent annuities[120] and up keep to the brahmanas who were considered to be the pillar of learning in the society. It has been suggested that the king should spend a portion of his income in settling the learned brahmanas who were performing their duties.[121] The *Visnudharmottara Purana*[122] like Manu,[123] Yajnavalkya[124] and *Nitiprakasika*[125] speaks that gifts offered to the brahmanas are imperishable treasure, so he should spend a certain part of his income in offering the gifts to the brahmana. According to the Puranic literature lands, hamlets, cows, villages and other various things were required to be offered to the brahmanas by the kin on important occasions, like coronation, propitiation of different calamities and planets and also particularly for gaining religious merits.[126] The *Matsya Purana*[127] throws much light on this subject and a detailed description on the gifts is made into thirty chapters. Like-wise the *Agni Purana,*[128] too, devoted six chapters on various types of gifts. The epigraphic evidence tells us that numerous land grants were made to the brah manas during the Gupta and the post-Gupta period and even afterwards.

The Puranic literature mentions the performance of the coronation ceremony of the king in details. It further lays down certain other religious and propitiatory rituals[129] like royal emblems, organisation of festivals in honour of goods,[130] worship of goddess Durga in the month of Asvina.[131] The king was, further more, required by the Puranas to construct the temples for the god and goddess and provision for painting, dance, music and purificatory bath of the images was to be made.[132] Epigraphic evidences clearly tell us that ancient Indian kings were fond of providing such annuities for temples. We are informed from the Chaulukyan inscriptions[133] that the king Bhogasakti granted eight villages for providing materials for the worship of gods, the repairs of temples and the maintenance of a sattra in the town of Jayapura. Certain rights, levies and taxes were assigned by him to the temples, and merchants of the town were exempted from octroi duties.

The *Visnudharmottara Purana*[134] informs us that the officer incharge of one, ten or hundred villages and the lord of Visayas were provided a share of offerings of revenue, which was made by villagers. The *Agni Purana*, further, lays down that the king was required to pay regular wages to the soldiers[135] and to arrange livelihood to his royal servants and also to bestow rewards and marks of distinction on them.[136] Though our Puranas do not help us in informing the scale of pay and emoluments as has been told by Kautilya[137] and Sukra.[138] But from the study of stray references in the Puranic literature we are told that a huge amount of king income was spent on different items of the state expenditure.

It is remarkable that the Puranas provide us some idea of revenue organisation. The *Visnudharmottara*,[139] the *Matsya*[140] the *Garuda*[141] and the *Agni* Puranas[142] mention the king's treasurer (Dhanadhyaksa) who was the head of the department of treasury. He was required by the same Puranas, to be wise, dexterous, clear-headed, free from laziness and avarice and able to evaluate things. The other officers who are known to us by the Puranic literature are Kosapala,[143] Kanakadhyaksa[144] and Aksaraksaka[145] (Officer-in-charge of royal mint). It is further said that the accountants of the treasury department were required to write neatly and legible. They were educated and clever enough to use sort phrases with pregnant meaning. The *Agni Purana* further lays down a department for fixing the boundaries of land. It is said that if a boundary is not well-marked the king is asked to demarcate it with the help of *Ksiticharinah* (Surveyors).[146] Besides two officers are incharge one incharge of land and tolls Sanskir and other incharge of ferry dues *(Tarika)*[147] are known from our text. It has also been said that the officer-in-charge of ferry charges shall be fined ten *panas* if he demands land tolls.[148] Hence the functions of these two officers were different. The *Agni Purana*[149] further states that the destroyer of the state custom-house situated on the sea shore (Samudragrha) should be punished with the fine of fifty *panas.* The *Visnudharmottara Purana*[150] informs us that the duties should be collected at one place and in coin only. So it appears that there was a separate department for customs duties. The *Nitivakyamrta*[151] elaborately discusses the name of five officers who mattered in the financial administration. Adayaka was the officer who realised customs duties and other taxes from the traders and peasants respectively. It was his duty to deposit the collected amount into the state exchequer. Apparently, his function was two-fold-collection of revenue and taxes and deposition of the amount collected for the state treasury. It is noticeable that this officer was assisted by Nibandhaka, who was interested with the work of putting into writing the accounts. Pratikantaka was another official who put the state seal over the amount deposited in the treasury by the Adayaka. Vinigrahana was the official-in-charge of the royal treasury.[152] Probably he seems to be the ancient version of the modern treasury officer. He had to keep an account of income and expenditure. All these officers worked under the direction, supervision and control of Rajadhyaksha. It further mentions to the appointment of auditors where there is discrepancy in the items of income and expenditure.

It is noticeable that our *Visnudharmottara* and the *Agni* Puranas[153] furnish a kind of budget, according to which half of the daily revenue of the state should be deposited in the king's treasury and rest should be distributed to the brahmanas. Yaun Chawang, too, informs us that Harsavardhana, the king of Kanauj, spent 50 percent of the land revenue on general administration and 50 percent on rewards for high intellectual eminence and gifts to various sects.[154] Somesvaradeva[155] made an attempt to provide a budget of expenditure for the state. According to him to total income should be divided into four parts. He further states that seventy-five percent of the income should be spent on promoting *dharma* (piety), *artha* (material resources) and *kama* (wordly pleasures), and rest 25 percent should be kept in treasury as reserve amount. Sukra prescribes that the king should save one-sixth of his total annual income and should spend half of the whole on the army and one-twelfth each on charity, (to the learned, the poor and helpless etc.) ministers, inferior officers and his private purse or expenses. Thus we find that our Puranic literature seems to have the idea of tentative budget.

It is appearent from the above description of the financial system as set-forth in the Puranic text without organisation of financial system on proper lines, it is very difficult if not impossible, to run the administration successfully. The Puranas appear to have realised its colossal importance. However, they fail to reveal us a complete picture of the fiscal system.

REFERENCES

1. AP. 224.42; NVM. 24.31.
2. Ibid; 224.10.
3. Chapt. 219. Raychaudhuri, H. *Political History of Ancient India*, 1953 p. 209.
4. *Dighanikaya*, II. 72.
5. Arth. 1.17.
6. NVM. 24. 72.
7. VI. 2. 152 and 155.
8. AP. 225.2-3, VDP. II. 65. 2-3.
9. *Ibid;* 223.30-32; VDP. II. 61.65-67.
10. II. 61. 63.64.
11. 223.29.31.
12. VDP. II. 61. 65-66, AP. 223.31.

13. Ibid; II. 32.17; AP. 222.18.
14. 215.58.61.
15. Ibid; 215, 61-62; AP. 225.25-26.
16. 173.7.
17. 292.1.
18. 227.32.
19. 225.26.
20. 24.34.
21. NVM. 7.2., 5.5.
22. 222.11-16; 2255.23.
23. II. 32.7; AP. 222.15-16.
24. AP. 223.9.
    223.9.
    III. 323.25-26.
25. II. 151. 19-20.
26. 235. 9-12.
27. I. 2.704.
28. 241.4, Arth. I. 15; I. 15; KNS. XI. 56; *Panchatantra* I, p. 85.
29. 241.3.
30. XI.62.
31. 241.5.
32. 122. 11.14.
33. AP. Chapt. 6.
34. *The Classical Age,* 1962, p. 101.
35. A.P. 220.3.
36. II. 24.16.
37. 215.16.
38. *Manasollasa* II.2. 127-130.
39. NVM. 32.2.
40. 4. 137.138.
41. Altekar, A.S., *State and Government in Ancient India.*
42. 1958. p. 171.
43. SN, II. 81.
44. Arth. V. 6; VIII. 1.
45. KNS. IV.48.
46. Ibid; IV.44.
47. SN. II. 74.

48. Arth. I.15.
49. SN. II.80.
50. Ibid. II. 247-49.
51. R.S. VI of Asoka.
52. *Divyavadana*. p.430.
53. E.I. VIII. p.44.II.16-17.
54. KNS.XI.59-61.
55. 215.2.
56. 241.12.
57. NVM. 13.19.
58. Yasas.III. 111.
59. NVM 24.26.
60. 242. 9-10.
61. AP. 241.11.
62. KNS. 12. 11.
63. Deo. Barnark Ins. of Jivita Gupta. II.
64. *The Age of Imperial Kanauj*, 1964. p. 242.
65. Ibid; 106.11.
66. 24.11 & 126.28.
67. 24.7.
68. 126.32.
69. II. 112. 17.
70. I. 8. 33.
71. KNS. Chapts. 4&12.
72. NVM. Chapts X (Mantri—Samuddesa) & XVIII (Amataya
73. Samuddesa)
74. P. 178.
75. 1.7.3. and 1.8.4.
76. I.A., XVIII. 238.V.5.
77. II. 65.39; 151.20.
78. 215.48.
79. 225.19.
80. XII. 85. 7-9.
81. XII. 85.11.
82. Arth. 1.15.
83. II.65.39; 40. 151.20.
84. 220.37.

85. 225.19.
86. *Manasollasa*. II. 2.57.
87. Ibid; 5.38.
88. 220. 1-12.
89. II. 65. 1-14.
90. 225. 1-7.
91. 220. 2-3; VDP. II. 65. 2-4.
92. 220.1; VDP. II. 65.3.
93. MP. 220.3., VDP.II. 65.4.
94. MP. 220.4; VDP. II. 65.5; AP. 225.3.
95. Ibid; 220.8; VDP. II. 65. 9-10; AP. 225.4.
96. Ibid; 220.9; VDP. II. 65. 11; AP. 225.5.
97. Ibid; 220.4; VDP. II. 65.6.
98. Ibid; 220.6; VDP. II. 65.7.
99. MP. 220. 19-20; VDP. II. 65-20-22; AP. 225. 11-12.
100. 18. 1-3.
101. MKP. 183-6.
102. V. 21. 18-24.
103. 18.25.
104. VSP. V.10.27-28; VDP. II. 65.46; AP. 225.21-22, 233.8.; MDS. VII.
105. 43; Santi. 59.33; Arth. 1.2; Yaj. 1. 311; Kamandaka II. 1.Sukrantil.
106. 152.
107. *Dasakumarcharita*, VIII. Para I, p. 202.
108. NVM. 5.55.
109. Arth. 1.2.
110. KNS. 2.3-6.
111. Arth. 1.3.
112. Ibid; 1.5.
113. NVM. 7.1.
115. VDP. I. 22. 129-133; AP. 219. 59-56.
116. 241.12.
117. NVM. 13.19.
118. Yasas.III. 111.
119. NVM 24.26.
120. 242. 9-10.

121. AP. 241. 11.
122. KNS. 12. 11.
123. Deo. Barnark Ins. of Jivita Gupta. II.
124. *The Age of Imperial Kanauj,* 1964. p. 242.
125. Ibid; 106.11.
126. 24.11 & 126.28.
127. 24.7.
128. 126.32.
129. II. 112. 17.
130. I. 8. 33.
131. KNS. Chapts. 4 & 12.
132. NVM. Chapts X (Mantri—Samuddesa & XVIII (Amataya
133. Samuddesa.
134. P. 178.
135. 1.7.3. and 1.8.4.
136. I.A., XVIII. 238.V. 5.
137. II. 65.39; 151.20.
138. 215.48.
139. 225.19.
140. XII. 85. 7-9.
141. XII. 85.11.
142. Arth. 1.15.
143. II.65.39; 40. 151.20.
144. 220.37.
145. 225.19.
146. *Manasollasa*. II. 2.57.
147. *Dighanikaya,* II. 72.
148. Arth. 1.17.
149. NVM. 24. 72.
150. VI. 2. 152 and 155.
151. AP. 225.2-3, VDP. II. 65. 2-3.
152. Ibid; 223.30-32; VDP. II. 61.65.67.
153. II. 61. 63-64.
154. 223.29.31.
155. VDP. II. 61. 65-66, AP. 223.31.

6

Foreign Policy and Inter-State Dealings

The Puranic records mention the diplomatic system and effective instruments through which a state may keep itself informed of the actions, opinions, resources and affiliations of the hostile elements with it, as well as the strength and inclination of foreign powers. Shri C.D. Burns, speaking about the diplomacy says "Diplomacy is the name for a method of negotiation, persuasion and conciliation for promoting the common interests of different nations, and adjusting those interests which are opposed .... without the diplomatic system war would be more frequent than it is. Behind the diplomatic system, however, lie the preparations of war: and in certain forms of policy, the threat of war is used as an instrument of diplomacy."[1] Here it will not be wrong to say that the history of diplomacy is commenced with from the chalcolithic period. There are numerous references in the Vedas, the *Ramayana* and the *Mahabharata* which prove the testimony to the system of espionage from the very ancient period. Even in a hymn of the *Atharvaveda*[2] it has been laid down that Varuna had a number of spies who were thousand-eyed and who went forth hither and thither. Thus we find that espionage as a system existed in India from very earliest times, and the art of employing spies was also thoroughly mastered by the ancient Hindu kings. Almost all authorities on polity have referred to this system and dealth with it somewhat exhaustively.[3] It is also clear that a king who was eager to outwit his enemy could not hope to attain success unless he employed spies to get secretly all necessary information about his enemy, his military installation his army strength attitude of his subjects and such other information as was likely to prove useful to him. Thus espionage in ancient India was an important institution as diplomacy and was sought to be governed by certain definite rules and usages.

Like other law books[4] the Puranas[5] also state the traditional six-fold policy or six-fold methods of diplomacy such as *Sandhi* or peace, *Vigraha* or War, *asana* or neutrality, *Yana* or expedition *Dvadhibhava* or duplicity and *Samsraya* or seeking shelter. Further our literature like the *Arthasastra*[6] defines these six methods as follows; Sandhi means making compact or agreemtn between two or more kings; *Vigraha* means taking up a hostile attitude;[7] *Yana* means marching by a king against his adversary,[8] Asana means halt by a king with his army before crossing over the border of his enemy country.[9] *Dvaidhibhava* means mobilisation of half an army in the enemy's country;[10] and *Samsrays* means an alliance with a king of the *Udasina* or the *Madhyama* class.[11] It is noticeable that the compilers of our Puranas[12] have made two major differences in the definitions advocated by other authorities like Kautilya,[13] Kamandaka[14] and Somadeva Suri.[15] First, the neutrality of the Puranic record is not the policy of indifference but is armed neutrality i.e. mobilisation within the kingdom. Secondly, the *Dvaidhibhava* is defined by Kautilya, Kamandaka and Somadeva Suri as making peace with one state and a hostile policy with other. But our literature states that *Dvaidhibhava* means taking expenditions with only half of the army. Other law books of ancient India like *Rajanitiprakasa*,[16] *Rajanitiratnakara*,[17] and *Mitaksara*[18] are also of the same opinion as has been discussed in our Puranic literature. Likewise our Puranas allow the king that under *Samsraya* policy he may take help more powerful or neutral king.[19]

Among six-fold policy, the policy of peace and war is considered as the important one by the *Agni Purana*. This is a frank and open procedure in diplomacy. In graphic language, the same text, elsewhere, states that Sandhi consists in a compact entered into by two foreign kings regarding a point at issue, whereas war means the settlement of a difference at the point of sword. It has also been laid down in the Puranic record that the king should make treaty either with his equal or with a more powerful king.[20] Further, the king is advised by the compiler of the *Visnudharmottara Purana* to wage war against the weak ruler and make efforts to conquer him.[21] Thus it is obvious that the treaties are only advocated for maintaining peace and to escape the invasion and the destruction of the state and its residents.

The *Agni Purana*[22] elaborately enumerates sixteen kinds of treaties which have been taken into consideration for the maintenance of peace. But, unfortunately, it does not define them as has been done by other authorities like Kamandaka.[23] These sixteen kinds of treaties are:

1. *Kapala-Sandhi* was that which was formed on equal terms between two equal sovereigns.
2. *Upahara-Sandhi* was that which was negotiated by one of the parties offerings presents to the other.
3. *Santana-Sandhi* was achieved by presenting daughter as hostage.
4. *Sangata-Sandhi* was concluded with declartaion of friendship between two contending parties.
5. *Upanyasa-Sandhi* aimed at terminating controversies.
6. *Pratikara-Sandhi* was concluded on mutual promise of doing benefit to each other.
7. *Samyoga-Sandhi* was concluded for joint venture

to achieve some aim.

8. *Purusantara-Sandhi* was concluded on the understanding that both the parties had to help each other by sending the arms.
9. *Adrstanara-Sandhi* was made with enemy through agreement.
10. *Adista-Sandhi* was the treaty secured by offering land.
11. *Atama-Sandhi* was concluded with the compact of his own army.
12. *Upagraha-Sandhi* required complete surrender on behalf of the vanquished.
13. *Parikrama-Sandhi* was that one in which the kingdom was protected by paying the money.
14. *Chhinna-Sandhi* was secured by ceding best land of the country.
15. *Paradusana-Sandhi* was the treaty which required surrender of all products and finally.
16. *Skandhopaneya-Sandhi* was a compromise for paying idemnity by installments.

But our Puranic literature suggests that among all above-mentioned treaties, the treaties made by after a consideration of benefit reciprocally or of mutual amity or common affinity or negotiations of being honoured with presents as a token of friendship should be considered as the four principal treaties. The history of ancient India is, undoubtedly, full of references of such type of treaties. The famous treaty concluded between the mighty king Chandragupta Maurya and his Greek rival Seleucus who was left by his master Alexander, the great, may be cited here. We are well acquainted with the fact that when Seleucus was defeated by Chandragupta Maurya, a treaty was concluded between the two belligerents, which was ratified by: *(i)* a matrimonial alliance, *(ii)* a surrender of the large portion of his kingdom, *(iii)* a gift of 500 white elephants by Chandragupta to Seleucus, and *(iv)* a receipt by Chandragupta of the satrapies of Paraganisadai, Aria, Gedrosia and Archsia, the capitals of which were known as Kabul, Herat, Makran and Kandahar[24] respectively.

It is interesting to note that our *Agni Purana*[25] enumerates twenty kinds of persons with whom *sandhi* (treaty) should not be made such as with a child, and old man, an invalid, a man deserted by his friends and relations, a coward, a terrified person, a greedy or a covetous sovereign, or the person who has renounced worldly concerns or excessively fond of earthly possessions. Similarly a king should never enter into an alliance with a king who devises many schemes at a time and does everything in a half-hearted way, or with those who speak ill of the gods and Brahmanas or with a king whose country has been suffering from famine or natural calamity, pestilence or discontented army, or with the king whose domain had been as under with civil dissensions, or had regained its peace after long time, or with the kings who are void of all sense of religion and truth. Thus we find that our Puranic record elaborately mentions the classification of the treaties and also the persons with whom the king should not make his treaties. But unfortunately we do not get any reference about the guaranteee of the said treaties and their methods of breaking. It is also evident that generally a treaty of peace was concluded by a sovereign in view of the fact that continuance of hostilitios would make him gradually weaker than his enemy. The *Agni Purana*[26] further reveals that hostile attitude *(Vaira)* is of five kinds viz., that of co-wife, that due to land, (seizure of or encroachment on lands or houses), that due to woman (carrying away one's wife or loving the same woman), that due to words (cutting speech and that due to wrongs). This *Purana* further informs us the sixteen ways in which the hostility springs, such as stealing away of a wife, encroachment upon the capital, kingdom, territory or the sovereign right of a king by his adversary, pride, harassment of subjects and so on.[27]

The application of the six methods of foreign policy through the seven means of *Sama, Dana, Bheda, Danda, Upeksa, Maya* and *Indrajala* is elaborately discussed in our Puranic record.[28] The *Matsya Purana*[29] clearly lays down that one and the same policy should not be pursued at all times with all persons. It, therefore, appears from our Puranas that the world is full of righteous and unrighteous persons so the application of policy should differ from person to person. The text of the same Purana speaks of a two-fold classification of the Sama or conciliation viz., *(i) Tathyasama* (policy of genuine conciliation) *(ii) Atathyasama* (perfedious policy of conciliation). It has been further referred to that the policy of genuine conciliation (*Tathyasama*) should be applied to righteous kings and the perfidious policy (*Atathyasama*) should be used towards the unrighteous kings. Furthermore, it is said that a righteous king is easily reconciled when an earnest appeal is made to his ancient family tradition. On the other hand if the same policy is pursued towards the unrighteous king, the bitter and aggressive feelings would be aroused. The *Visnudharmottara,*[30] further, recommend that the policy of conciliation can be applied with the persons who are of noble family, having acquired a perfect control over their senses and of a righteous temperament. On the other hand the false policy may be applied towards the persons who are rough and misbehaved like a demon. It is remarkable that the *Matsya Purana*[31] specifically mentions that the principle of Sama policy should be applied with those sovereigns who are born in good family, and are noble, simple, virtuous, truthful and modest.

The Puranic record[32] further enumerates that *Tathyasama* may be applied by narrating of the high pedigree and description of the deeds done for one's benefit and acqknowledging the one's gratitude and using of sweet and lively words etc. through which religious persons may be controlled under the subjection. The *Agni Purana*[33] speaks in the similar tone and states that the policy of conciliation may be applied by four means such as: *(i)* the expression of gratitude for benefit done by each other, *(ii)* the recollation of old relationship existing between two hostile monarchs, *(iii)* use of soft and lovely words in the presence of an antagonist, and lastly *(iv)* a complete surrender with all possessions in a formal meeting. It is noticeable that the conquering king is asked by Kautilya,[34] the father of politics, to observe this policy of conciliation by promising of protection of villages and forests, of seeps and cattle, of the roads of traffic, of the restoration of the banished and of the run away people. He further recommends that this policy should be applied towrds the conquered king so that latter may remain loyal. Unfortunately, our Puranas do not throw much light on this subject as Kautilya laid down.

The other important policy of diplomatic utility is Dana or gift. The *Matsya Purana* states that even the god may be influenced and conquered through gifts of wealth and other presentations.[35] It further enumerates that the men who are free from avarice and are grave like ocean and who never accept presents even they may be won by offering gifts.[36] Therefore, our Puranic literature[37] speaks that the policy of gifts is the best one in the matter of foreign policy and it is stated that gift is indeed highly beneficial to the sovereign who wanted to win his enemy. Undoubtedly, the men who give gifts are known to be the best men in the world. In such a way the king not only conquers this world but also wins the realms of Indra.[38] The *Agni Purana,*[39] further lays down the five shapes of gifts through which the stronger adversary may be appeased. These gifts consists of: *(i)* the return of what has been received, *(ii)* of accepting a thing by the latter out of his own choice, *(iii)* of making monetary presents as has never been offered before, *(iv)* of paying all to other what has been captured, and lastly *(v)* of granting remission in taxes. Similar ideas of gifts are advocated by the *Arthasastra,*[40] the *Nitisara,*[41] the *Nitiprakasika*[42] and the *Manasollasa.*[43] This policy of *Dana* is also supported by other law givers like Manu[44] and Kautilya.[45] Kautilya recommends the policy of conciliation and of gifts of weak kings.

The next policy of diplomatic relations, according to our literature, is Bheda or dissension, which plays very important role in the matter of inter-state relations. The *Matsya Purana*[46] states tha tthis policy should be pursued towards the unrighteous king. It further lays down that the policy of divide and rule which is known as *Bheda* should be employed with the class of the people who are hostile and wicked to one another, and insulted and afraid. The *Agni Purana,*[47] too, is of the same view and states that the policy of dissension can be created between two monarchs who are inimically disposed afraid and insulted by each other. It further speaks that policy may be easily created among the officers, aggrieved and discontented people of the enemy's country by a proper and judicious use of conciliatory measures and also by honouring and buying off the allegiance of the principal men of his government.[47] In very graphic language the Agni Purana speaks that a sovereign surrounded by false friends is destroyed like a piece of timber eaten away insects dwelling in holes incised into its body.[48] The *Matsya Purana*[49] lays down that the policy of dissension should be applied when a certain class of the people becomes displeased to each other due to vices and weaknesses of the ruling monarch. The *Agni Purana*[50] suggests the king to compel them to fall out with each other even by showing threat. It if further said that variance may be created either by raising high hopes or territorial acquisition. Under these circumstances their own faults and defects should be explained and they should be frightened by the opposite party. Thus, that class of people may be gradually and easily be divided from their party and then would be brought under submission.[51] It has been further laid down that the poor and the greedy can be pleased with the money while other allies by showing danger. On the other hand, sons and brothers of the enemy can be kept under proper control by means of conciliatory measures. It is further suggested by our literature that the victorious sovereign should keep leaders of his own army, provincial governors, vassals and foresters by means of money gifts. According to the *Matsya*[52] *Purana* the policy of *Bheda*, however, should not be launched by the sovereign personally, but should be acted upon by the persons appointed for the purpose. The king is required to protect them into all hazards.

The *Agni Purana*[53] elsewhere, lays down that expedient of dissension consists of the three factors of destroying amity or friendship between two monarchs or producing a thrill of fear or inducing a party to betray the secrets confided in him by the other. It is suggested by our literature,[54] that the king should send his spies in the enemy's country and they should ascertain the weakness of the ruling king, the state of treasure, army and allies. They should also try to know the personal liking and disliking of the king. The spies are further required to acknowledge the feelings of subjects and number of allies of sovereign who may help him in the time of war.

According to the *Matsya Purana*[55] a sovereign, wishing to use the policy of divide and rule in case of his compeers should create disunion in their communities, and kith and kin, and then the royal regards and gifts should be provided for the distressed kith and kin and those suffering from ill-treatment. But the king is further advised by our Puranic literature[56] that he should very cautiously prevent these happenings amongst his own brothers and distressed kith and kin. Therefore, it is evident that in launching a policy of either aggression or defence, internal peace is essential. The *Matsya Purana*[57] speaks that a king can be victorious over his enemies, but internal dissension even destroys a powerful king like Indra. From the Puranic text now it is clear that this policy of *Bheda* should be applied only to conquer an enemy by creating division amongst his kinsmen or amongst his subjects and to attack him when they are disunified. We are well acquainted with the fact that during the life time of Budha the famous democratic state named Lichchhavi was conquered by Ajatasatru of Magadha by introducing the policy of Bheda only. Thus we find that under this policy, a king is apt to be troubled by internal dissension as well as by external aggression.

Danda or punishment is the last resort of the four traditional policy of diplomacy. Danda is not actual punishment or opening of hostilities but it is a diplomatic war which is applied as the last resort before actual commencement of fighting. Kautilya is of the opinion that this policy of punishment should be employed in the case of stronger powers. Our Puranic literature as well as other writers on *Nitisara* state that a king should adopt this policy when he finds that the other three do not yield the good result.[58] The other authorities[59] have also echoed the same sentiments and opine that Danda is to be applied as the last resort, when the victory is not certain. Similarly Brhatparasara lays down that a prudent ruler should not resort to fighting and *Danda* is to be resorted only when there is not other way left.[60] In the Udyoga Parva of the *Mahabharata*[61] we find that Krisna informs Yudhisthira how he first employed conciliation, then dissension, then gift and how only punishment was the proper recourse in the case of wicked Kauravas. The *Visnudharmottara*[62] and the *Agni* Puranas[63] mention two-fold division of punishment. The first is to be applied in one's own country and other should be applied in the foreign state. The latter punishment is further divided into two categories—open and secret (*Prakasa* and *Aprakasa*). The *Prakasa* punishment consists of looting villages, destroying the towns, crops or setting fires. Poisoning the wells and murdering the people come under second punishment *(Aprakasa)*. The punishment is further divided into three classes by our Puranic literature such as murder, fine or loss of money and infliction of corporal punishment.[64] A detailed list of punishment is mentioned by Somesvaradeva[65] who is of the opinion that the enemy should be punished by the destruction of the forests, ponds, setting fire to the villages, cutting nose and ears of the people, seizure of the cattle and the harvest, imprisonment of the relatives, householders and rich people, annexation of the territory, plunder of gold etc. by soldiers, destruction of houses by setting fire to the palace, residential buildings, markets, stables etc. driving away the enemies to hills and forests and finally kill them in the battle. He further states that destruction of property, corporal punishment and murder are to be applied only to weak enemy. Thus it appears that Somesvaradeva opines for the total annihilation of property of the enemy king so that he should not be able to regain his power and prowess in an easy way.

Our Puranas not only mention the policies adopted by the stronger power in the open warfare but also provide the policy of *Upeksha* (indifference) for an inferior power. It may be well realised that application of *Danda* policy cannot be resorted to by all monarchs. Therefore, our literature envisages that a king should be indifferent to his enemy when he would find that he is neither in agreement with nor at war with his enemy. This policy should also be applied when the king would find that war would not decide the supremacy of either of the parties engaged in the contest. The *Visnudharmottara*[66] and the *Agni* Puranas[67] inform us that whenever the king finds that it is not possible to create dissension among his enemies or to punish them, he should apply the policy of indifference. Under these circumstances the kings are required to see that both are unable to do any harm to each other.

It is interesting to note that the *Agni Purana* states that in the policy of indifference *(Upeksha)* the king may adopt injustice, personal vices or a battle, as the case may be, as exemplified in the conduct of Hidimba who did not prevent her brother from measuring arms with her beloved Bhima. We are, further told that Bhima killed Kichaka in the disguise of a woman.[68] Thus it appears that our Puranic literature allows injustice in the fulfillment of indifference policy. Kautilya,[69] on the other hands, asks a neutral power to cultivate the virtue of indifference towards his neighbours, whether they are his allies or foes.

The other two diplomatic attitudes *Maya Indrajala* are added by our Puranic literature. *Maya* means illusion and therefore, it suggests that the invader would put to use all illusory powers to deceive the enemy and strike him at his weak point. Undoubtedly, this policy consists of counningness and intrigue. Some interesting details can, however, be gathered from the *Visnudharmottara*[80] and the *Agni* Puranas[81] which mention the measures of illusion to be utilised by a king in frightening away the hearts of a hostile army. According to these Puranas the birds of strong and extensive plumage should be reared in the camp and let them fly over the enemy's line with lighted wicks attached to their tails, so that the soldiers of the enemy take them to be so many meteors falling down from the skies. The other physical disturbances should be simulated to scare away the enemy. The ascetics and astrologers should be appointed to proclaim the pre-ordained fail of the enemy. Further, it has been laid down that an invading monarch should put his enemies to utter rout, by proclaiming that his cause had been favoured with the blessing of the immortal gods and their wrath had been alighted upon the heads of the enemies. Moreover, he should give out that he had been reinforced by the opportune arrival of fresh allies, whereby the enemy be surely and utterly routed. War-whoops and jubilant shouts of victory should be caused to be raised, and it should be publicly proclaimed that the enemy had been irretrievably beaten. Thus a king backed by divine favour and equipped with the help of the gods, should met his enemy in battle, and fill the minds of his enemy's forces with the fear of incurring the wrath of gods, by practising tricks of magic in the following way. An army consisting of the four essential divisions of cavalry, car-warriors, foot-men and elephant-men, should be exhibited so as to delude the vision of the enemy and so as to make believe that they had been sent by the gods to strengthen the already victorious arms of the invading monarch. Similarly the quarters of the enemy should be denuded with showers of simulated blood, and a similar severed head of the adversary should be exhibited at the terrace of the palace.[82] The *Agni Purana*,[83] elsewhere, states that hostile army should be frightened away by practising such illusions as the apparitions of horrible ghosts and Vetalas or other shadow of male figures clad in female costumes, by simulating of showers of meteors, blood, stones, fire and the fall of columns of water from the sky and similar other spectacles of divine wrath and also by formation of clouds and the wreaths of smoke and other physical phenomena. It shows that the people of this period had a deep faith in omens, portents and magical rites and rituals. Similarly, the conqueror is asked by Kamandaka to get himself dressed as a god, or a pillar, and when the enemy comes to worship to slay him. If we believe the story of *Devi Chandra Guptam* then we are told that Chandra Gupta II killed Saka ruler Kudrasimha III in disguise of a woman.

The last policy which has been accepted by our Puranic literature is *Indrajala* through which a victorious king may conquer his enemy. Prof. Dikshitar is of the opinion that it must have come into being after a Mauryan epoch, for it is not among the accepted principles of the Kautilyan diplomacy.[84] According to the *Agni* Purana[85] the expedient of Indrajala (magic) consists in scaring away the enemy's forces by showing the artificial clouds, darkness, rains and hills or by exhibiting them the banners of alarge army from the distance as if coming to meet them in the battle field or a mirage-like picture of their future reverses and entire annihilation. It further states that the policy of Indrajala should be practised to make the soldier of hostile army depressed and stricken with fear. It is well known fact that in the Second World War Japan had applied the policy of Indrajala and she arrayed the artificial soldiers from her side and succeeded in her policy. Thus it shows that our Puranic literature believes in artificial things and magic rites and rituals through which an ambitious king may get success in the battlefield.

Diplomatic Agent

The instruments of carrying on inter-state relations in a circle were known as Dutas or envoys in Ancient India. The functions performed by these envoys in the matter of diplomacy were the same as modern plenipotentiaries of states do in the foreign countries. In fact states in ancient India were inclined to regard spies as highly indispensable. Due to the importance of this post the ambassadors in general occupied a very high and honoured place among the state functionaries. The Puranic record[86] lays down very high qualifications of this important official. The *Visnudharmottara*[87] and the *Matsya* Puranas point out that an ambassador is required to possess the knowledge of different languages of various countries as well as the languages of his own country, *(Desabhasavisaradah)* to speak frequently and to bear troubles. He is further asked to state the facts without fear and to tender advise about the Niti to the king at proper time. It is further said that the man who is appointed as a spy should be intelligent, learned, free from avarice, able to keep secrets and to put with hardship, incapable of being recognised by the subjects, simple in habits able to mix with people and to disguise himself in the garb of merchants, ministers, astrologers, physicians and ascetics. According to *the Agni Purana*[89] an ambassador must be intelligent, ingenuous, accurate in memory, eloquent, accomplished in the arts of war, well-versed in sastras, well-exercised in all sorts of work and well-accustomed to the works of espionage. The other authorities have also echoed the same qualification. Manu, for example, holds that he must be well-versed in all sciences of diplomacy and should possess the knowledge of physiognomy, to enable to read the deeper intention of the enemy from facial expressions. He should be honest, clever and devoted to his master. Further, he should be born of good family, should possess retentive memory, have strong physique and should be devoid of fear and eloquent in speech.[90] Bhisma[91] mentions seven essential qualifications of an ambassador. They are as follows that an ambassador should be of noble line, belonging to a high family, be skilful, eloquent in speech, dexterous, true in delivering the mission and of excellent memory. Sukra[92] points out that an ambassador is one of the ten principal ministers and he should be capable of reading signs demeanor, and behaviour of the adversery, well-versed in all arts and sciences, eloquent and devoid of fear.[93] The *Agni Purana*[94] like other authorities on ancient polity, mentions three classes of envoys—*Nisrstartha*, *Mitartha*, and *Sasanaharaka*. The *Nisrstartha* or plenipotentiaries were those who were invested with preliminary powers of discussing and concluding terms with foreign powers and even issuing ultimatums. The *Mitartha* or ambassadors were those who enjoyed restricted powers, yet had some rights of initiative. The *Sasanaharaka* or the third class of envoys were those who merely carried errands of their masters and had to repeat the message word for word only, without a change of comma even. They were of lowest rank.

The *Agni Purana* at one place, speaks that diplomacy is better than the expedient of war and this could be affected only by spies. An ambassador is but an open spy and a spy is but an envoy roaming about the enemy's country in the guise of trader, a mendicant or a strolling physician or some other person to get at the truth.[95] Thus the duties of an ambassador are numerous and varied. The *Agni Purana* lays down the explicit functions of this functionary. Firstly, he is asked to ascertain the weak points of an enemy with the position of his treasury. Secondly, he has to ascertain the nature and scope of the enemy's strength, his allies and followers. He is further required to know the personal liking and disliking of enemy from his looks and gestures.[96] The envoy is also required to eulogise both his master and his adversary so that he shall be able to judge the true feelings of the subjects and to asserting the actual strength of his allies. In this way the king would be able to utilise the said information in the time of war.[97] The other law-givers like Manu[98] and Kautilya[99] mention the similar duties of an ambassador though with little difference. Thus it is obvious that our Puranic literature has followed the old tradition envisaged by Manu and Kautilya. It is also clear from the Puranas that during the time of stay in the foreign state, an ambassador is required to mix freely with all classes of the people in the realm so that he should be able to understand the degree of loyalty of the subjects. It is further said that if he is not in a position to collect the reliable information by open means then he should put on various disguises like those of a physician, a beggar, an ascetic, a merchant etc. In brief, the delivering of the message in to-to, issuing ultimatums, sowing dissensions among the enemy's friends and subjects, carrying away the actual position of treasury and secrets of the army of the enemy and collecting secrets when necessry, were the main functions of an envoy by our Puranic literature. Thus we can infer that the office of an envoy was full of onerous responsibilities on which the international relations depended.

The history of Ancient India is full of examples in which we find that these envoys were freely used by kings to carry on their diplomatic relations. Seleucus Nicator, a Greek contemporary ruler of the Mauryan King, sent his envoy Megasthenes in the court of Chandra Gupta. Asoka, too, continued the same policy and he sent his own son and daughter Mahendra and Samghamitra to Ceylon in the court of Devanampiyatissa as his ambassadors to propagate his Buddhist mission. Dr. Bhandarkar has really remarked in this connection which is worth quoting here that "what we have really to understand from the Rock edict VIII, is that Asoka was already in the habit of sending ambassadors to the Greek courts but that he now thought of propagating his faith through these officers in the Greek kingdoms, just as he did in his own empire through his other officers. The Selecudian monarchy, we know, sent two ambassadors one after another to the Mauryan court."[100]

From the account of Ma-twan-lin, we are informed that in the year A.D. 641, the king Siladitya (Harsa) of Magadha sent an ambassador with a letter to the emperor of China. In return the Chinese king also sent Liang-hoai-king as an envoy in the court of Siladitya. Further, after two years (A.D. 643) a second Chinese embassy came to Magadha under Li-y-piao and Wang-hiuen-tse.[101] Similarly a Muslim historian Tabari (AD 838-923) records that in the year A.D. 625-26 the Chalukya king Paramesa or Parameswara sent an embassy in the court of Khusru II (A.D. 570-628), the king of Persia, carrying a letter and presents for him and his sons.[102] An inscription[103] of a Chola king Virarajendra records ample and eloquent testimony to this practice. According to it the Chola king despatched a letter to the Chalukya prince through a messenger with an ultimatum for war. This letter bears: "He who does not come to the appointed Kudal through fear, shall be no king but a liar and disgrace in war." This letter was handed over to the Chalukya king. The Chalukya King resented the action of Chola. We are further told that numerous kings like Bimbisara, Ajatsatru at Magadha, Chandragupta I, Samudra Gupta and Chandra Gupta II of the Gupta dynasty had maintained diplomatic relations with other states through matrimonial alliances. Thus, from the both literary and epigraphic evidences it is evident that a useful part was played by the ambassadors in the policy of diplomacy and warfare in the history of ancient India. It will be useful here to give some illustrations from our Puranic literature. The *Visnu Purana*[104] informs us that king Vasudeva of Pundra, claimed a divine status for himself and sent an ambassador to Krisna, the king of

Dvaraka. The message, which was delivered by him to the king, is as follows: "Leave off your Chakra, oh foolish person and come and accord me your homage and I shall forgive you and grant you means of subsistence." The lord Krisna laughed and sent a fitting reply "I shall even tomorrow go with my Chakra and yield it to you". Krisna set out Mount Garuda against Paundraka and the king of Pundra helped by the ruler of Kasi came to meet him. Further, are told from the *Markandeya Purana*[103] that when the fourth son of Madalasa named Alarka was ruling, his elder brother Subahu wished to usurp the throne. So he took help from the king of Kashar sent an ultimatum through his own envoy. As befitted Kshatriya Alarka offered battle and being defeated fled for life. This *Purana*, elesewhere, again lays down another instance for this of a messenger. We are informed that two great Asuaras named Sumbha and Nisumbha, completely defeated the gods. Only the goddess Durga was left unconquered. Therefore, Sumbha sent a messenger named Souriva to the goddess with the message: "I want you have quickly. So do come without delay". The envoy reached her all among the mountains and delivered the message in toto. The gods received it and sent the reply that if he would conquer her in the battlefield would be her husband and hence Sumbha accepted the challenge to fight with her. Sumbha sent his mighty generals drag her by the hair to his abode. They were all completely destroyed when Durga sent the celestial messenger Siva with the ultimatum for war. Therefore, Sumbha marched with his army with eighty-six different weapons and eighty-four different clubs, all of whom she destroyed utterly. The *Agni Purana*[106] cites another instance that after arriving on the shores of Lanka, Rama sent Angada as an envoy to Ravana with message "Give up Sita or fight". Ravana replied that he would fight. Then Rama with his all forces consisting of generally monkeys marched the citadel. Such details indicate the importance of ambassadors and spies through whom the victorious king could collect the information of the enemy as well as of his own country. The ancient India which was full of wars and aggressions the espionage system played very important role in the daily life of the state. We find that in later period, however, the Indian rulers seems to have neglected this important branch of administration, with the result that they were often taken unawares by the foreign invaders. It would not be far from truth to suggest that once of the potential cause of of their defeat. Towards the close of ancient period, was the inefficient espionage system, otherwise it would not have been possible for Mohammad-bin Bakhtiyar Khilji to overthrow the Palas and Senas, merely with a handful of soldiers disguised as horse-dealers. Kamandaka's dictum that a king "who does not watch the movements of his enemies is asleep, although he may be wide awake, and he never wakes up from such a sleep" is as true today as it was when he wrote his *Nitisara.*

Mandala Theory

Another striking feature of diplomacy, according to the Puranic literature, is the development of Inter-state relations on hypothetical trounds. Like other authorities[107] on polity our literature[108] enumerates the circle of twelve state with allies and enemies. It consists of twelve kings, who according to the Puranas are *Vijigisu, Ari, Mitra, Amitra, Mitramitra, Arimitramitra, Parsnigraha, Akaranda, Parshigrahaşara* and *Akarandasara.* Behind it there was the *Madhyama* and the *Udasina.*

Thus our Puranic literature reveals the old traditional theory of Mandala advocated by Kautilya for the first time. The *Visnudharmottara Purana* clearly lays down that the kingdom governed by the king directly is considered to be the first Mandala[109] and the feudatory or the dependent estates of an empire should be known as the enemies. But is they are fondly attached to their paramount lord they should be regarded as allies.[110] Our literature relates that the kings of the neighbouring countries should be arranged as friendly, hostile to the friend of friendly monarch and so on, in succession with the kings who are ruling the bordering countries of the dominion of the king in the front.[111] The *Agni Purana* further speaks that invading king should create friends and enemies among the rulers of contiguous countries lying on the rear of his own domain. The hostile king, whose kingdom lies bordering on the posterior boundary of an invading sovereign, was called a *Parsnigraha*. An invading king should enter into an alliance with a friendly monarch *(Akranda)* whose territory would be contiguous to be realm of the latter, who would thus serve as a check against his own forces with those of his allies, in the time of war against his central kingdom. The hostile king, whose dominion would be beyond those of an *Akranda* sovereign, is known as *Asara* who would be an ally of the *Parsinigraha* king. The ruler, whose kingdom would be contiguous to that of an Asara monarch, is known as the *Akrandasara,* an ally of the *Akranda* king.[112] The other two members of the Mandals are *Madhyastha* and *Udasina*. The *Madhyastha* state is described as one which is close to both the conqueror *(Vijigisu)* and his immediate enemy *(Ari)* in front and who is capable of punishing both the kings. The *Udasina* state is described as the most powerful kingdom,[113] which is located outside of the circle of the state and capable of helping or punishing to other states as the case may be. Sri P.V. Kane is of the opinion that the *Vijigisu,* the enemy, the *Madhyama* and the *Udasina* are independent categories, while four out of the remaining eight other viz. *Mitra, Mitramitra, Akranda, Akrandasar* can be grouped under *Vijigisu* while other four viz. *Arimitra, Arimitramitra, Parasnigraha* and *Parasnigrahasara* may be grouped under *Ari.*[114]

It is noticeable that our *Visnudharmottara*[115] and the *Agni Puranas*[116] lays down three sorts of enemies i.e. ancestral, personal and artificial. It is said that each preceding enemy is more dangerous than the one immediately in succession. The *Parsnigraha* of a hostile king, as well as his enemies, should be considered as friends and allies by an invading king. Thus an invading king is suggested by the Puranic record to conquer his own *Parsnigraha* by means of political expedients. It is further laid down that a friend may turn inimical on account of his enforced vassalage to an invading Monarch or from other causes. Therefore, the invading King should exterminate his enemies himself if possible. The sovereign who is trusted by all and is follower of *Dhrama Vijaya* can rule over the whole world.[117]

REFERENCES

1. NVM. 13.19.
2. Yasas. III. 111.
3. NVM 24.26.
4. 242. 9-10.
5. AP. 241.11.
6. KNS. 12. 11.
7. Deo. Barnark Ins. of Jivita Gupta. II.
8. *The Age of Imperial Kanauj,* 1964. p. 242.
9. *Ibid;* 106.11
10. 24.11 & 126.28.
11. 24.7.
12. 126.32.
13. II. 112. 17.
14. I. 8. 33.
15. KNS. Chapts. 4 & 12.
16. NVM. Chapts X (Mantri—Samuddesa) & XVIII (Amataya
17. Samuddesa)
18. P. 178.
19. 1.7.3 and 1.8.4.
20. I.A., XVIII. 238.V.5.
21. II. 65.39; 151.20.
22. 215.48.
23. 225.19.
24. XII. 85. 7-9.
25. 241. 12.

26. NVM. 13.19.
27. Yasas. III. 111.
28. NVM 24.26.
29. 242. 9-10.
30. AP. 241.11.
31. KNS. 12. 11.
32. Deo. Barnark Ins. of Jivita Gupta.II.
33. *The Age of Imperial Kanauj,* 1964. p. 242.
34. Ibid; 106.11.
35. 24.11 & 126.28.
36. 24.7.
37. 126.32.
38. II. 112. 17.
39. I. 8. 33.
40. KNS. Chapts. 4 & 12.
41. NVM. Chapts X (Mantri—Samuddesa) & XVIII (Amataya
42. Samuddesa).
43. P. 178.
44. 1.7.3 and 1.8.4.
45. I.A., XVIII. 238.V. 5.
46. II. 65.39; 151.20.
47. 215.48.
48. 225.19.
49. XII. 85. 7-9.
50. XII. 85.11.
51. *Arth.* 1.15.
52. II. 65.39; 40. 151.20.
53. 220.37.
54. 225.19.
55. *Manasollasa.* II. 2.57.
56. Ibid; 5.38.
57. 220. 1-20.
58. II. 65. 1-14.
59. 225. 1-7.
60. 220. 2-3; VDP. II. 65. 2-4.
61. 220.1; VDP. II. 65. 3.
62. MP. 220.3. VDP. II. 65.4.

63. MP. 220.4; VDP. II. 65.5; AP. 225.3.
64. Ibid; 220.8; VDP. II. 65. 9-10; AP. 225.4.
65. Ibid; 220.9; VDP. II. 65. 11; AP. 225.5.
66. Ibid; 220.4; VDP. II. 65.6.
67. Ibid; 220.6; VDP. II. 65.7.
68. MP. 220. 19-20; VDP. II. 65-20-22; AP. 225. 11-12.
69. 18. 1-3.
70. MKP. 183-6.
71. V. 21. 18-24.
72. 18.25.
73. VSP. V. 10.27-28; VDP. II. 65.46; AP. 225.21-22, 233.8.
74. MDS. VII. 43; Santi. 59.33; Arth. 1.2; Yaj. 1. 311; Kamandaka II.
75. *Sukraniti*. 152.
76. *Dasakumarcharita*, VIII. Para I, p. 202.
77. NVM. 5.55.
78. Arth. 1.2.
79. KNS. 2.3-6.
80. Arth. 1.3.
81. Ibid; 1.5.
82. KNS. 2.13.
83. NVM. 7.1.
84. VDP. I. 22. 129-133; AP. 219. 59-56.
85. AP. 238.9.
86. MP. 220.44. VDP. II. 65-73.
87. 241.12.
88. NVM. 13.19.
89. Yasas. III. 111.
90. NVM 24-26.
91. 242. 9-10.
92. AP. 241.11.
93. KNS. 12. 11.
94. Deo. Barnark Ins. of Jivita Gupta. II.
95. *The Age of Imperial Kanauj*, 1964, p. 242.
96. Ibid; 106.11.
97. 24.11 & 126.28.
98. 24.7.

99. 126.32.
100. II. 112. 17.
101. I. 8. 33.
102. KNS. Chapts. 4 & 12.
103. NVM. Chapts X (Mantri—Samuddesa) & XVIII (Amataya
104. Samuddesa).
105. P. 178.
106. 1.7.3. and 1.8.4.
107. I.A., XVIII. 238.V. 5.
108. II. 65.39; 151.20.
109. 215.48.
110. 225.19.
111. XII. 85. 7-9.
112. XII. 85.11.
113. Arth. 1.15.
114. II. 65.39; 40. 151.20.
115. 220.37.
116. 225.19.
117. *Manasollasa*. II. 2.57.

7

Conclusion

The foregoing critical study of the various topics bearing on Governance as described in the Puranas clearly shows the importance of the Puranas in the political history of ancient India. Since the importance of this source being unknown to us its study was neglected at the hands of the scholars. But in the light of the facts mentioned in the preceding pages, it is obvious that without properly and critically studying them, a study of the Hindu political thought would remain incomplete. The Puranas are indebted to various texts compiled between the 6th century B.C. and the tenth century A.D. Sometimes it has been found that they have borrowed verse verbatim but sometimes they are summarised. Most probably the compilers of the Puranas have borrowed the material from different branches of Sanskrit literature like the *Ramayana*, the *Mahabharata*, the *Smrtis*, the *Arthasastra*, the *Nitisara* etc. in order to make them encyclopaedia.

From the study of the contents given in the Puranas it is obvious that the compilers of the Puranas were in favour of a strong central government. Thus the kingship being the only form of government was known to the

Puranas. Keeping in view the other ancient definitions of the government, the traditional seven elements theory (Saptanga) continued to be popular with the Puranas. As regards the theories of origin of the government, reference to the divine origin theory seems to be popular in the Puranic period. The various stages in the development of this theory extending over more than thousand years, mark progressive development in the life of the people. The traditional account of the government of Natural and the circumstances leading to the rise of coercive authority, the conditions obtaining in kingless society are a unique contribution to the Hindu political thought.

The notion of the divinity was prevalent among the kings. They showed themselves to be vested with super human qualities and liked to use titles before their names indicative of their divine character. But this divinity did not make them to be irresponsible and tyrannical. The doctrine of the divinity was preached to inspire respect to the office of the kingship and to exact unfliching obedience and loyalty from the subjects. It may, however, be noted that the sovereigns were learned people and they fully understand the sprit of the Sastras. Very high and sound qualifications were laid down for them. Not only the kings but even the princes were required to be highly qualified and trained in the different branches of knowledge and the art of the government. For the training of princes the Puranas lay down that well qualified brahmanas should be appointed and after completing the study the crown-prince was required to undergo a formal consecration. The duties and functions of the king were varies. The king was required to extend his empire and to realise the ideal of universal monarchy. But he still enjoyed certain rights and privileges.

The ministers were supposed to be very highly qualified persons. Numerous qualifications of the ministers are laid down in the Puranas. The king is advised to appoint them after taking their test of their noble birth, education etc. The king is also asked to take advice from his ministers on all important matters relating to the government policy. The exact number of the ministers is not laid down but it appears that their numbers were left to be determined by the king. The ministers were regarded as parents of the king which shows their importance in the government administration.

War played an important role in the life of the government in ancient period. The traditional four-fold division of the army was prevalent but the use of chariot was in deteriorating position. The Puranas give greater importance to the foot soliders, than the rest three archery was considered the most important to the king; the princes, the officials and soldiers in general. The ethics of war is also laid down in the Puranas. The construction of forts and king's capital was also known which shows that the kings were well acquainted with the fact that sound planning of the construction make the government healthy.

There can be no doubt that the Puranas have evolved excellent principles of taxation. The king is advised by the text together taxes like the bee, which sucks the honey without damaging the flower, that an article should not be taxed twice. The principles of exemption advocated by the literature were also sound. The dumb, the deaf, the blind and the widows were free from taxation, as they were usually poor. The students, learned scholars and brahmanas were also exempted from the taxes. The taxes were usually determined by the local customs and traditions.

In the matter of Inter-state relations the Puranas have accepted the old traditional theory of Mandala advocated by Kautilya for the first time. The Puranas have also enumerated a list of seven political expedients, namely, Sama, Dana, Bheda, Danda, Upeksha, Maya and Indrajala with their application at great length.

The local administration is not described fully. A fragmentary and very him picture of it is provided. The village headman was assisted by a village council consisting of five members. The epigraphs of the period prove its testimony.

The political organisation discussed in the Puranas proves the ideals of ancient Indian government. It sought to promote the moral material aesthetics and spiritual progress of the people. The king is asked to protect them like a pregnant mother who sacrifices her own desires and pleasures for the child to be born. The body of the king was menat for enjoyment of pleasure but it had to put up with great trouble while carrying out the royal duty of protecting the subjects and fulfilling his dharma.

If the Government is supposed to originate as a grater force to suppress the unbridled violence of Matsyanyaya and to restrain men primarily impelled to it by nature, it becomes the arbitrary promulgator of the standers, aims and ideals that govern human life. But if it is taken to originate, as we have tried to show, in the pious resolve of self control, its functions are to be determined with a reference to the ends of human life as conditioned by his nature. Balanced as it was, by the recognition of the repeated emphasis of Hindu thinkers on the point that the State is not above dharma, the attempt of Dr. Bhandarkar to infer the functions of the government by a reference to the conditions of are *arajaka* or *matsyanyaya* though leading to almost identical conclusions[1] necessarily suffers from a sort of self-contradiction when logically examined. How can there be a dharma independent of the government, it may be asked, if everything noble and spiritual, may even religious, man owes to the Government of and if the material moral religious and, spiritual ideals of man are laid down by the government, and not by his nature which is funamentally opposed to these, how can the principle of dharma embodying all these be placed above and beyond the government?

Obviously these questions cannot be effectively answered unless we give-up the old theory that human nature is fundamentally bad is illustrated by the conditions of *matsyanyaya* and that the state originates to suppress and restrain man's heritage of such a nature for one contending that human nature is basically good and the state originates in a pious resolve to check temporary lapses of the society into *arajaka*. But as the true anti-*arajaka* principle is *dharma* state originates to implement it on the principle of coercion to the extent to which it is possible and feasible on social level. Dharma is hene above the government and represents the principles that the inherently pure nature of man leads him to formulate from time to time. These principles seek to fulfill the aims and ends if human life as determined by his nature and as the mission of the government is to implement dharma to the extent to which it is necessary to check the tendency of *arajaka* it is in the fitness of things to visualise the functions of the government with a reference to the ends of human life.

As we have already seen, the ultimate aim of human life as conceived in the Puranas is the consummation of ones being or moksa. But the temporal self obliges him to seek the satisfaction of hunger and the gratification of his desires calling for the enjoyment of the objects of senses. But as this temporal obligation of his being makes him amenable to the lapses of *arajaka,* however, temporarily, it calls for the righteous mediation of dharma lest the entire society composed of such individuals may fall a prey to *arajaka* due to the weakness of a few and the government originates to ensure the implementation of dharma to the exten to which it is necessary to save the society though not each and every individual from lapsing into *matsyanyaya*. Summarised as those principles of material and spiritual pursuits are in the twin concepts of *bhukti* and *mukti* in the Puranas, their statement in these texts amounts to saying that the functions of the government are confined mainly to the regulation of *bhukti*.

Before proceeding further it may be worth while to noticed that the Puranas do not condemn *bhukti* as something begetting sin and making salvation a hard affair.

On the contrary they some times contend that it is difficult, even impossible, to achieve *mukti* without a successful zpursuit of bhukti as unsatisfied senses of the aspirant oblige him to covet the objects of desire.[2]

The pursuit of *bhukti* however, is not allowed to outweigh that of *mukti* and it is proclaimed with much emphasis that indulgence begets more desires and desires in turn a greater indulgence.[3] If allowed to expand unbridled this unending chain of cause and effects envelops the entire life of man till it becomes entirely mechanical without a shred of peace. It is probably such an imbalance in favour of bhukti in the character of modern age that impelled thinkers like Gandhi to exclaim: "I do not want growth, I do not want self-determination, I do not want freedom, but I want all these for the soul. I doubt if the stielage is an advancement over flintages. I am indifferent. It is the evolution of soul to which intellect and all our faculties have to be devoted. I have no difficulty in imagining a man armoured after a modern style making some lasting and new discovery for manking but I have less difficulty in imagining a man having nothing but a bit of flint and dail for lighting his path or his matchlock, ever singing a new hymn of praise and delivering to an acting world a message of peace and goodwill upon earth."[4]

With this funamental note of harmony and balance between the material and spiritual pursuits of man in view, when we look for the functions of the Government in the Puranas they crystallize themselves into twin principle of *raksana* and *palana* with a general inclination towards the spiritual motive of material supervision, which we may name as moral.

The principle of *raksana* has been repeatedly emphasized in the Puranas. Thus it is said in one of them that of what use sacrifices and penance are for one whose subjects are not well protected for heaven is like his own house for his whose people are well protected. But *naraka* is invariably the abode of one who fails to protect one's subjects. As the king acquires one sixth both from the merit and demerit of the subjects he should devote himself to the duty of protection as it is the source of dharma as against oppression which is source of sin.[5] The king, states another Purana, who obliges his kingdom by efficient protection and earns his livelihood from the kingdom, wealth, vegetation and earth thus protection acquires no doubt a great success. The kingdom is to be protected from internal as well as external enemies with a great effort and so doing the king acts like the father and mother of the people.[6] Enumerating the five great sacrifices of the king the Visnudharmottara, names them and the chastisement of the wicked, regard of the righteous, earning of wealth by lawful means, protection of the kingdom and impartiality in the law court.[7] Of these as noted by Brhaspati the protection of the government from external enemies comes in the sphere of foreign policy as it is to be effected through the upayas or expedients which we shall notice at its proper place. What remain in the sphere of *raksana,* according to him, are *caurabhaya* i.e. fear from thieves and the fear from the strong,[8] for the government, as we have seen stands not only for the survival for the weakest but for their life on a par with the strong. *Markandey Purana* expresses similar ideas in a much shorter manner. It says that a king should rescue whosoever is threatened by any fear besides waging war with the enemies.[9]

Palana or sustenance the inevitable concomitant of raksana is also a much lauded principle. It is this principle from which the word *raja* is derived and it is again, as we have already seen, at the root of the name of our country. It is thus the central tenent of Indian polity. This is why it is said that the *palana* of the people by the king alone is equal in merit to a thousand of *asvamedha*.[10] It casts upon the king the severe liabilities almost identical with those of a mother who bears an unborn child.[11] The birth of the king, asserts *Markandeya Purana,* is not for the sake of enjoyment but for enduring a great deal of suffering entailed upon him by a sincere observation of his *svadharma* and sustenance of the earth.[12]

In the material functions of the government are included the formulation of such benevolent economic policies as may ensure the livelihood of all. This is why it is often said that it is the king who provides livelihood to all.[13] This he does by his policy of taxation. Only he who sustains the people well through his righteous and judicious policies, we are told, is entitled to his share of revenue.[14] Just as the sun soaks the accumulated water on earth to return it in the form of equally distributed rains even so the king takes away the excess of wealth of the earnings of every one to return it in the form of service, remunerations, gifts and public works.[14] He thereby provides livelihood to many of the who do not till the land or rear the cattle or transact business themselves.[15] But the policy of taxation should be judicious and the conferring of the livelihood upon those not engaged in the process of production should be directed towards the deserving among them. The principle that the king should devise the yoga ksema of the subjects put the Puranas more in line with Manu who lays down that the policy of taxation should be so implemented as to allow the producers and the dealers enjoy the full benefit of their labour.[16] Invoking the analogy of a be in order to explain the principle of the policy of taxation the *Garuda Purana* says that the king should suck the wealth of his people little by little without sapping the vitality of the subject.[17]

Besides the funds that are needed for providing the livelihood of those not engaged in the process of production directly a substantial part of the revenue collected is to be spent in the maintenance and further expansion if possible of the eight fold sources of income viz. Agriculture, trade routes, capital town or forts, dams bridges, capture of elephants, mines and minerals, briging wealth forcibly from and other countries and reclamation of the land lying waste all works of public utility.[18] This statement of *Agni Purana* parallels an observation of Kamandaka to the effect that 'the treasury leads to the construction of dams and bridges, expansion of trade and commerce, receipt of loyalty from the subjects as well as allies and success in moral, temporal and financial pursuits of life.'[19]

By way of gift the king is to provide sustenance to righteous but orphan women for dana given to them is always known as eternal.[20] He has moreover to fetch oil, pots and food to the asramas in person without disregarding those who are respected. The obligation of the king when put face to face with another well known tradition that to providing *Guru daksina* on demand by those Brahmacarians, who have finished their studies,[21] indicates the extent to which to government promoted education for *asramas* were the chief centres of education and learning in ancient India. Promotion of education and learning through a policy of gift and encouragement as one of the functions of the State is brought home more clearly when we are told that the king is to provide 'decent amenities' to learned brahmanas after duly inquiring about their learning and erudition. It is further laid down that the king is to repectfully bring the learned brahmanas already surrounded by disciples over to his capital and after sparing a suitable place to lodge them beside ensuring their livelihood is to ask them to observe their *svadharma*.[22] The king has further to sustain those who are poor, destitute, widow and women in general.[23]

Mora: The social and material functions of the government have a moral basis inasmuch as by regulating the mundane affairs of mankind it assists the individual to reach to consummation of his being the ultimate aim of his life. State control of immorality has been regarded as a supplement to the sum of morality which is also constituted by the deterrent apprehension of punishment of Yama, and the fear of one another.[24] But it is the negative contribution of the State to the cause of morality. Did it take any positive step to promote a moral sense among those amenable to immoral ways? It certainly did but it is necessary to point out before noticing them particularly that the spheres of both religion and morality are fused together in the concept dharma in the Puranas. Moral functions of State, therefore, also include religious.

This State as expressed through the king, has to place the ideal of noble behaviour before the people. The king should never annoy, disregard or insult those women, it is said, who are righteous and given to conjugal chastity for it is such women who bear all the three worlds. The miseries endured by them in this world beget a number of pleasures in the next. Their power is great and their teja unbearable. Such women should not be called to law courts or subjected to punishment as it is their husband who has to be punished for them. An insult to such pious ladies results in the total destruction of the entire *kula*.[25] The king has, moreover, to generate a wholesome respect for cows, the bedrock of *varta*, by taming cows himself.[26] In his coronation ceremony the king has to offer worship publicly to the bull, calf and cow.[27] The State as represented by the king has further to protect with a great effort the inheritance, wealth, and servants of the old temples created for the worship of various gods in his own country. The gods, we are told, protect the earth being themselves protected by the king. This entire surface of the earth is, indeed, pervaded by gods who are to be worship the mankind with age, glory, prosperity and heaven besides bestowing on men the desire they have in mind. Even should worship all the gods and depute brahmanas for conduction their worship as said down in the Vedas.[28] The king, the Mahabharata says in a similar spirit, should construct stay houses, establishments for supplying water to the travelers, and temples and has to patronise the brahmanas in general.[29] Besides temple building the *Agni Purana* also alludes to the provisions for painting, dance, music and both of the images as among the functions of the State.[30]

Obviously all these recommendations for the king are envisaged as the functions of the State that aims at instilling a moral and religious consciousness among the people by creating a religious atmosphere in the country. This environment is also to be created by the celebration of a various ceremonies and performing a number of sacrifices prescribed in the Puranas.[31]

The Hindu view of life as delineated in the scheme of varnasrama appears to uphold the view that moksa or salvation the ultimate end of human life to which all roads of morality, religion, society and material prosperity lead resides not in the indulgence of the enjoyment of desires but in the sacred penance of wilderness. This is why the wantless tapasas to whom gift is meaningless patronage a useless formality and desires a dried up river are the objects of the highest reverence and veneration in the Puranas. They are the living source of inspiration for the people to be righteous. The king is asked to dedicate all his business, kingdom and himself to them and worship them like a gods.[32] The efficacy of moral function of the State with righteous king at its head to judiciously regulated its social and material functions is clearly stresed when it is said that fear from such more or less natural phenomena as epidemics, famine, fire, theft and serpents do not threaten them who hae a righteous monarch.[33]

REFERENCES

1. MP. 220.3., VDP. II. 64.4
2. MP. 220.4; VDP. II. 65.5; AP. 225.3.
3. *Ibid;* 220.8; VDP. II. 65. 9-10; AP. 225.4.
4. *Ibid;* 220.9; VDP. II. 65. 11; AP. 225.5.220. 2-3; VDP. II. 65. 2-4.
5. 220.1; VDP. II. 65.3.
6. MP. 220.3., VDP. II. 65.4.
7. MP. 220.4; VDP. II. 65.5; AP. 225.3.
8. *Ibid;* 220.8; VDP. II. 65. 9-10; AP. 225.4.
9. *Ibid;* 220.8; VDP. II. 65. 11; AP. 225.5.
10. *Ibid;* 220.4; VDP. II. 65.6.
11. *Ibid;* 220.6; VDP. II. 65.7.
12. MP. 220. 19-20; VDP. II. 65. 20-22; Ap. 225. 11-12.

13. 18. 1-3.
14. MKP. 183-6.
15. V. 21. 18-24.
16. 18.25.
17. VSP. V. 10.27-28; VDP. II. 65.46; AP. 225.21-22, 233.8; MDS. VII.
18. 43; Santi. 59.33; Arth. 1.2; Yaj. 1. 311; Kamandaka II. 1. *Sukraniti*.
19. 152.
20. *Dasakumarcharita*, VIII. Para I, p. 202.
21. NVM. 5.55.
22. Arth. 1.2.
23. KNS. 2.3-6.
24. Arth. 1.3.
    Ibid; 1.5.
    KNS. 2.13.
    NVM. 7.1.
25. II. 112. 17.
26. I. 8. 33.
27. KNS. Chapts. 4 & 12.
28. NVM. Chapts X (Mantri—Samuddesa) & XVIII (Amataya
29. Samuddesa).
30. P. 178.
31. 1.7.3 and 1.8.4.
32. I.A., XVIII. 238. V. 5.
33. II. 65.39; 151.20.

Bibliography

1. Original Sources

(a) Puranas

Agni	:	Anandasrama
Brahma	:	Anandasrama
Brahmanda	:	Venketesvar
Brahgavata	:	Gitapress
Bhavisya	:	Venkatesvar
Brhaddharma	:	Bib. Indi.
Brahmavaivarta	:	Anandasrama
Devibhagavata	:	Venkatesvar
Garuda	:	Venkatesvar
Harivamsa	:	Gita Press
Kalika	:	Gita Press
Kurma	:	Bib. Ind.
Linga	:	Venkatesvar

Markandeya : Venkatesvar & Bib. Ind.

Matsya : Venkatesvar

Naradiya : Venkatesvar

Nilamata : Ram Lal Kanji Lal

Padma : Anandasrama

Skanda : Venkatesvar

Siva : Venkatesvar

Samba : Venkatesvar

Saura : Anandasrama

Vayu : Venkatesvar, Anandasrama, : Bib. Ind.

Visnu : Venkatesvar

Visnudharmottara : Venkatesvar

Varsha : Bib. Ind.

Vamana : Venkatesvar

(b)Epics

Ramayana : Gita Press

Mahabharata : Gita Press, Critical and Kumbhakonam

Apastamba Dharmasutra : Ed. by Buhler

Baudhayan Dharmasutra : Ed. by E. Hultzsch

Gautama Dharmasutra : Anandasrama

Manusmrti : Ed. by Ganganath Jha

Naradasmrti : Ed. J. Jolly.

Yajunavalkyasmrti : Trivendram Sanskrit Series with Viramitrodaya and Mitaksara, Banaras.

Visnusmrti : Ed. by J. Jolly.

Krtyakalpataru of Laksmidhara : Gaekwad Oriental Series Poona.

Parasaramadhaviya : Bombay Sanskrit Series Bombay.

Rajanitiratnakara of Candesvara : Ed. by K.P. Jayaswal

Viramitrodaya of Mitramisra: Chowkhambha Sanskrit Series, Banaras.

(c)*Arthasastra* of Kautilya : Ed. by R. Shamasastry R.P. Kangle T. Ganapatisastri.

: Trivendram 1912

: Calcutta 1882

Nitisara of Kamandaka : Ed. by Ludwik Sternback

Sukraniti

Chanakya Rajanitisastra :

(d) Vedic Literature : Ed. by S.P. Pandit Bombay

Artharvaveda : Ed. by F. Max Muller (Second Ed.)

Rgveda : Anandasrama

Aitareya Brahmana : Ed. by R. L. Mitra and S. Vidyabhusana, Calcutta.

Gopatha Brahmana : Ed. by A. Weber, London.

Satapâtha Brahmana : Anandasrama

Taittariya Brahmana Br-Hadarangaka Upanisad : Anandasrama

Chandogya Upanisad : Anandasrama

Kathopanisad : Anandasrama

Mundaka upanisad : Gita Press

Principal Upanisads : S. Radhakrishnan

Svetasvatara Upanisad : Gita Press

Sankhyayana Srautasutra : Ed. by A., Hidlebrandt, Calcutta

Taittariyopanisada : Gita Press

2. Modern Works

Abhilasitarthachintamani, Ed. R. Shamasastry, Mysore, 1926.

Acton, Lord, *History of Freedom and Other Essays*, London, 1909.

Agni Purana, Guru Mandala, Calcutta, 1957.

Agrawal, V.S. *Markandeya Purana eka Sanskrtika Adhyayana*, Hindustani Academy.

Agrawal, V.S., *India as Known to Panini*, Lucknow, 1953.

Agrawal, V.S., *Kadambari: Eka Samskrita Adhyayana*, Varanasi, 1958.

Agrawal, V.S., *Matsya Purana a Study*, Varanasi.

Agrawal, V.S., *Harsacharitaeka Samskritika Adhyayana*, Patna, 1953.

Agrawal, V.S., *Vamana Purana a Study*, Varanasi.

Aiyanger, K.V.R., *Aspects of the Social and Political System of Manusmrti*, Lucknow, 1949.

Aiyanger, K.V.R., *Considerations on Some Aspects of Ancient Indian Polity*, Madras, 1935.

Aiyanger, K.V.R., *Indian Cameralism*, Madras, 1949.

Aiyanger, K.V.R., *Some Aspects of Ancient Indian Polity*, II. ed. Madras University, 1935.

Aiyanger, S.K., *Hiṇdu Administrative Institutions in South India*, Madras, 1936.

Aiyer, Sivaswami, *Evolution of Hindu Moral*, Kamla Lecture, Calcutta, 1935.

Allan J., Catalogue of Coins in the British Museum, London.

Altekar, A.S., *History of village communities of Western India*, Bombay, 1926.

Altekar, A.S., *State and Government in Ancient India*, Banaras, 1955.

Altekar, A.S., *State and Government in Ancient India*, Delhi, 1958.

Altekar, A.S., *The Rastrakutas and their Times*, Poona, 1934.

Amarkosa (Namalinganusasana)., With Poona, 1941.

Anjaria, J.J., *The Nature and Ground of Political Obligation in Hindu State*, Bombay, 1935.

Arthasastra, Mysore, University, 1960.

Awasthi, A.B.L., *Rajaputa Polity*, Lucknow 1964.

Awasthi, A.B.L., *Studies in Skanda Purana*, Lucknow 1965.

Bandhopadhyaya (Banerjea) P.N., *International Law and Custom in Ancient India*, Calcutta, 1920.

Bandhopadhyaya, N.C., *Development of Hindu Polity and Political Theories*, Calcutta, 1938.

Banerji, P.N., *International Law and Custom in Ancient India*, Calcutta, 1920.

Banerji, P.N., *Public Administration in Ancient India*, London, 1920.

Barhaspatyasutra, Ed. F.W. Thomas, Lahore, 1921.

Barker, E., *Greek Political Theory*, London, 1951.

Barker, E., *Political Thought of Plato and Aristotle*, Oxford 1961.

Barker, E., *Principles of Social and Political Theories*, Oxford, 1956.

Barnett, L.D., *Antiquities of India*, London, 1913.

Basak, R.G., *The History of North-Eastern India,* Calcutta, 1934.

Basham, A.L., *The Wonder that Was India,* London 1956.

Basu, P.C., *Indo-Aryan Polity,* London, 1925.

Basu, P.C., *Indo-Aryan Polity,* Lucknow, 1925.

Beal, S. *Travels of Hiouen-Tsang,* Vols. J. IV, Now ed. Calcutta, 1957-58.

Beni Prasad, *The Theory and Government in Ancient India,* Allahabad, 1927.

Bhandarkar, D.R., *Some Aspects of Ancient Hindu Polity,* Banaras, 1929.

Bhandarkar, D.R., *Some Aspects of Ancient Indian Polity,* Varanasi, 1920.

Bhargav, P.L., *India in the Vedic Age,* Lucknow, 1956.

Bluntschli, *Thoery of State,* Oxford, 1892.

Brahaspati Smrti, Reconstructed and Ed. K.V. Rangaswami Aiyangar, Gos, Baroda, 1941.

Chakrawarti, P.C., *The Art of War in Ancient India,* Dacca University, 1941.

Chatterjee, Hiralal, *International Law and Inter-State Relations in Ancient India,* Calcutta, 1958.

Chaudhary, H.K. *Studies in Ancient Indian Law and Justice,* Patna, 1953.

Choudhary, R.K., *Select Inscriptions of Bihar,* Patna, 1958.

Crindle, M.C., *Ancient India as described by Megasthenes and Arrian,* Calcutta, 1906.

Dasakumaracharita, Bombay Sanskrit Series Chaukhamba.

Data, G.T., *The Art of War in Ancient India,* 1929.

(Miss) Dharma P.C., *Ramayana Polity,* Madras, 1941.

Dikshit, P.K., *Mahabharata Mai Rajyayavastha*, Lucknow, 1970.

Dikshitar, V.A.R., *Hindu Administrative Institutions*, Madras, 1952.

Dikshitar, V.A.R., *Mauryan Polity*, Madras, 1932.

Dikshitar, V.A.R., *The Gupta Polity*, Madras, 1952.

Dikshitar, V.A.R., *The Matsya Purana—A Study*, Madras, 1935.

Dikshitar, V.A.R., *Purana-Index* in 3 volumes, Madras, 1936.

Dikshitar, V.R.R., *Hindu Administrative Institutions*, Madras University, 1929.

Dikshitar, V.R.R., *Mauryan Polity*, Madras, 1955.

Dikshitar, V.R.R., *Purana-Index*, Vol. I, Madras University, 1951.

Dikshitar, V.R.R., *The Gupta Polity*, Madras University, 1952.

Dikshitar, V.R.R., *The Matsya Purana-A Study*, Madras University, 1935.

Dikshitar, V.R.R., *War in Ancient India*, Macmillan and Co. 1944.

Dutta, M.N., *The Garuda Puranam*, Calcutta, 1903.

Dutta, M.N., *Translation of Agni Purana*, 2 Volumes, Calcutta 1903-1904.

Dutta, S., *Problem of Indian Nationality*, Calcutta, 1926.

Early Arab Geographers. II ed. Culcutta, 1956.

Elloit and Dowson, *History of India as told by its own Historians*, London, 1866-77.

Fick, A., *The Social Organization in North Fastern India*, Calcutta, 1920.

Figgis, J.N., *Divine Right of the Kings,* Cambridge University Press, 1914.

Fleet, *Corpus Inscriptionum Indicarum,* Vol. III, London, 1888.

Fleet, J.F., *Corpus Inscriptionum Indicarum,* Vol. III.

Ganguly, D.C., *History of the Paramara Dynasty,* Dacca, 1933.

Garner, J.W., *Political Science and Government,* Calcutta, 1955.

Garuda Purana, Venkateswar Press, V.E. 1963.

Gautama Dharmasutra, Ed. Hari Narain apte ASS, Poona, 1910.

Gettell, Raymong G., *Political Science,* Calcutta, 1954.

Ghoshal U.N., *A Treatise on Hindu Law and Usage,* 1922.

Ghoshal, U.N., *A History of Hindu Political Thought,* Calcutta, 1923.

Ghoshal, U.N., *A History of Hindu Public Life,* Oxford, 1923.

Ghoshal, U.N., *A History of Indian Political Ideas,* Oxford, 1959.

Ghoshal, U.N., *A History of Political Ideas,* Bombay, 1959.

Ghoshal, U.N., *Contributions to the History of Hindu Revenue System,* Calcutta, 1929.

Ghoshal, U.N., *Corporate Life in Ancient India,* Calcutta, 1922.

Ghoshal, U.N., *Hindu Revenue System,* Calcutta University, 1929.

Ghoshal, U.N., *Studies in Indian History and Culture,* Orient Longmans, 1957.

Gierk, Otto, *Natural Law and Theory of Society (1500-1800).*

Gopal, M.H. Yani, H., *Mauryan Public Finance,* Lond. 1935.

Gopal, M.H. Yani, H., *Studies in the Agni Purana*, Banaras, 1964.

Gyani, S.D., *Studies in the Agni Purana*, Banaras, 1964.

Hammond, M., *City State and World State in Greek and Roman Political Theory until Agustus*, Harvard University Press, 1951.

Harsa Charita of Banabhatta, Ed. by A.A. Further, Bombay, 1909.

Hazra, R.C., *Studies in the Upapuranas*, Vol. I (1958) and II (1963), Calcutta.

Hazra, R.C., *Studies in the Puranic Records on Hindu Rites and Customs*, Dacca, 1940.

Hazra, R.C., *Studies in the Puranic Records on Hindu Rites and Customs*, Dacca, 1940.

Hazra, R.C., *Studies in the Upapuranas*, Vol. I, Calcutta, 1958.

Heesterman, J.C., *The Ancient Indian Royal Consecration*, Hague, 1957.

Indra, *Ideologies of War and Peace in Ancient India*, Vishveshvaranand Institute Publications, 1957.

Jayaswal, K.P., *Hindu Polity*, Bangalore, 1943, Manu and Yajnavalkya, Calcutta, 1930.

Jayaswal, K.P., *Hindu Polity*, Calcutta 1924: Second and enlarged edition, Bangalore 1943, 3rd and enlarged edition, 1955.

Jolly, J., *Hindu Law and Customs*, Calcutta, 1928.

Kamandakiya Nitisara, Ed. I. Ganapati Sastri, TSs. Tivandrum, 1912.

Kamandakiya Nitisara, Venkateswar Press, Bombay, V.E. 2009.

Kane, P.V., *History of Dharmasastra*, Vols. I & II, Poona, 1930.

Kane, P.V., *History of Dharmasastras,* Vol. I, Poona, 1930 Vol. III Poona, 1946.

Kangle, R.P., *Kautiliya Arthasastra,* Pt. III. A Study Bombay, 1965.

Kathasaritasagra of Somadeva, With Hindi Tr. Kedar Nath Sharma Saraswat, Patna, 1960.

Kavyamimamsa Ed. C.D. Dalal, Baroda, 1934.

Keith, A.B., A History of Sanskrit Literature, Oxford, 1928.

Kosambi, D.D., *An Introduction to the Study of Indian History,* Bombay, 1956.

Krishna Rao, M.V., *Studies in Kautilya,* Delhi, 1958.

Law, N.N., *Aspects of Ancient Indian Polity,* Oxford, 1921.

Law, N.N., *Inter-State, Relations in Ancient India,* Calcutta, 1920.

Law, N.N., *Studies in Ancient Indian Polity,* Longmans Green & Co.

Law, S.N., *Aspects of Ancient Indian Polity,* Oxford 1921 eprinted in 1960.

Law, S.N., *Inter-State Relations in Ancient India,* Calcutta, 1950.

Law, S.N., *Studies in Ancient Hindu Polity,* London, 1914.

Mahabharata, 6 Vols. Gita Press, 2016, V.S.

Mahabharata, With the Commentary of Nilakantha ed. R. Kinjawadekar, Poona, 1929-1933, Critical edition, Poona.

Mahalingam, T.V., *South Indian Polity,* Madras, 1950.

Maine, H., *Ancient Law,* London: Oxford, 1954.

Maithai, J., *Village Government in British India,* London, 1915.

Maity, S.K., *Economic Life of Northern India*, Calcutta, 1957.

Majumdar and Altekar, *The Vakataka-Gupta Age*, Lahore, 1946.

Majumdar, A.K., *Chaulukyas of Gujarat*, Bombay, 1956.

Majumdar, B.C., *Corporate Life in Ancient India*, 2nd ed., Calcutta, 1922.

Majumdar, B.K., *The Military System in Ancient India*, Calcutta, 1955.

Majumdar, R.C., *The Age of Imperial Unity*, Bombay, 1968.

Majumdar, R.C., *The Age of Imperical Kanauja*, Bombay, 1964.

Majumdar, R.C., *The Classical Age*, Bombay, 1962.

Majumdar, R.C., *The Struggle for Empire*, Bombay, 1956.

Manu Smrti, Venkateswar Press, Bombay V.E., 1980.

Manu Smrti, With the Commentary off Kullukabhatta, Gujarata Printing Press, Bombay, 1913.

Markandeya Purana, S.V. Press.

Matsya Purana, Anandasrama Aanskrit series, 1907.

Matsya Purana, Gurumandala Granthamala, Calcutta, 1954.

Matsya Purana, Translated into English by A Taluqdar of Oudh, Vol. 1 & 2 Allahabad, 1917.

Max Muller, F., *A History of Ancient Sanskrit Literature*, II. ed. London 1960.

Mayne, *A Treatise on Hindu Law and Usage*, Madras, 1953.

McCrindle, *Ancient India as Described by Megasthenes and Arrian*, Calcutta, 1905.

Mcdonell, *History of Sanskrit Literature*, London, 1909.

Minakshi, C. *Administration and Social Life Under the Pallavas*, Madras, 1938

Mirashi, V.V. (Ed), *Corpus Inscriptionium Indicarum*, Vol. IV-two parts (Ootacmund 1955).

Mishra, B.B., *Polity in the Agni Purana*, Calcutta, 1965.

Mishra, Rambahadur, *Polity in the Agni Purana*, Calcutta, 1965.

Mookerji, R.K. *Asoka*, Delhi, 1955.

Mookerji, R.K. *Chandragupta Maurya and His Times*, II. ed. Oxford, 1926.

Mookerji, R.K. *Local Government in Ancient India*, Oxford, 1920.

Mookerji, R.K., *Glimpses of Ancient India*, Bhartiya Vidya Bhawan, 1961.

Mookerji, R.K., *Local Self Government in Ancient India*, 3rd.ed., Calcutta, 1922.

Mrchachhakatika, Haridasa Sanskrit Series, Banaras, 1954.

Mudraraksaka of Visakhadata., E.d. k.T. Telang, Enghth Edition, Bombay Sanskrit Series, Bombay, 1935.

Munshi, K.M., *Glory that was Gurjara Desa*, Vol. I & II., Bombay, 1955.

Munshi, K.M., *Indian Inheritance*, Vol. I & III Bhartiya Vidya Bhawan, 1957.

Naisadhiyacharita, With Hindi Translation Chandrika Prasad Shukla, Dehradun, 1951.

Narada Smrti, Ed. J. Jolly, Calcutta, 1885 Engl. Tr. J. Jolly, Oxford, 1889.

Natyasastra, K.M. Series, Bombay, 1956.

Nilakanta Shastri, K.A., The Theory of Pre-Muslim Indian Polity, Madras, 1912.

Nitiprakasika of Vaisampayana, Government Press, Madras, 1953.

Nitivakyamrta, Granthamala, Bombay, 1923.

Niyogi, Roma, *History of the Gahadavala Dynasty*, Calcutta, 1959.

Oppert, Gustav, *On the Weapons, Army Organisation and Political Maxims of the Ancient Hindus*, Madras, 1880.

Panchatantra, Ed. and Tr. Saryu Prasad Pandey, Banaras, V.E. 1959.

Pande, Rajabali, Sircar, D.C., *Historical and Literary Inscriptions*, Varanasi, 1962.

Pande, Rajabali, Sircar, D.C., *Select Inscriptions*, Vol. 1, Calcutta 1965.

Pandey, R.B., *Historical and Literary Inscription*, Varanasi, 1962.

Pandey, R.B., *Subject Index of the Puranas*, Pt. I. (Politcal) Banaras, 1957.

Pandey, V., *Harivansa Purana eka Sanskritka Vivecana*, Prakasana sakha Sucana Vibhaga, Uttar Pradesh, 1960.

Pandey, Veenapani, *Harivamsa Purana Ka Samskrtik Vivechana*, Prakasana Sakha, Suchana Vibhaga, Uttar Pradesh, 1960.

Panda, C.C., *Studies in Origins of Buddhism*, Allahabad, 1957.

Panikkar, K.M., *Origin and Evolution of Kingship in India*, Baroda, 1938.

Pargiter, F.E., *Ancient Indian Historical Tradition*, Delhi, 1962.

Pargiter, F.E., *The Purana Text of the Dynasties of the Kali Age*, Oxford, 1913.

Pargiter, F.E., *Translation of Markandeya Purana*, Calcutta, 1904.

Patil D.R., *Cultural History from the Vayu Purana*, Poona, 1927.

Prabandhachintamani of Merutingacharya, C.H. Tawney, Calcutta, 1899.

Pradhan, Sitanath, *Chronology of Ancient India*, Calcutta, 1927.

Prasad, Beni, *The State in Ancient India*, Allahabad, 1928.

Prasad, Beni, *The Theory of Government in Ancient India*, Allahabad, 1927.

Pratapagiri, R., *Problems of Ancient Indian Polity*, Bombay, 1935.

Puri, B.N., *History of Indian Administration*, Vol. 1, Bombay, 1968.

Puri, B.N., *The History of the Gurjara Pratiharas*, Bombay, 1957.

Pusalker, A.D., *Studies in Epics and Puranas of India*, Bombay, 1955.

Raghuvamsa.

Raghuvan, V., Sanskrit Literature, Delhi 1961.

Rajadharmakanda of Krtyakalpataru, E.d K.V Rangaswami Aiyangar, Gos. Baroda, 1943.

Rajaniti Prakasa.

Rajaniti Ratnakar of Chandesvara, Bihar and Orissa Research Society, second Edition, Patna, 1936.

Rajatarangini of Kalhana, Eng. Tr. M.A. Stein, London, 1900.

Ramaswami, T.N., *Essentials of Indian State Craft*, Asia Publishing House, 1962.

Ramayana of Valmiki, Gita Press, V.E. 2017.

Rao, Venkata, V., *Ancient Political Thought*, S. Chand & Co., 1961.

Rapson, E.J., Cambridge History of India, Vol. 1, 1922.